CONFESSIONAL FICTIONS

A Portrait of the Artist in the Canadian Novel

Confessional Fictions is a study of the *Künstlerroman* – the artist-novel – and its evolution in Canada from the inheritors of Wilde and modernist followers of Joyce and Proust to the postmodern revivalists of the Decadence. Through close readings of nine classic authors David Williams traces the transformations of British and American models to offer a uniquely Canadian portrait of the artist.

He is concerned with three versions of the artist-novel: fictional autobiographies which play with the idea that life recreates art (by Grove, Davies, and Laurence); explicit fictional portraits of the artist (by Ross, Buckler, and Roy) which criticize concepts of art as autonomous form; and postmodernist metafictions which reveal links between parody and photography (by Munro, Kroetsch, and Findley) and reaffirm the novel as an eccentric 'camera' for capturing the modern experience.

Williams analyses the use of the aesthetic vision – not only in Wilde and Joyce, but also in Moore, Pound, Proust, and Thomas Wolfe – while insisting on the relevance of postmodern theories of structural mimesis and parody to the contemporary Canadian writer. Through Williams's method, surprising new light is cast upon, for example, Hagar's self-creation in *The Stone Angel*, art for art's sake in *As For Me and My House*, feminist humanism in *Badlands*.

Finally closing the circle between decadent and postmodern aesthetics, Williams exposes the roots of poststructuralist thinking about the crisis of subject and the absence of truth in language. By tracing the line from Joyce through Mikhail Bakhtin to Timothy Findley, from Oscar Wilde to Alice Munro, *Confessional Fictions* ends by showing how contemporary reports of the death of humanism may be greatly exaggerated.

DAVID WILLIAMS is Professor of English at the University of Manitoba. He is the author of *Faulkner's Women: The Myth and the Muse* and editor of *To Run with Longboat: Twelve Stories of Indian Athletes in Canada*. He has also had three novels published; the most recent is *Eye of the Father*.

David Williams

CONFESSIONAL
FICTIONS
A Portrait of the Artist
in the Canadian Novel

University of Toronto Press
Toronto Buffalo London

University of Toronto Press 1991
Toronto Buffalo London
Printed in Canada

ISBN 0-8020-5878-7 (cloth)
ISBN 0-8020-6807-3 (paper)

∞

Printed on acid-free paper

Canadian Cataloguing in Publication Data

Williams, David, 1945–
Confessional fictions

Includes bibliographical references.
ISBN 0-8020-5878-7 (bound). – ISBN 0-8020-6807-3 (pbk.)

1. Canadian fiction (English) – 20th century – History
and criticism.* 2. Artists in literature. I. Title.

PS8191.A78W54 1991   C813'.5409'3527   C90-095199-0
PR9192.6.A78W54 1991

This book has been published with the help of a grant
from the Canadian Federation for the Humanities, using funds
provided by the Social Sciences and Humanities
Research Council of Canada.

For Daisy, Doris, Stuart, and Xiaoping

league of nations 1987–1988

and for Martin

deconstructing an evil empire

Contents

Acknowledgments

Grateful acknowledgment is made for permission to reprint the following essays in more or less revised form:

'Oscar Wilde and a Swede from Nebraska: Masks of Autobiography in *Settlers of the Marsh* and *In Search of Myself*,' from *Canada and the Nordic Countries: Proceedings from the Second International Conference of the Nordic Association for Canadian Studies, University of Lund, 1987*, 365–75. Edited by Jørn Carlsen and Bengt Streijffert. Copyright © 1988 by The authors and Studentlitteratur 1988. Reprinted by permission of The Nordic Association for Canadian Studies.

'The Confessions of a Self-Made Man: Forms of Autobiography in *Fifth Business*,' from *Journal of Canadian Studies* 24 (Spring 1989): 81–102. Reprinted by permission of the *Journal of Canadian Studies*.

'Jacob and the Demon: Hagar as Storyteller in *The Stone Angel*,' from *Crossing the River: Essays in Honour of Margaret Laurence*,' 81–98. Edited by Kristjana Gunnars. Copyright © 1988 The Authors. Reprinted by permission of Turnstone Press.

' "Looking into a Void": The Clash of Realism and Modernism in *As For Me and My House*,' from *Canadiana: Studies in Canadian Literature/Etudes de Littérature Canadienne*, 25–42. Edited by Jørn Carlsen and Knud Larsen. Copyright © 1984 Canadian Studies Conference, University of Aarhus. Reprinted by permission of The Nordic Association for Canadian Studies.

'After Post-Modernism,' from *Trace: Prairie Writers on Writing*, 275–84. Edited by Birk Sproxton. Copyright © 1986 The Authors. Reprinted by permission of Turnstone Press.

The excerpt from 'The Waste Land' in *Collected Poems 1909–1962* by T.S. Eliot, copyright 1936 by Harcourt Brace Jovanovich, Inc., copyright © 1964, 1963 by T.S. Eliot, is reprinted by permission of Harcourt Brace Jovanovich, Inc., and Faber and Faber, Ltd. The excerpts from Ezra Pound's *Hugh Selwyn Mauberley (Life and Contacts)* in *Personae*, copyright 1926 by Ezra Pound, are reprinted by permission of New Directions Publishing Corporation and in *Selected Poems of Ezra Pound*, by T.S. Eliot, by permission of Faber and Faber, Ltd.

I am personally grateful as well to Professor Jørn Carlsen and the Nordic Association for Canadian Studies for invitations to address international conferences in Denmark (1984) and Sweden (1987). Not only did the themes of both gatherings help to supply me with a motive for writing, but comparatist assumptions about the place of Canadian writing in world literature supplied a healthy model of critical procedure.

Finally, an 'Award for Outstanding Research in the Humanities' from the RH Institute of Winnipeg brought me into the remarkable world of Macintosh computers. I find such generous support of the humanities by colleagues in medical research no less remarkable.

Introduction

1

From Aestheticism to Postmodernism: The Artist-Novel Tradition

The concept of a 'Canadian tradition' is not easily established. In literary terms it is, I believe, neither an abstraction like a sense of identity nor a theme like survival. It evolves gradually from the achieved literary works that have been written by its people.

W.J. Keith, *Canadian Literature in English*

Much of Can Lit is the invention of academics and remains their preserve ... Loony and spurious literary traditions have been invented.

John Metcalf, *The Bumper Book*

The immigrant writer has every reason to feel uneasy about tradition. Even that high priest of modernist tradition, T.S. Eliot, lacked a local language, once he settled in Britain, that could carry poetic echoes going back and back. And so he chose to become a polyglot and a cosmopolitan, turning poetry in the process into something resembling ventriloquism. Still the individual talent was not content to play a highbrow Mortimer Snerd to the Edgar Bergen of European tradition: 'Whoever has approved this idea of order, of the form of European, of English literature will not find it preposterous that the past should be altered by the present as much as the present is directed by the past' (Eliot 50). His not quite preposterous hope that he might change the past, if ever so slightly, is immensely significant to the immigrant poet who seeks a way to inscribe the self (or make it present) in the very past which threatens to exclude him or her.

The writer who is an immigrant to Canada may, on the other hand, recognize no literary tradition which antedates his own arrival on the scene. F.P. Grove is a case in point; John Metcalf may be another. (In comparison to Grove's relative artistic failure, any lack of art in the latter-day saint must be attributed to his extreme belatedness.) And yet it may also be, as Sam Solecki says, 'that Metcalf *must* offer a high valuation of short fiction – the fiction he excels in – if he is to recast the Canadian tradition in such a way that he will have a place in it' (222). In either event, Metcalf seems bent on inscribing himself within a dead tradition of international modernism which he and his party have managed to bear safely out of burning Troy. The modern Aeneas must look again to a future Augustan age in the past, even as he seeks to embody it in his own words and deeds.

The immigrant *critic* more modestly refuses to hold any brief for himself, unless it should be as a historical man yearning for a 'native tradition' (Keith x). And yet this very need to emphasize the 'native' leads, in general, to cultural insularity and, in particular, to serious distortions of judgment, such as when 'Ernest Buckler's finest achievement, *The Mountain and the Valley* (1952),' is said to bear 'a decided if superficial resemblance to *Who Has Seen the Wind*' (Keith 146). In fact, Buckler's work depends upon a very different model of romantic egoism – Thomas Wolfe's *Look Homeward, Angel* – and a highly sceptical mode of parody to expose the pitfalls of American transcendentalism for Canadian artists and audiences. So an insular concept of tradition might really obscure, rather than explain, our artists' true achievements.

Keith is none the less aware that books as well as persons have emigrated to other countries, if with mutual difficulties. The general principle of his own literary history is to show how 'outside influences have been assimilated, transformed into a new and distinctive combination. This poised balance between British and American models will ultimately be recognized as a quintessentially Canadian – and independent – stance' (116). Yet nothing in the summary practice of literary history can show *how* the verbal process of transformation actually occurs or how its ideology – both aesthetic and social – differs from that of its presumptive models.

It was that latecomer Virgil who first showed the world how to 'assimilate an outmoded form and content to a contemporary subject; he could thus Augustanize Homer and revive heroic myth in truly successful poetry, because he consistently adapted Homer to a thoroughly un-Homeric ideology, always converting the objective narrative of *Iliad* and *Odyssey* to one that was both subjective and symbolic' (Otis 221–2). Parody is not quite the word to describe Virgil's technique, though ironic inversion is central to his method of narration as well as to his vision. For 'the distinction between Aeneas and any genuinely Homeric hero is quite fundamental. His ethos is utterly different from that of Achilles, Hector or Odysseus. Aeneas' goal and object in life is not merely in the near but in the remote future, in Augustan Rome itself. Thus all the intelligible goals of Homeric epic or Greek tragedy, indeed of all Greek literature, are not available to him.'

The aim of this book is to explore the assimilation in the Canadian novel of an 'intelligible goal' which has not been as readily available to belated modernists and postmodernists as it was to Americans such as Sherwood Anderson or Ernest Hemingway, who wrote as contemporaries of Joyce. The 'goal' or 'theme' – what might be called the modernist 'matter of Troy' – is the portrayal of the artist's growth in the *Künstler-roman* or artist-novel. But even in 1916, Joyce's *A Portrait of the Artist as a Young Man* was not the first *Künstlerroman* in English, though it was surely the best modernist example of the type. Rather, the artist-novel appears to be an inevitable outgrowth of aestheticism, from its incipience in Pater's *The Renaissance* (1873) and *Marius the Epicurean* (1885) to its decadent flowering in George Moore's *Confessions of a Young Man* (1888). To this day, the type has escaped obsolescence through radical changes in the ideology of art and artist in each new generation. So our first concern in tracing its development in Canadian fiction from modernism through to postmodernism must be to supply an aetiology of the form.

In *Aestheticism and the Canadian Modernists: Aspects of a Poetic Influence*, Brian Trehearne concludes that 'our poets found a middle ground between the extremes of experiment and conservatism' precisely because they 'themselves provided the Aestheticism that so many critics have suggested to be a necessary preliminary to Modernism. So necessary is Aestheticism to the birth of Modernism that, in a country where no significant Aesthetic period had existed, one had to be created before Modernism could occur' (318, 314). Much the same thing may be said of modernism in the Canadian novel, since the autobiographical fiction of Frederick Philip Grove, including *In Search of Myself*, is as nearly derived from aestheticism as anything in Canadian poetry. Grove is a late aestheticist, however, closer to George Moore and to Oscar Wilde than he is to Walter Pater. If – to make a momentary (because provisional) use of Trehearne's definitions – 'Paterian Aestheticism is, at root, a doctrine of the removal of art and the artist from all other human activity and of pursuit in his specialized realm of affective beauty in objects commonly recognizable as "art," ' then 'Decadence begins ... when creative personalities too active to persist in the ethereal contemplation of timeless art seek to unite that life of Paterian contemplation with the life of worldly experience – to perceive all of life as an art work yielding, potentially, moments of extreme aesthetic pleasure' (Trehearne 12). Grove's 'life,' from *A Search for America* (1927) to the late fiction of his artistic 'autobiography,' is filled with a similar pressure which 'is thus brought to bear upon the late Aesthetic artist to create intensity and beauty, while consciously or unconsciously recognizing the incompatibility of his enterprise with reality' (Trehearne 12).

The first ideological shift from aestheticism to modernism is thus apparent in the decadence, though not necessarily in the formalist terms peculiar to modernist aesthetics. Citing J.E. Chamberlin's 'From High Decadence to High Modernism,' Trehearne says that 'the formal breakdown we tend to associate with Modernism is inherent in the "dissolution" of form apparent in the literature of the Decadence ... and this preoccupation was passed on to the next generation: "The disunity, the separateness, the disintegration, that seemed to define decadence both fascinated and bothered the artists who moved from decadence to modernism, and few escaped the ambivalence" ' (20). Yet the example of Joyce's *Portrait* points to an opposite tendency in the ideology of 'high' modernism: an emphasis upon wholeness, proportion, and order which are evidently meant to reify (and even to totalize) the personality of the artist. For the self-proclaimed 'priest of eternal imagination' promises to transubstantiate 'the daily bread of experience into the radiant body of everliving life' (*Portrait* 221). Art thus turns into the one and only reality as transient (and mundane) 'experience' is transmuted into the everliving portrait of the artist.

Wilde, of course, had already set the fashion when he said, 'I treated art as the supreme reality and life as a mere mode of fiction' (*De Profundis* 46). Characteristically, the Irish apostle of the decadence had held 'art to have two basic energies, both of them subversive. One asserts its magnificent isolation from experience, its unreality, its sterility.' The other affirms that 'The artist may be criminal and instill his work with criminality' (Ellmann, 'Critic' 100–1). While the energy of unreality 'undermines things as they are,' affirming the superiority of art to nature, the energy of criminality promises its own 'liberation of personality' which is the true 'goal of man' (Ellmann 101). Whether one seeks a 'magnificent isolation from experience' or the intense individualism of experience, one moves toward freedom. For Wilde's 'private equation is that sin is the perception of new and dangerous possibilities in action as self-consciousness is in thought and criticism is in art' (Ellmann 102). As he wrote in 'The Critic as Artist,' 'What is termed Sin is an essential element of progress ... By its curiosity Sin increases the experience of the race. Through its intensified assertion of individualism, it saves us from monotony of type' (*Intentions* 134). And so the criminal becomes an artist every bit as much as the artist is a criminal, though a criminal sort of life is but one of many modes of 'fiction' available to the artist.

To the author of 'The Decay of Lying,' the 'fine lie' is one of the more creative criminal acts, since the cultured liar alone offers freedom from 'Nature's lack of design, her curious crudities, her extraordinary monotony, her absolutely unfinished condition' (Wilde, *Intentions* 6, 3). 'Life,' in the terms of Wilde's famous slogan, thus 'imitates Art far more than Art imitates Life' (56). In such a context, even the name of Joyce's artist-hero must recall another artist's criminal subversion of nature. For Daedalus, Ovid's mythic artificer, panders to a queen's unnatural lusts, then hides her monstrous offspring in the Cretan labyrinth before fashioning wings to escape his own incarceration. Joyce's epigraph from the *Metamorphoses* also anticipates the judgment of nature on all such Icarian careers: '*Et ignotas animum dimittit in artes*' – 'So then to unimagined arts/ He set his mind and altered nature's laws' (Melville 177). And we instantly recognize the fallen Wilde as the most recent – and most relevant – example of such 'unnatural' artists.

Yet, contrary to Wilde, Joyce's artist also remains a mere spectator, determined to separate his art from the common life of Ireland and to refuse any action save his own exile into art. In other words, the only life which Stephen can allow himself now consists of his act of self-portraiture; only in such fashion does the artist's written *life* become his supreme mode of living. Now, too, the Dedalean theory of *integritas*, *consonantia*, and *claritas* might well turn into the paradigmatic reification of personality for which *The Waste Land* stands as the modernist icon: 'These fragments I have shored against my ruins.' But Joyce's presentation of a theory of art developed in dialogue with several different interlocutors tends in fact to undercut Stephen's aesthetic renunciation of life for a timeless (and hermetically sealed) art of stasis. Here, even the interruptions in the 'artist's' monologue call into doubt Joyce's supposed faith in pattern and wholeness which would turn the self-contained work of art into an analagon of the self-sufficient individual (Murdoch, 'Sublime' 259). For Joyce, as we shall see in the next section of this chapter, is really the only artist in *A Portrait* who could look beyond the icon of art for the artist's sake 'to forge in the smithy of [his] soul the uncreated conscience of [his] race.'

Dedalus, on the other hand, is Joyce's parody of the decadent poet, even as *A Portrait* parodies the self-enclosing icons of aestheticist beauty. 'While it is easy to mistake the Decadent version of Aestheticism for a wilfully perverse approach to aesthetics and to life, a deliberate effeminacy of spirit that seeks decay and failure where they need not be found, such a sense of decay and falling off was a manifestation of a keenly felt cultural impasse' (Trehearne 13). A more recent way out of the impasse of the 'verbal icon' and self-contained form appears, in the postmodern *Künstlerrroman*, to be the author's creative collaboration with the reader. This further ideological shift away from 'Paterian contemplation' to 'worldly experience' involves a deconstruction of both 'timeless art' and the self-sufficient artist, laying bare the actual process of creation. Yet deconstruction, like the aesthetics of the decadence, has managed, in its profound scepticism about meaning and its utter loss of faith in language, to create a new cultural impasse quite as serious as the one of the 1890s.

First and foremost, deconstruction asks to be viewed as a metaphysics, or more precisely as an anti-metaphysics, of freedom. Jacques Derrida, who 'equates the conventions of literary study with the rules that govern – and repress – society as a whole' (Fischer 90), mounts a furious attack on the old metaphysics of the centre, exposing as its 'contradictory coherence' the idea that 'the center, which is by definition unique, constituted that very thing within a structure which governs the structure, while escaping structurality' (Derrida 248). The idea of the centre, in other words, conceals a fiction of authority, since power of any sort, whether political or theological or literary, is necessarily arbitrary. Only after 'the structurality of structure had to begin to be thought,' that is, 'in the absence of a center or origin,' could 'everything bec[o]me discourse,' and so 'everything became a system where the central signified, the original or transcendental signified, is never absolutely present outside a system of differences. The absence of the transcendental signified extends the domain and the interplay of signification *ad infinitum*' (Derrida 249). The supplementary character of language supposedly offers one of the best means to freedom – a 'joyous affirmation of the freeplay of the world and without truth, without origin, offered to an active interpretation' which also '*determines the non-center otherwise than as loss of the center*' (Derrida 264). Inasmuch as a 'text ... "ramifies" or "disseminates" an author's intent,' readers are forced 'to see multiple possibilities and not a fixed "center" that governs the production of meaning' (Fischer 116).

What this ultimately means is 'that the ineluctable fictiveness of discursive structures keeps them from becoming truthful assertions' (Fischer 95). Yet such an idea hardly seems new to anyone who has read Wilde's 'The Decay of Lying.' Thus Roland Barthes, writing that 'life never does more than imitate the book, and the book itself is only a tissue of signs, an imitation that is lost, infinitely deferred' (Barthes, 'Death' 146), goes out of his way to identify poststructuralism with decadent aesthetics, even as he extends the implication that art (or textuality) *is* the universe.

In a similar fashion, Barthes's *The Pleasure of the Text* (1973) offers a contemporary equivalent of the decadent pursuit of 'aesthetic pleasure,' although it now requires us to 'play with texts ... uncovering the possibilities that "society" suppresses' (Fischer 119). The poststructuralist project of exposing 'the omnipresence of "patriarchal" or "logocentric" authority' (Mahaffey 2) thus gains a social purpose that the early aesthetic movement, in its pursuit of beauty, never found. But 'the arguments advanced by deconstructionists and others against the referentiality and determinacy of literary texts' (Fischer 111) have also turned language against itself and made the ludic possibilities of criticism jaded, if not positively futile. While 'the transience of beauty, the brevity of impressions, [were] largely responsible for the Decadent's misery' (Trehearne 15), the joy of the deconstructionist also turns to misery, since, as J. Hillis Miller writes, 'The most heroic effort to escape from the prisonhouse of language only builds the walls higher' (cited in Fischer 53). Because 'language has died "as the natural medium of truth"'

(Fischer 103), the reader becomes trapped in a labyrinth which goes nowhere. And, as Miller unhesitatingly concedes, 'One can never escape from the labyrinth because the activity of escaping makes more labyrinth, the thread of a linear narrative or story' (Miller 420). But one cannot concede the artist's story-making power to the critic without making it 'another *mise en abyme*, both a mapping of the abyss and an attempted escape from it, criticism as cure' (Miller 420). For the infinite regress of language must, in the eyes of the postmodern decadent, turn everything into a *mise en abyme*. So art, for him, can no longer be a road through to action – or to life – as it could be for his 'criminal' predecessor a century before.

The question is, how have art and artist arrived at such an impasse? Fischer suggests that the problem, at least in literary criticism, begins with Matthew Arnold. The positivism of nineteenth-century science so 'corroded the authority of Christian dogma' that it 'could also jeopardize the social claims [Arnold] wanted to make for the study of literature' (8). But 'by weakening the "truth-telling function," ... [b]y making the discovery of new ideas the exclusive "business of the philosopher," Arnold threatened the ability of poetry to fulfill the social functions that he wanted it to assume' (6–7). Quite unintentionally, then, Arnold's position hastened that separation of art from life which was to become an article of faith for such aesthetes as Pater who shifted attention away from aesthetic objects in themselves to the impressions they might create in perceivers. But then, given the social functions that a later impressionist such as Wilde wanted art to assume, the deceased Arnold would have been likely to urge a further separation of life from art.

Fictional portraits of the artist have still tended, ever since the age of the decadence, towards this autonomous image of the self-made 'life' – towards the eternally youthful face, if not the aging picture, of Wilde's Dorian Gray. But 'Arthur Rimbaud's "systematic derangement of the senses," ' much less the crimes of the Wildean hero himself, necessarily involved the decadent in 'more direct conflict with social codes than was brought to bear upon the more spiritual Paterian aesthete' (Trehearne 12). The 'typical' modernist solution to this unwinnable 'conflict with social codes' is subsequently offered by Stephen Dedalus: 'I will try to express myself in some mode of life or art as freely as I can and as wholly as I can, using for my defence the only arms I allow myself to use – silence, exile, and cunning' (*Portrait* 247). The Canadian postmodernist, who refuses the apparent rootlessness of international modernism, also refuses Stephen's condition of exile, if not his strategy of cunning. For life and art, it seems, continue to be equivalent terms for him, too, if on radically different grounds. Now that everything becomes a text, even external reality is hardly more than a 'pre-text.' Such 'pervasive artistic self-consciousness in contemporary fiction' (MacLulich 237) privileges the *Künstlerroman* as one of the more worthwhile types of the novel in postmodern writing about writing, since it opposes the heroic writer to a world still blinded by the false 'transparency' of language.

Because of such radically different assumptions about art, artist, and audience in each era and because of the changing imperatives of criticism, the methodological problem of this study must then be how to make sense of a literary type which is so diverse in form and in ideology. Mere literary history has proved to be insufficient to the demands of texts which self-consciously 're-inscribe' prior texts. For this reason, the work of Mikhail Bakhtin, who bases his whole theory of literary development upon a general theory of linguistic parody, can be seen as underwriting my method, even when he is not referred to directly. Yet only the whole spectrum of theoretical models appropriate to the novels themselves can ever allow us to see them singly, as well as in relation, since their art-ideologies range from aestheticism to formalism to inscribed reader-response, and more recently, from deconstruction to the writings of the poststructural and 'semiotic Freud.'

My project is still not completely at odds with the methods of a J. Hillis Miller: 'The deconstructive critic seeks to find, by this process of retracing, the element in the system studied which is alogical, the thread in the text in question which will unravel it all, or the loose stone which will pull down the whole building' (Miller 423). But my difference from the deconstructive critic is that I assign to a narrator or to a dramatic persona the burden of a system which he locates in language itself. In other words, I acknowledge the need to master the textual 'aporia' (421) without having to deny an author's intent, or a text's own context, or even language's reference to a world outside itself. In the 'absence of the transcendental signified' (Derrida 249), I take 'truth' to refer to the *ethos* of a text which is ultimately discoverable in the sort of ethical choices it presents in the reading act. My view of the text and the act of reading thus approaches Stanley Fish in his recent essay on 'Truth and Indeterminacy in Milton's *Areopagitica*,' where he says that, 'if the

Areopagitica is to be faithful to the lesson it teaches, it cannot teach that lesson directly; rather it must offer itself as the occasion for the trial and exercise that are necessary to the constituting of human virtue; it must become an instrument in what Milton will later call "knowledge in the making" ' (Fish 242).

Such a concept of ethical function grows out of Milton's own pronouncement about the benefits to be had from 'promiscuous reading': 'Good and evil we know in the field of this world grow up together almost inseparably.... Assuredly we bring not innocence into the world, we bring impurity much rather; that which purifies us is trial, and trial is by what is contrary' (Hughes 728). What has changed in Fish's reception theory from work he did on Milton twenty years ago – work which was still quite conservative, perhaps even authoritarian – is precisely his changed view of the text which, in its 'self-effacing' way, plays a 'part in the fashioning of another vehicle, the heart of the reader,' although the scattered body of truth may not be recoverable ' "till her Master's second coming" ' (Fish 242, 243, 246).

As Fish admits, he may still be taken to task for trying to 'recuperate both the unity of the text and the totalizing power of the author's intention,' though in fact 'it is precisely my method to find tensions and discontinuities where others before me had found only the steady unfolding of a classic liberal vision' (248). Such a method is ironic, in the root sense of the word, since the text serves as a self-effacing Socratic *eiron*, offering but an occasion to the reader for 'knowlege in the making.' In reading acts 'by which the self is refined and purified' (Fish 244), literature can finally escape its self-enclosure to provoke choices which do not end once the reader has stopped reading. Implicitly, this is to affirm a larger mode of mimesis containing the mode of diegesis privileged by postmodern aesthetics, since, 'Like any other discourse ... a poem affects our conduct if and only if we respect what it says about the "real nature of things" ' (Fischer 9).

The marginal reader of self-effacing cultural artefacts might still perform one political function unavailable to the critic from an imperial culture, trapped as he is within a 'centre' and a history which inevitably threaten closure. Away from the centre, out on the margins where traditions are never fully monumentalized, both the artist and critic are free to dissent from, or radically to alter norms which have never included them. Much of what follows offers such a revisionist view of the early aesthetic and modernist tradition of the artist-novel, as well as its multiform reception in Canada. But what really matters in the brief literary history which follows are the ways in which 'revisionism' can release new energies in supposedly moribund forms, can even offer new possibilities for artistic 'immigration' in a post-colonial literature.

Northrop Frye once remarked how, 'when we find that a technical discussion of a theory of aesthetics forms the climax of Joyce's *Portrait*, we realize that what makes this possible is the presence in that novel of another tradition of prose fiction' (308). In Frye's taxonomy, that other tradition is the 'confession,' so named by 'St Augustine, who appears to have invented it, and Rousseau, who established a modern type of it... After Rousseau – in fact in Rousseau – the confession flows into the novel, and the mixture produces the fictional autobiography, the *Künstler-roman*, and kindred types' (307).

George Moore, whose *Confessions of a Young Man* (1888) might be said to inaugurate the artist-novel in English fiction, later claimed that he had not read Rousseau's *Confessions* before composing his own artistic autobiography: 'It is barely credible that I could have lived into early manhood without having heard of him, but "The Confessions of a Young Man" testifies that I never read him; a page of Jean Jacques would have made the book I am prefacing an impossibility; another book more complete but less original might have been written. I wrote without a model' (Preface to the American edition of 1917 – Moore 42). Yet in the Preface to the second English edition of 1889, Moore had already identified the model which he was most intent on parodying: 'St Augustine ... wrote the story of a God-tortured soul; would it not be interesting to write the story of an art-tortured soul?' (35). At a single stroke, Moore converts the religious confession into an aesthetic one.

Hereafter, the redemptive quest of spiritual autobiography turns into the governing story of the aesthetic movement: the artist, holding to 'a doctrine of the removal of art and the artist from all other human activity' (Trehearne 12), opposes himself to his age in order, paradoxically, to redeem the bourgeois society he rejects. Yet, in terms which also locate Moore's aestheticism nearer to the decadence, his narrator says, '[T]he life of the artist should be a practical protest against the so-called decencies of life' (Moore 139).

It is, in fact, the decadence of Moore's *Confessions* which makes it anything but tortured in 'its exuberant artist's defiance of orthodoxy and its often undetected self-mockery' (Jeffares 1). Moore's conflation of the opposing terms of 'timeless art' and 'worldly experience' into an *artistic life* has not yet been undermined by the 'withering self-consciousness' of later decadents who would write 'a poetry obsessed with failure, since desire for unceasing intensity and beauty must inevitably leave the poet embittered' (Trehearne 15). Accordingly, Moore offers 'a portrait of a pagan and patrician Aesthete, glorying in beauty, form, and flesh and announcing his scorn of humanity' (Chaikin 25). In other words, the aesthetic confession is from the outset an artistic pose as well as a biographical fiction. But then even Walter Pater, the more passively 'receptive' aesthete, knew better at the time than to take literally 'so satiric a book' (cited in the 'Preface' to the third English edition, 1904 – Moore 38).

Pater, of course, had already published a different sort of aesthetic confession in *Marius the Epicurean*, a novel which would strongly influence both Moore and Wilde, as well as Joyce, for it was the fictional biography of an aesthetic temperament, if not of an accomplished artist. Even in this highly refracted, almost faceless account of 'His Sensations and Ideas,' Marius the aesthete is drawn to the confessional form of a journal in one of the final chapters of the novel: 'It was become a habit with Marius – one of his modernisms – developed by his assistance at the Emperor's "conversations with himself," to keep a register of the movements of his own private thoughts and humours; not continuously indeed, yet sometimes for lengthy intervals, during which it was no idle self-indulgence, but a necessity of his intellectual life, to "confess himself," with an intimacy, seemingly rare among the ancients; ancient writers, at all events, having been jealous, for the most part, of affording us so much as a glimpse of that interior self, which in many cases would have actually doubled the interest of their objective information' (II, 172). This concern for subjectivity becomes the hallmark of Pater's own aestheticism, inasmuch as 'we are all under sentence of death but with a sort of indefinite reprieve ... For our one chance lies in expanding that interval, in getting as many pulsations as possible into the given time. Great passions may give us this quickened sense of life ... Of such wisdom, the poetic passion, the desire of beauty, the love of art for its own sake, has most. For art comes to you proposing frankly to give nothing but the highest quality to your moments as they pass, and simply for those moments' sake' (*Renaissance* 238–9). Pater's *l'art pour l'art* turns out to be much less art for the sake of art than it is for the sake of the viewer's fleeting moments.

The 'confession' of Marius still 'brings to life a decisive feature missing or perhaps even deliberately omitted from the "Conclusion". There he had put forward the aesthetic moment as a theoretical guideline for conceiving human life, whereas in *Marius* he spotlights the spiritual problems arising from such an aesthetic conceptualisation of life by revealing the moment as the genesis of longing and anxiety' (Iser, *Pater* 141). In fact, it is transience and death which finally end Marius's several attempts to realize 'what it is the chief function of all higher education to impart, the art, namely, of so relieving the ideal or poetic traits, the elements of distinction, in our everyday life – of so exclusively living in them – that the unadorned remainder of it, the mere drift or *débris* of our days, comes to be as though it were not' (*Marius* I, 53–4). Through Marius, Pater can himself confess that 'there is a certain grief in things as they are, in man as he has come to be, as he certainly is, over and above those griefs of circumstance which are in a measure removable – some inexplicable shortcoming, or misadventure, on the part of nature itself – death, and old age as it must needs be, and that watching for their approach, which makes every stage of life like a dying over and over again' (II, 181–2).

A major difference, however, between the personal and the fictional confession becomes evident in Pater's stylistic attempt to arrest the flow of time and to extract from it 'the ideal or poetic traits, the elements of distinction, in our everyday life.' For it is a style which is 'static, pictorial. It resembles the highly inflected structure of the classical languages in that it permits a more arbitrary order of words so that the sentence seems to present to the reader all of its parts simultaneously' (Monsman, *Portraits* 57). Still, the author does not insist that because time is frozen into art by this artifice of simultaneity, it has lasting power in life. In the quest of his hero Pater finally demonstrates with 'admirable integrity' 'the failure built into the aesthetic attitude' (Iser, *Pater* 141): 'On the one hand he wishes to orientate himself by the moments that race by completely out of his control, but on the other he seeks something quite specific in this passing stream: an ideal of totality. So long as he lives only by experience, he remains passive and receptive, but his desire to find wholeness requires action. The only action he can perform, though, is to move from one set of ideas to another: the philosophy of the moment, ethics, religion. He is for ever halfway – distancing himself from the secular experience, hoping to find totality, unable to commit himself' (Iser, *Pater* 148–9). Were he to commit himself but once, he would surrender that total openness to experience which he has taken for his only creed.

Though Marius, after his death, is mistaken for a Christian martyr, he has hardly given himself to that creed either, not even though he had once sensed, in a requiem mass for a child, an answer to his most besetting problem, since the participants 'were still under the influence of an immense gratitude in thinking, even amid their present distress, of the hour of a great deliverance' (II, 190). As long as he is cloistered in St Cecilia's house, he feels how 'very forcibly' its hope contrasts 'with the imperial philosopher's so heavy burden of unrelieved melancholy. It was Christianity in its humanity, or even its humanism, in its generous hopes for man, its common sense and alacrity of cheerful service, its sympathy with all creatures, its appreciation of beauty and daylight' (II, 115). But in its other-worldly zeal for martyrdom, the Christian faith negates not only the humanity, but the very beauty, which its light has brought into the world: 'To him, in truth, a death such as the recent death of those saintly brothers, seemed no glorious end. In his case, at least, the Martyrdom, as it was called – the overpowering act of testimony that Heaven had come down among men – would be but a common execution: from the drops of his blood there would spring no miraculous, poetic flowers' (II, 214). For Marius, the death of the martyr fails the aesthetic sense just as surely as his own sense of the aesthetic moment is unable to 'expand the interval' beyond the moment of death.

Pater's loss of faith in a cult of art as 'the "virtue" that takes [experience] out of the "permanent flux" and enables it to defy time by freezing the transient into a permanent image' (Iser, *Pater* 37) does not leave him, however, quite without hope at the end of *Marius the Epicurean*. Only his hope, as revealed in his final analogy, has shifted from a world of 'autonomous art' (Iser 35) to a community of generations throughout time: 'Yes! through the survival of their children, happy parents are able to think calmly, and with a very practical affection, of a world in which they are to have no direct share; planting with a cheerful good-humour, the acorns they carry about with them, that their grand-children may be shaded from the sun by the broad oak-trees of the future. That is nature's way of easing death to us. It was thus too, surprised, delighted, that Marius, under the power of that new hope among men, could think of the generations to come after him ... In the bare sense of having loved he seemed to find, even amid this foundering of the ship, that on which his soul might "assuredly rest and depend" ' (II, 221–2, 223). In fact, this consolation hardly differs from 'The Religion of Numa' with which the novel began. But even if it is true that a man survives in his heirs, Marius dies childless; only his author survives in his readers. The moral test of the author's aesthetic philosophy thus ends in an admission of art's dependence on life; neither art nor the artist can ever be truly autonomous.

By contrast, Moore's *Confessions* attempts to show how the spiritual problem of Pater's novel is his unacknowledged confusion of art with life in his demand that art should somehow make up in intensity for the brevity of human existence. Moore, like Gautier, the father of French aestheticism, actually 'demanded a total separation of art from life ... [whereas] Pater saw the one as a "consummate extract" of the other ... [For] the slogan of "art for its own sake" is meant to indicate that it is not subservient to any overriding reality' (Iser, *Pater* 31). Given such a premise, the fatal flaw in Pater's view of art had to be that it served only the moment – art for the sake of heightened experience, instead of art for the sake of art. As his essay on the Mona Lisa further suggested, the observer could indulge a perfect solipsism were he to 'imaginatively *become* those people, as the Mona Lisa "was," among others, "the mother of Helen of Troy." By means of this conception of fulfillment through vicarious experience, Pater sought at once to advance beyond, and yet to retain, his observer's status' (Cohen 114). Such 'an imaginative form of participation' through art would later give 'perfect expression to an impulse in Wilde. Both men [would] cease to distinguish between life and art, action and contemplation ... Wilde and Pater approach art – and history – not for their own sakes, but as substitutes for life, as means to act out, in a sense, impulses that would ordinarily find expression in reality' (Cohen 114).

Moore's strategy for freeing art from life thus adapted some of Pater's methods for confusing the two: though art might offer a viewer the 'multiplied consciousness' (Cohen 115) of a Leda *and* a Saint Anne in the Mona Lisa, it could also become, as it were, a *life* of the artist apart from his actual living of it. For only art 'makes permanent pleasures which, in experience, cannot satisfy because of their fleetingness'; and only art makes permanent a life which has been transformed into an aesthetic object: 'this is the great discovery made by the Irishman after his attempts to balance the appeal of Marius and the challenge of Natural-ism – "Art is eternal!" ' (Farrow 66).

Evidently the primary aim of Moore's satiric portrait of the artist was, 'as he later said, to establish the "aesthetic novel" in England ... By "aesthetic novel" Moore meant a novel free from moral lessons and reflective of the true spirit of the age it grew out of' (Dick 6). Of course, the age that grew out of the book suggests that art for Moore, as later for Wilde, is to have priority over life: '*Confessions* ushered in a decade which was fast to become infamous. The aestheticism, the taste for decadence, the celebration of French poetry and painting, and the irrever-ence and contempt expressed for the powerful villa in *Confessions* all became hallmarks of the 1890s' (Dick, Introduction 16).

Dismissing the ideals of his age, Moore tried as much as Wilde to shock his reader with his aesthetic indifference to conventional morals. For example, there is his opening portrait of the young impressionist: 'I came into the world apparently with a nature like a smooth sheet of wax, bearing no impress, but capable of receiving any; of being moulded into all shapes. Nor am I exaggerating when I say I think that I might equally have been a Pharaoh, an ostler, a pimp, an archbishop, and that in the fulfillment of the duties of each a certain measure of success would have been mine' (49). Even so, 'With his emphasis on the individual, Moore would hardly endorse a theory that stresses the overwhelming influence of the environment to the total extinction of personal force; his formula-tions here owe something to Schopenhauer ... [a]ccording to [whom] will is objectified in the world, which affords a mirror to the man who will look into his life and see the manifestation of self under the various guises presented by experience' (Farrow 60). That the self could be *both* a pimp and an archbishop was as much Moore's Paterian confession of the need for 'a full or complete life, a life of various yet select sensation' (*Marius* I, 142) as it was a satire on the potential hypocrisy of moral refinement. What he became in life was neither, though the *artist* needed to imagine himself containing both of them. But Moore was not pre-pared to go as far as Wilde in conceiving of life as a 'mode of fiction.' Just as his art was not finally a Paterian 'extract' of life – or a means to heighten his impressions – neither was his living a pose or a 'performance.' Rather, the artist's 'life' was itself 'for art's sake,' a new and independent aesthetic creation.

In a sense, what Moore then managed to do was to import a foreign mentality into Victorian traditions of the morally responsible artist which Pater had first outraged in his (later suppressed) 'Conclusion' to *The Renaissance* and had finally tried to mollify in *Marius*. For the narrator of *Confessions*, recently arrived in London from Paris, is really the citizen of a separate nation of art, 'as covered with "fads" as a distinguished foreigner with stars. Naturalism I wore round my neck, Romanticism was pinned over the heart, Symbolism I carried like a toy revolver in my waistcoat pocket, to be used on an emergency' (Moore 149). The result would not seem quite so comic a scant decade later when Oscar Wilde descended into Reading Gaol. But Moore's confession is both less and more aesthetic, the record of the naturalization of an idea of art more than of Wilde's literalization of Pater's idea of 'treat[ing] life in the spirit of art' (cited by Cohen 110). In Moore's 'aesthetic novel,' Gautier and Baudelaire and Balzac become, as it were, fictional British subjects, while Wilde, in his doctrine that 'life imitates art,' seems bent on turning literary history into social reality.

In another sense, however, Moore's portrait of the artist as a young man is a story, very much like Wilde's, of self-creation. Describing his dominant emotion at his father's funeral, Moore says: 'My father's death freed me, and I sprang like a loosened bough up to the light. His death gave me power to create myself – that is to say, to create a complete and absolute self out of the partial self which was all that the restraint of home had permitted; this future self, this ideal George Moore, beckoned me, lured like a ghost; and as I followed the funeral the question, Would I sacrifice this ghostly self, if by so doing I should bring my father back? presented itself without intermission, and I shrank horrified at the answer which I could not crush out of mind' (second English edition of 1889 – Dick, Variorum Notes 196). Moore here anticipates Wilde's advice to a friend to 'Create yourself. Be yourself your poem' (O'Sullivan 223), though the latter would be loath to admit to such influence. For 'Wilde disapproved of artists treating art as if it were merely "a mode of autobiography," and the total absence of Moore's name from his work, even from the list of Realist miscreants in "The Decay of Lying" (a position to which several of Moore's early novels fully entitled him), is perhaps in itself an eloquent denial of influence' (Shewan 106).

In a later statement to Charles Morgan, his biographer, Moore would none the less uphold his own mode of aesthetic autobiography: 'Your story is of a man who made himself because he imagined himself, and you must discover when his imagination went with his nature and when against it' (cited in Chaikin 21). Moore's need to invent an artist whose 'life' could stand apart from his social world, its own autonomous work of art, thus puts him somewhere between the aesthete Pater and the more decadent Wilde, both of whom wanted to blur – if from opposite sides – the formal distinctions between art and life.

The unusually long and precise title of Joyce's *A Portrait of the Artist as a Young Man* (as compared to his customary one- or two-word titles) might now be more legible as an ironic inversion of *Confessions of a Young Man*. For Stephen's own aesthetic ambition parodies Moore's attempt to make his life into a self-existent work of art. Yet recent emphasis in critical theory on the self-reflexive character of all writing would tend to universalize what the decadent once claimed for himself alone: 'Joyce indicates within the text the task performed by every serious writer: the act of revision that is at once the author's writing and reading (as interpretation) of his self-made image in language' (Riquelme 51). In this sort of poststructuralist reading, Joyce's concluding quotation from Stephen's journal becomes an act of narrative doubling 'in which Stephen completes the transforming of the journal into a book that is the simulacrum of Joyce's ... When the character's role as son is over after the final page, his fatherly role as teller is born phoenixlike to return home on the first page. Character transforms himself into artist as the son becomes his own father' (Riquelme 62–3).

Quite unwittingly, the current critical climate duplicates Stephen's ambition without recognizing as objects of parody these familiar decadent doctrines of art and artist:

> The artist, like the God of the creation, remains within or behind or beyond or above his handiwork, invisible, refined out of existence, indifferent, paring his fingernails.
> – Trying to refine them also out of existence, said Lynch.
> (*Portrait* 215)

On the one hand, Joyce is obviously echoing Gustave Flaubert's definition of the artist's impersonality.[1] On the other hand, he exaggerates it, much as Wilde had done, into a doctrine of self-authorization (thus linking *A Portrait* as well with *The Picture of Dorian Gray*). Here, the parody of Flaubert as proto-aesthete and Moore and Wilde as decadents is now played out in the terms of Stephen's reluctance to disappear into the handiwork of his creation; he wants to be like God himself, transcending the whole creation. So, instead of merely separating art from life, or of making life itself into another art form, Dedalus seeks a way to make his life 'outlive' his art.

At least two other factors serve to obscure Joyce's parody of the decadent artist in *A Portrait*: the usual identification of Pater as the source of his 'esthetic impressionism' (Levin 50), and the vexed question of the relation of Stephen's theory to 'the Thomist sources from which it derives' (Beebe 273). One of the better surveys of the development of Joyce's own aesthetics goes so far as to conflate the two (with certain reservations): 'an aesthetic theory formulated on Thomistic principles will clearly result in a theory identical in all important respects with the idea of *l'art pour l'art* if aesthetics is divorced from metaphysics. Joyce could not accept Aquinas' total philosophy of experience and selected only those aspects conducive to his personal use, welding them into an aesthetic of direct contemporary applicability, in harmony with the conditions of his temperament and environment' (Block 184). But, as Kenner first saw, 'Stephen's esthetic is not Joyce's' ('Perspective' 154). While the young rebel claims an authority for himself which is 'a transcendent and primarily spiritual one' (Mahaffey 10), he is – even in revolt – 'an idealistic perfectionist whose unfulfillable hunger is for God' (Kenner, 'Perspective' 172). Thus 'the complicity of such rebellion with the obedience it claims to displace' (Mahaffey 1) implicates him in a

1 Flaubert's description of the god-like artist in his letter of 18 March 1857 to Mlle Leroyer de Chantepie, reads: 'L'artiste doit être dans son oeuvre comme Dieu dans la Création, invisible et tout-puissant, qu'on le sente partout mais qu'on ne le voie pas' (*Correspondance de Gustave Flaubert*, Troisième Série [Paris: Bibliothèque-Charpentier 1913], 80. One should not undervalue Joyce's confidant, Frank Budgen, who 'recounts [that] "of all the great nineteenth century masters of fiction, Joyce held Flaubert in highest esteem," having read every line of his works and committed whole pages of them to memory' (Richard K. Cross, *Flaubert and Joyce: The Rite of Fiction* [Princeton: Princeton Univ. Press 1971], v).

structure of power which he does not really wish to change. For 'it is virtually impossible to criticize such authority without usurping it or reproducing its negative image, and both alternatives perpetuate the very system the critique was designed to uproot' (Mahaffey 23). As a negative image of the God he wants to replace by his own verbal creation, Stephen will then have more than a merely aesthetic interest in theories of stasis.

Of course, the 'priggish, humorless Stephen of the last chapter of the *Portrait*' (Kenner, 'Perspective' 153) is also indebted to aestheticism (not just the decadence) for ideas about stasis in art. Pater, we recall, sought to arrest the stream of sensations in the aesthetic image which could yield the 'fruit of a quickened, multiplied consciousness' by expanding the interval, by 'getting as many pulsations as possible into the given time' (*Renaissance* 238). Stephen also speaks of 'a stasis of the mind' (*Portrait* 208) in front of the work of art in terms which, if different from Pater's, are meant to free him from 'the spiritual problems arising from such an aesthetic conceptualisation of life by revealing the moment as the genesis of longing and anxiety' (Iser, *Pater* 141). The aesthete who says, 'Aristotle has not defined pity and terror. I have,' offers definitions which consistently locate the aesthetic response outside the actual moment of longing or desire: 'Pity is the feeling which arrests the mind in the presence of whatsoever is grave and constant in human sufferings and unites it with the human sufferer. Terror is the feeling which arrests the mind in the presence of whatsoever is grave and constant in human sufferings and unites it with the secret cause' (*Portrait* 204). Of course, such a representation of the aesthetic moment has not gotten outside the moment of longing or desire if what is represented is the structure of the mind itself:

– This hypothesis, Stephen repeated, is the other way out: that, though the same object may not seem beautiful to all people, all people who admire a beautiful object find in it certain relations which satisfy and coincide with the stages themselves of all esthetic apprehension ...

To finish what I was saying about beauty ... the most satisfying relations of the sensible must therefore correspond to the necessary phases of artistic apprehension. Find these and you find the qualities of universal beauty. Aquinas says: *ad pulcritudinem tria requirun-*

tur, integritas, consonantia, claritas. I translate it so: *Three things are needed for beauty, wholeness, harmony and radiance.* Do these correspond to the phases of apprehension? (209, 211–12)

Wilde, who had first dramatized the autonomy of the work of art in Dorian Gray's changing portrait, ventured a related theory of reader-response in 'The Critic as Artist' which Stephen has followed up to a point: 'It is through its very incompleteness,' Wilde had said, 'that Art becomes complete in beauty, and so addresses itself, not to the faculty of recognition nor to the faculty of reason, but to the aesthetic sense alone, which, while accepting both reason and recognition as stages of apprehension, subordinates them both to a pure synthetic impression of the work of art as a whole' (*Intentions* 153). Only the 'stages of apprehension' for Wilde are to be transcended in the final, unifying impressions of the viewing subject, whereas for Stephen the 'necessary phases of artistic apprehension' are to be objectified in both the art object and in the mind of the 'critic.' In Stephen's sense, the art work merely embodies the aesthetic operations of the mind itself, as critics have often noted: 'Joyce secularizes the Thomist insistence on the moral obligations of the artist by demanding instead intellectual or psychological obligations' (Beebe 283). But in another sense, Stephen is even more impressionistic than Wilde who did not deny that 'the meaning of any beautiful created thing is, at least, as much in the soul of him who looks at it, as it was in his soul who wrought it' (*Intentions* 148). For the author disappears entirely in Stephen's formulation, leaving only the mind of the viewer to complete the sum of the 'qualities of universal beauty' found in the aesthetic object. In other words, the 'apprehending' mind becomes, in the absence of any creator, both the source and end of 'the supreme quality of beauty' which has nothing to do with 'a light from some other world.' All 'that is literary talk,' as Stephen says. 'I understand it so' (*Portrait* 213).

Joyce none the less signals his own parody of Wilde's critical impressionism by hinting that the theory of stasis might be a joke which is lost on the young 'artist' speaking of 'the luminous silent stasis of esthetic pleasure, a spiritual state very like to that cardiac condition which the Italian physiologist Luigi Galvani, using a phrase almost as beautiful as Shelley's, called the enchantment of the heart' (213). In fact, Galvani's 'enchantment' had prompted a 'cardiac condition' in an experimental frog by inducing an electrical current between the two ends of a nerve. And so the self-enclosing circuit of Stephen's aesthetic theory promises to be 'enchanting' in art much in the same way it had been in (frog) life.

Stephen's ulterior purpose, of course, is like Wilde's, to free art from any moral considerations whatsoever: 'You see I use the word *arrest*. I mean that the tragic emotion is static. Or rather the dramatic emotion is. The feelings excited by improper art are kinetic, desire or loathing. Desire urges us to possess, to go to something; loathing urges us to abandon, to go from something. These are kinetic emotions. The arts which excite them, pornographical or didactic, are therefore improper arts. The esthetic emotion (I use the general term) is therefore static. The mind is arrested and raised above desire and loathing' (205). In the published fragment of *Stephen Hero* (1944), Stephen had still been forced to face overt moral objections to his project:

> – Your argument is not so conclusive as it seems, said the President after a short pause. However I am glad to see that your attitude towards your subject is so genuinely serious. At the same time you must admit that this theory you have – if pushed to its logical conclusion – would emancipate the poet from all moral laws. I notice too that in your essay you allude satirically to what you call the 'antique' theory – the theory, namely, that the drama should have special ethical aims, that it should instruct, elevate, and amuse. I suppose you mean Art for Art's sake.
> – I have only pushed to its logical conclusion the definition Aquinas has given of the beautiful. (*Hero* 100)

Yet, 'when, in the process of revision, the audience of many becomes the single auditor Lynch,' the reader still cannot assume that 'the ethical objections disappear altogether' (Beebe 279). For the 'ethical objections' are now at least anticipated by the dean of studies who, in asking Stephen, 'When may we expect to have something from you on the esthetic question?' (*Portrait* 186), goes on to limn the crucial distinctions that the young aesthete will fail to make: 'And to distinguish between the beautiful and the sublime, the dean added. To distinguish between moral beauty and material beauty. And to inquire what kind of beauty is proper to each of the various arts. These are some interesting points we might take up' (189–90). Stephen's refusal to take up these 'interesting points' does not invalidate any one of them so much as it reveals the partial nature of his dogmatic theory.

His later attempt to distinguish among 'the various arts' – but not among the kinds of beauty 'proper to each' – further exposes his theoretical ignorance as well as his contradictory logic, both of which render absurd the 'psychological obligations' of stasis. For in an apparent *non sequitur*, Stephen refers to the work of the eighteenth-century German aesthetician, Gotthold Ephraim Lessing, presumably wanting to have the last word on an absent interlocutor: ' Goethe and Lessing, [Donovan had said], have written a lot on that subject, the classical school and the romantic school and all that. The *Laocoon* interested me very much when I read it. Of course it is idealistic, German, ultraprofound' (211). Stephen's subsequent act of oneupmanship exposes his ignorance of the standard definition of the laws of perception which are proper to both the temporal and the spatial arts: 'Lessing, said Stephen, should not have taken a group of statues to write of. The art, being inferior, does not present the forms I spoke of distinguished clearly one from another' (214). Since his own aesthetics is based upon the process of perception in aesthetic experience, this ignorance of Lessing's perceptual theory can only be ironic. For Lessing writes about 'a group of statues,' as his subtitle points out, precisely to essay 'the Limits of Painting and Poetry.'

To complete the dramatic irony, Joyce makes the succession of forms which Stephen lays out – the progression of the lyrical, epical, and dramatic from the personal to the impersonal – a further reminder of the fundamental laws of aesthetic perception: 'The rule is this, that succession in time is the province of the poet, co-existence in space that of the artist' (Lessing 109). The literary arts are thus inescapably temporal, 'composed of a succession of words proceeding through time; and it follows that literary form, to harmonize with the essential quality of its medium, must be based primarily on some form of narrative sequence' (Frank 223). Since time is the inevitable medium of all language, the theory of 'aesthetic stasis' in poetry has to be a contradiction in terms.

Sculpture, on the other hand, can never represent successive actions since it is the nature of the medium to freeze the moment in space. At best, sculpture 'can use but a single moment of an action, and must therefore choose the most pregnant one, the one most suggestive of what has gone before and what is to follow' (Lessing 92). But this is merely to say that, wherever action is represented, even visual art will imply a narrative sequence. Thus, in terms of viewer response, not even frozen forms can induce an aesthetic stasis but must imply a before and after.

The villanelle which Stephen, the apprentice poet writes, is one such attempt to 'freeze' an emotion, to arrest a form of speech which must nevertheless go on speaking:

> *Are you not weary of ardent ways,*
> *Lure of the fallen seraphim?*
> *Tell no more of enchanted days.*

And yet the succession of words denies the possibility of formal 'arrest' to which the poet aspires:

> *Our broken cries and mournful lays*
> *Rise in one eucharistic hymn.*
> *Are you not weary of ardent ways?*
>
> *While sacrificing hands upraise*
> *The chalice flowing to the brim,*
> *Tell no more of enchanted days.*
>
> *And still you hold our longing gaze*
> *With languorous look and lavish limb!*
> *Are you not weary of ardent ways?*
> *Tell no more of enchanted days.* (223)

The careful sequence of rising cries and upraised hands, culminating in the speaker's longing gaze, punctures the whole pretence of artistic renunciation.

If the before and after of the *lyric* 'narrative' reveal the speaker's pose as little more than 'sour grapes,' the before and after of the *dramatic* narrative expose a poet writing in anger and in lust: 'Rude brutal anger routed the last lingering instant of ecstasy from his soul. It broke up violently her fair image and flung the fragments on all sides' (220). We are hardly surprised, then, that his final gesture of refusal in the quatrain should come in a rush of erotic desire: 'A glow of desire kindled again his soul and fired and fulfilled all his body. Conscious of his desire she was waking from odorous sleep, the temptress of his villanelle. Her eyes, dark and with a look of languor, were opening to his eyes. Her nakedness yielded to him, radiant, warm, odorous and lavishlimbed, enfolded him like a shining cloud ...' (223). Obviously, his fantasy reveals the poet as being anything but weary of 'ardent ways.' Neither is the poem so weary; there is nothing in it to support his claim of being at rest from '*languorous look and lavish limb!*' As Kenner says, it is 'a poem of which Wilde might perhaps have acknowledged the paternity' ('Cubist' 183). For everything about it smacks of the decadents' self-conscious pose, much less of 'stylistic qualities' which 'bring their poetry to a trembling standstill, a quiet hush as the thin lines whisper by' (Trehearne 16). The following remarks on a poem by Dowson could just as well refer to Stephen's production: 'The style itself seems to have achieved a superlative tension, so that one drop more of despair would collapse the whole thing in upon itself in utter failure. A situation roughly similar to Rossetti's, the passing of some beautiful beloved, produces an entirely different style, the only end of which is to express pain, emptiness, and bitterness' (Trehearne 17).

The 'artist's' parodic role in Joyce's decadent drama – 'dramatic' because impersonal, removed from the character of the author – is more fully exposed in his response to the actual world: 'His mind, when wearied of its search for the essence of beauty amid the spectral words of Aristotle or Aquinas, turned often for its pleasure to the dainty songs of the Elizabethans. His mind, in the vesture of a doubting monk, stood often in shadow under the windows of that age, to hear the grave and mocking music of the lutenists or the frank laughter of waistcoateers until a laugh too low, a phrase tarnished by time, of chambering and false honour, stung his monkish pride and drove him on from his lurking-place' (176). 'Since the transience of beauty, the brevity of impressions, is largely responsible for the Decadent's misery, a hatred and fear of natural processes, of inescapable decay, is also central to decadent literature' (Trehearne 15). Evidently Stephen is one of those decadents who can take no real pleasure in life. He is dead to the world, but also cut off from finding life in the stasis of an art which can prevent life's transience only by transfixing it.

If, therefore, 'Joyce modeled, as seems likely, the name of the hero of his novel on the pseudonym of the fallen Oscar Wilde [Sebastian Melmoth],' he seems to have been 'invoking a Wildean parallel for Dublin

readers to recognize' (Kenner, 'Cubist' 176). For Stephen ironically
champions 'the creed of beleaguered beauty' in the very city which 'had
already extruded the arch-bohemian of a generation, Oscar Wilde, who
had completed the Icarian myth by falling forever' (176). The later
Icarus's refusal of a moral purpose in art may link him even more
profoundly with the fallen archangel of the decadence. Speaking of
Wilde's dialogue, 'The Critic as Artist,' Frank Kermode concludes: 'The
object of the artist is to produce pleasure, though pleasure is a somewhat
inadequate term; better to say that he has nothing to do with anything
useful. "All the arts are immoral except those baser forms of sensual or
didactic art that seek to excite to action of evil or of good." The word
"immoral" here represents a coarsening of the aesthetic in the interests of
paradox; but the descent of the idea is obvious enough, and Wilde is
concerned, in modern terms, to distinguish art from propaganda and
entertainment, and to hang on it the sign "No road through to action".
His opinion is exactly that of Stephen Dedalus in The Portrait' (Kermode 44–5). Ironically, however, Stephen wants to view his pending
departure from Ireland in terms of 'the white arms of roads' (Portrait
252) which seem to loom as another 'road through to action.' For, as his
diary concludes, 'I go to encounter for the millionth time the reality of
experience and to forge in the smithy of my soul the uncreated conscience
of my race' (253) – in seeming forgetfulness of his previous denial of a
didactic purpose for art.

In a further contradiction, the aesthete of stasis still dreams of soaring
free of an earthbound world that would forever arrest and fix his identity: 'When the soul of a man is born in this country there are nets flung
at it to hold it back from flight. You talk to me of nationality, language,
religion. I shall try to fly by those nets' (203). At this point, he is most
clearly identified with George Moore who, in his Confessions, had
claimed to be 'not an indifferent spectator, but an enthusiast, striving
heart and soul to identify himself with his [exile's] environment, to shake
himself free from race and language and to recreate himself as it were in
the womb of a new nationality, assuming its ideals, its morals, and its
modes of thought' (129). Stephen, the self-created citizen of an autonomous province of art, will also try to have it both ways, though 'the final
chapter is to image painstakingly the spiritual pride and autonomy that
are to come to comprehensive grief in Ulysses' (Kenner, 'Perspective'
172).

The final chapter also 'makes it clear that Stephen's struggle is the struggle between an individual and his context, a struggle that also defines the process of reading' (Mahaffey 97). And so the ultimate difference between the author and his creation proves quite profound. For 'Joyce represents authority as inherently double, a doubleness that takes as its two poles an individualistic model of authority on the one hand, and a communal model on the other' (Mahaffey 13). In his brilliant exposé of the authoritarian values of both the decadent *and* his rejected society, Joyce is the only artist in the novel who could reasonably hope to 'forge in the smithy of [his] soul the uncreated conscience of [his] race.' But he might do so only because 'His authority is provisional ... his every point contingent upon its ability to engage readers – living in one sense and unliving in another, like Joyce himself – in a mutually animating dialogue' (Mahaffey 5). Here, at last, the solipsistic and static 'authority' of Stephen's aestheticism gives way in Joyce's own work to an interactive process.

The first section of this study, 'Confessions of a Self-Made Man,' examines the work of three writers whose fictional autobiographies are on the verge of turning into artist-novels. In a sense, each of these writers maintains as deep a kinship with nineteenth-century realists as with twentieth-century formalists or postmodernists; not one of them even shows much sign of the direct influence of Pater's or Moore's or Joyce's 'confessional' aestheticism. And yet the one who was actually formed in the period of late nineteenth-century decadence, the German writer F.P. Greve, did manage to assimilate such an aesthetics from translating, not to say emulating, the life and art of Oscar Wilde, that other literary son of Walter Pater. F.P. Grove, the pseudonymous immigrant to Canada, obviously had more compelling reasons than Greve's own social and literary imitations to invent himself anew. Yet Grove's early literary career in Canada was mostly preparation for his ultimate, if undetected, *Künstlerroman, In Search of Myself* (1946). In fact, both his more autobiographical *A Search for America: The Odyssey of an Immigrant* (1927) and his 'realist' *Settlers of the Marsh* (1925) are displaced confessions which serve, in a way that concerned neither Wilde nor Moore, to justify the self-invention of his fictional autobiography. Of course, the 'real' confession proves to be a fiction in much the same sense that Edwin Dayne, later renamed George Moore, is a fictional invention of the writer

George Moore. Still, the need to justify himself leads Grove to confess himself as much as to translate himself into a self-existent *objet d'art* like Wilde or Moore.

The fictional autobiography of Dunstan Ramsay in Davies's *Fifth Business* (1970) is a similar *apologia*, though it is made by a narrator, not an author, who seeks through self-invention to be free of any overriding reality. Ramsay's fondness for magic and his faith in miracles suggest an ultimate longing, like Wilde or Moore's, to inhabit an exclusive world of art. And yet the various forms of confession which he uses to invent an autonomous self are inherently contradictory. Frank confession on the model of St Augustine and poetic self-expression on the model of Rousseau turn into an *apologia pro vita sua* which fails to paper over his lasting guilt for what amounts to a terribly destructive aestheticism. The example of John Henry Newman's *Apologia* finally exposes what, for Davies, is wrong with the modern devotee of the *Arabian Nights*. For Ramsay's own subjectivism is actually much closer to the decadents than it is to Newman's; Padre Blazon, Ramsay's Jesuit mentor, sketches a contrary 'egoism,' like Newman's, which would make the self more like a ground of apprehension of something beyond the self. The magian world-view, which begins in Paterian aestheticism, is thus exposed as an aesthetics descended from Wilde's 'The Decay of Lying,' while the autobiographer's self-portrait comes more and more to resemble Wilde's picture of Dorian Gray.

Margaret Laurence's successful retreat to the Victorian era of her grandparents in *The Stone Angel* (1964) suggests that she too is closer to the nineteenth century, in most respects, than to the aesthetic world-view which follows from the period of the moderns. *The Stone Angel* is not even an artist-novel as such, though in many ways it anticipates and even transcends *The Diviners* (1974). Once again, it reveals a fictional autobiography on the point of turning into the *Künstlerroman*, for the narrator, who compulsively tells her story to *herself*, is the one who longs to be a 'self-made man' like her father. Hagar's motive is hardly aesthetic, however, and her particular form of confession is not even equipped to question her own methods of telling. All the same, her need to invent an autonomous self is born of her refusal to be mortal like her mother and, thus, to be subject to nature. She is even driven by the same desire for freedom as an aesthete like Pater, if for less obvious reasons than his. Since '*l'art pour l'art* means the triumph of art over reality' (Iser, *Pater*

35), Hagar's 'confession' shares most basically in this aesthetic hope to master death itself. Only the presence of an unacknowledged truth – Hagar's refusal of life out of her fear of death – gives design to her life in a way that the more programmatic 'confession' of the writer in *The Diviners* cannot. Morag's story of the aesthetic processes of her life and of her writing turns out to be rather more static and closed, a more modernist version of Pater's idea of 'autonomous art' (Iser 61). As Linda Hutcheon has also noted, Laurence's final novel reveals 'more a *modernist* search for order in the face of moral and social chaos than a *postmodern* urge to trouble, to question, to make both problematic and provisional any such desire for order or truth through the powers of the human imagination' (*Postmodern* 2). And so Hagar's 'confession,' unlike the ostensibly more aesthetic one made through Morag, the author's artistic double, produces a more dynamic type of artist than the actual *Künstlerroman* with which Laurence ended her career as a novelist.

The later sections of this study, 'Portraits of the Modernist' and 'Snapshots of the Parodist,' are focused on genuine artist-novels which have been shaped by the ethos of both the modern and postmodern eras. Though a postmodernist such as George Bowering might delight in tarring 'modernist realist fiction' (29) with one brush, modernism was hardly a movement which was devoted to the aims of realism. The greatest single limitation of modernist aesthetics, we now realize, was its concretization of Pater's idea of the autonomy of art, of the notion that it could 'expand the interval' by arresting time in the aesthetic object. And yet Joyce's *Portrait*, as we have also seen, works against many of the assumptions about modernist art which have been extracted from it. Stephen's theory of aesthetic stasis identifies him and him alone with the solipsism of autonomous form, while Joyce's ironies align him with the satiric – and healing – arts. Even Stephen's own mother 'prays now, she says, that I may learn in my own life and away from home and friends what the heart is and what it feels' (*Portrait* 252–3). But Joyce leaves the reader to learn from the fall of his latter-day Icarus.

Formally, Sinclair Ross's *As For Me and My House* (1941) takes over where *A Portrait* left off: in the diary of an aesthete who records her total alienation from her social world. Morally and aesthetically, however, Ross's novel reverses the role of the artist in the *Portrait*, since the writer in exile is alienated from her husband and their community precisely because his art expresses a sympathy she refuses to feel. In two essays, I undertake to show how the 'confession' of the diary offers another version of aesthetic self-creation – since the diarist's form requires her to impose a 'plot' upon the future and so to play God with events – while the modernist 'formalism' of the preacher serves to literalize Joyce's figure of the 'priest of eternal imagination,' making him the servant of his people. As the minister says to his wife, 'Religion and art are ... almost the same thing anyway. Just different ways of taking a man out of himself, bringing him to the emotional pitch that we call ecstasy or rapture. They're both a rejection of the material, common-sense world for one that's illusory, yet somehow more important' (112). Because we have to 'read' the work of two artists in this text, the confessional mode of the diary, with its own questions about the sincerity and morality of the narrator, looks not only backward to forms of confession, but ahead to a whole new set of questions about the morality and sincerity of the artist. Finally, both the irony of Mrs Bentley's technique as a professed realist and the formalist 'religion' of Philip's drawings help to transpose some of the aesthetic issues raised by Joyce into terms which not only question the self-sufficiency of modernist form but also redefine the relations between the artist and his community and, ultimately, between art and religion.

Ernest Buckler's *The Mountain and the Valley* (1952), which has already been mentioned as a parody of Thomas Wolfe in particular, and of American transcendentalism in general, explores in similar terms the defining problems of the artist-novel – the artist's use of language and his sense of himself in relation to his audience – both of which reveal why David Canaan has to fail. Buckler's novel adds another dimension to the shadow cast by Joyce's *Portrait* over the whole aesthetic façade of modernism, since Wolfe's novel, as the author himself confesses, slavishly follows the Joycean pattern of the artist as a sensitive, wounded creature in conflict with his society. In this respect, *The Mountain and the Valley* treats romantic icons quite as iconoclastically as Joyce's *Portrait* ever did, while parodying the master's 'illegitimate' offspring. For David Canaan's moment of 'aesthetic arrest' on the top of Altamont actually leads to cardiac arrest – to the sort of 'enchantment of the heart' which Dedalus had ironically associated with Luigi Galvani.

Lastly, but perhaps most eloquently, Gabrielle Roy's *The Road Past Altamont* (1966) gives us, at the very close of the modernist era, an equivalent of the imagist novel, achieved early on in the short-story sequences of Anderson's *Winesburg, Ohio* (1919) and Hemingway's *In Our Time* (1925) – both descended directly from Joyce's artist-novel – but rarely knit into longer forms. Pound's imagism and Proust's method of photographic juxtaposition are also transformed in Roy's novel into a method of tapestry whereby the frozen moment and the flow of time are both made 'eternally' present. In a temporal succession of figures, the present gives the past a voice with which to speak in the most personal of terms: the female modernist learns that 'We give birth in turn to the one who gave us birth when finally, sooner or later, we draw her into our self' (*Altamont* 129). By contrast, the 'impersonal' male modernist can only imagine himself as being 'a shred of platinum' or the 'catalyst' (Eliot 54) between past and present, and so impervious to touch.

The third section of this study, 'Snapshots of the Parodist,' brings together the influences of photography and parody as defining features of the postmodern artist-novel. Here, a typically modernist self-consciousness about art has been largely reshaped by technological developments. George Bowering has most clearly grasped how the video camera, for those who are photographically literate (i.e., are not just photographic realists), has 'changed the way we look at the world' (Bowering 81). Evidently the camcorder not only changes our epistemology (82), but helps as well to put the reader in the place of the author:

> Look at it this way. You are watching television, & the sun bumps out from behind the afternoon's cloud, & now you see your reflection & the reflection of nearby objects on the screen along with the electronic figures there. This is slightly post-modern. If you pull the blinds or turn off the picture, you will just get the modern.
>
> If you had a video camera on your shoulder, ah, reader, you would be writing this next word.   (82–3)

The reader, it seems, is presumed to have entered into the 'position' of the author in postmodern writing, to have put his eye to the viewfinder in the place of an absent artist. And so the writer, if he exists at all, does so only to empower the reader. You want to know how it's done? The postmodern writer smiles his most conspiratorial smile. Well, then, let me tell (not show) you, for, let me tell you, those old-fashioned dramatic methods will never let you see who's really in charge. Why, you, dear reader, of course.

At the beginning of this same essay ('Modernism Could Not Last Forever'), Bowering betrays another sort of hypocrisy in the literary politics of postmodernism: 'Among serious novelists who garner both solemn essays on their work & listings on the lit parade are Alice Munro, Margaret Laurence, & Margaret Atwood, good writers all, who tell the normal realist story of sensitive child growing up to be disillusioned but wisely maladjusted adult, the most personal proof of cause & effect' (77). What might be called the surrealism of photography in *Lives of Girls and Women* (1971) and the mocking, doubling strategies of *Who Do You Think You Are?* (1978) – by which the stories begin to question their own form – show Munro to be as postmodern as Bowering himself, though her 'narcissistic' fictions turn out to be far less flattering to narcissistic tellers. In fact, her frequent recourse to deconstructive strategies of undecidability shows up a character trying to escape self-knowledge.

While the *telling* in both these 'snapshots' of the artist is largely epistemological, Munro's quotidian (and very female) content still shows that the 'how' of knowing must be balanced by the integrity and the independence of what is known. Here, the folk-saying could be updated to read: *A son is a son till he writes his own life; a daughter's a daughter even though she's a wife.* For Munro's female metafictions work, at their deepest level, to interrogate an ideology which is quintessentially male in its rejection of influence.[2] To a daughter, the inescapable (because shared) body of the mother makes it a much more immediate, and less selfish, model of the creative act; she can never distance herself from the poetic 'corpus' of the mother without doing violence to herself. Munro's scepticism thus seems to be open-ended enough to question her own motives for scepticism, and to offer, in a sophisticated parody of metafictional strategies, a remarkable feminist challenge to the whole project of male postmodernism.

Once again, literary history serves to remind us that contemporary theories of art are heir to late nineteenth-century aesthetics. For the

2 In *A Map of Misreading* (New York: Oxford 1975), Harold Bloom elaborates his Oedipal reading of the 'anxiety of influence' in spatial terms. The idea that 'Milton re-writes Spenser so as to *increase the distance* between his poetic father and himself' (128) actually depends upon a prior 'misreading' (or repression) of the biological experience of continuity which, though it may be an overt fact of life for mothers and daughters, is more easily denied by sons and (putative) fathers.

beginning of Pater's break with Victorian conceptions of art was his 'reaction against a dogmatism that imposes a structure on the world' (Iser, *Pater* 16). To him, 'The sceptical, relative spirit' offered 'a countervailing force' (17) which might keep open 'a vastly wider range of connections than the absolute, which constantly imposes restrictive patterns on what is' (15). Better yet, 'the quality of the interesting as a subversive force against hierarchies of any kind is that it seeks to rescue all human possibilities from being subsumed under overriding concepts' (40). As Linda Hutcheon says in a very different context, 'This phenomenon does betray a loss of faith in what were once the certainties, the "master" narratives of our liberal humanist culture. But that loss need not be a debilitating one. In postmodern literature, as in architecture, it has ... been marked by a move away from fixed products and structures to open cultural processes and events' (*Postmodern* 23).

And yet Pater, a century before, was already moving in essay form away from 'fixed products' to open-ended processes: 'In presenting intimate observations, inarticulate emotions, fleeting impressions and disjointed observations, the essay appears to be the form of formlessness, which makes it necessary for Pater to contrast it with the treatise as a paradigm of the closed form. The essay, then, is a form which deconstructs itself in order to represent open-endedness, unrelatedness and endlessness as facts of experiential reality' (Iser, *Pater* 19). So, too, in Pater's fiction, it has been recently argued, we find a more familiar contemporary manner: 'When Pater's youthful readers (the novel was addressed to the young men possibly misled by the Conclusion) encountered in Marius's truant reading of Apuleius's *Golden Book* a mirror of their own activity of reading and responding to Pater's novel, the text is [sic] clearly depicting the process of its own making and of its being read' (Monsman, *Autobiography* 52).

Again like the postmoderns, Pater in his writing does not 'propose to be openly autobiographical, to allow himself what would be, even were it justified, a very painful form of direct self-revelation. Instead, he discarded conventional mimetic assumptions in favor of a reflexive textual model' (Monsman, *Autobiography* 6). In that sense, he 'succeeded, by heroic force of intellect spurred on by the most painful of psychological urgencies, in giving a new emphasis to the point of view involved in the act of artistic creation; that is, to the processes and problems of consciousness and to the activities of reading and composition as themselves the subjects of fiction' (Monsman 4–5). Such a sentence virtually sums up the aesthetic attitude of that unlikely studhorse Pater, Robert Kroetsch.

Badlands (1975) has to date been understood largely as a version of the artist who must parody, and ultimately destroy, the sources of her art to be free of a dead tradition. Yet, in this one novel at least, Kroetsch's view of history entails more than simple rejection or even deconstruction of the past. The final stages of the female narrator's thrice-told story (so different from his male-voiced novels) turn to parodic synthesis and even to sympathetic re-creation of her inherited documents, just as Kroetsch himself rewrites through parody Sinclair Ross's *As For Me and My House*.

Likewise, the artist-novel which is most explicitly indebted to Pater, Moore, and Wilde – Timothy Findley's *Famous Last Words* (1981) – turns to the re-creation of private documents in the narrator's very public last testament. But Findley's novel, which is also a confession writ large as well as a parody of Pound's *Hugh Selwyn Mauberley*, is a less happy instance of work which fails to transform its models. Findley's Mauberley, as his 'prose kinema' reveals, is another decadent son of Oscar Wilde, much like Pound's original impressionist, who is temperamentally unable to distinguish between beauty and truth. And so the moral confusions of the novel make it a belated, if self-nominated, target of Pound's own great parody, one final sign that successful 'immigration' is no more easily achieved in literary terms than it is in the social and political world.

A word about principles of selection is by now overdue. *Caveat lector* will have to do. For these are not disinterested readings, though they are offered with all the 'objectivity' that a man who is also a writer and a university teacher may offer. The essays in the first section were written (and appeared elsewhere) before I fully realized the design of a book in the making. In that sense, each chapter maintains its local focus, though I am hopeful that earlier sections of this 'Introduction' might resonate in the gaps between succeeding chapters, much as a polyphonic novel can be made to echo in its vocal stops, in the speaking silence among its competing voices.

Each of the nine authors discussed shows signs, if only in a single narrative, of upholding that most traditional (and imperilled) of Delphic and Socratic maxims, know thyself. I confess my bias for this branch of the humanist endeavour not as an anachronism but as the necessary response both to a series of texts and to an aesthetic movement which continues to exploit the self-reflexive possibilities inherent in Pater's kind of subjectivism. Ironically (and somewhat portentously), much post-structuralist thinking denies any possibility of self-knowledge on onto-logical, as well as epistemological grounds, maintaining that the only known self is a linguistic self. Especially in autobiography, 'the very project of writing, the act of signification itself, alienates the writing self from his subject. Roland Barthes goes so far as to say that there is no referent in the field of the subject; according to Barthes, the self, so called, can at most be written, but not represented' (Martens 40). In all of this, the Delphic wisdom should sound more urgently than ever.

In fiction, the first-person pronoun is increasingly recognized as a shifty piece of business, if only because of the 'semiotic' rereading of Freud by Jacques Lacan and others. Lacan's radical decentring of the subject has re-situated the ego within a largely unconscious discourse: 'In the end, there exists a kind of mirror relation between the subject-individual and the decentred subject, the subject beyond the subject, the subject of the unconscious' (Lacan 210). In consequence, the literary text itself becomes a textual unconscious – a linguistic system – born out of an 'ongoing process of marking and supressing differences, a process which, as Ferdinand de Saussure and others have suggested, is the basis of signification' (Con Davis 247). And so the ego, or the speaking 'subject, in this semiotic model is not a "thing" but an "inscription" in a psychic (and linguistic) discourse – in effect, one of the messages the unconscious subject sends itself' (Con Davis 221). As Lacan's reading of Poe's 'The Purloined Letter' shows, the text (or in this case the letter) is for each of the characters 'his unconscious. It is his unconscious with all of its consequences, that is to say that at each point in the symbolic circuit, each of them becomes someone else' (Lacan 197).

Even if psychic identity were to prove so fluid, the project of constituting the self in and through language would not be free of ethical criticism. Lacan himself cannot avoid speaking in terms of the psychoanalyst's responsibility 'to assist the subject in the revelation of himself to himself' (Lacan 206), though the *self* is no longer synonymous with ego-consciousness. Of course, literary works in this century have long portrayed the self-deceptions involved in first-person utterance, even giving rise to a formalist preoccupation with 'unreliable narrators.' Davies's narrator in *Fifth Business* offers a most blatant example of the way in which a psychologically sophisticated man masks himself as both a saint and a devil to forestall a 'revelation of himself to himself.' Dunstan Ramsay is even intent on inventing a self that is free of all antecedents – free, that is, of a controlling 'author,' whether that should happen to be a biological mother or some other 'language' of his begetting – although the strain of supporting and confirming such self-invention is what finally leads to his schizophrenic evasion of responsibility. Human beings, Davies implies, have to be responsible for their actions, no matter what new forms of determinism are offered in the place of Calvinist theology. Actions, as the old folk-saying has it, still speak louder than words. And so the *act* of writing must itself be louder than the words, must presume a writing subject of the grammatical action, no matter what written *mise-en-abyme* reflects an infinite regress of the reader in the place of the absent author. To assume differently would be to make language the author, as well as the subject and object, of the story. Or, in terms borrowed by the structuralists from de Saussure, it would be to make *langue* the actual speaker of *parole*, to find a kind of linguistic determinism overriding any possible speech act.

Given my bias, I am unable to deal adequately with books which are wholly consumed by doubt or by the treacheries of language. Even the metafictions I have chosen are *centred* in this problem of self-knowledge. Other novels still testify to various strengths in the *Künstlerroman* as an evolving type of Canadian writing: A.M. Klein's *The Second Scroll* (1951), for example, or Elizabeth Smart's *By Grand Central Station I Sat Down and Wept* (1945); Bill Harlow's *Scann* (1972); Audrey Thomas's *Latakia* (1979); Michael Ondaatje's *Coming Through Slaughter* (1976) and *Running in the Family* (1982); Clark Blaise's *Lunar Attractions* (1979); and George Bowering's *Burning Water* (1980), to name the most obvious. But many of these novels would require a different book, given more to poststructuralist problems of language than to the problem of self-knowledge.

While the list could be extended to include Jack Hodgins's *The Invention of the World* (1977), Bill Percy's *Painted Ladies* (1983), Guy Vanderhaeghe's *My Present Age* (1984), or even Margaret Atwood's *Lady Oracle* (1976), I have not tried to write a history of the *Künstlerroman* in English-Canadian fiction. What follows, then, cannot be fairly termed a 'tradition' of the artist-novel in Canadian fiction. It is more like a narrative 'before and after' that I have chosen for myself, a sort of larger critical 'novel' whose 'plot' is made up of other novels to represent the continuity of humanist values in work even by postmodernists like Robert Kroetsch. Of course, this is to see Kroetsch as he is rarely represented (though his work is large enough and diverse enough to contain such normally hostile contraries). It is also to discover 'humanism' in the very citadel of Canadian postmodernism, a mode whose imperializing ideology is part and parcel of a new (though rarely self-effacing) anti-humanism. As such, my selection is open to the criticism that Solecki makes of Metcalf as a writer-critic for attempting 'to restructure the canon in order to make it accommodate his own writing and, incidentally, to assert the primacy or superiority of his own genre' (Solecki 222).

The final essay in 'Post-Script' was written at the invitation of Birk Sproxton for *Trace: Prairie Writers on Writing* (1986) as a way of locating myself against various 'schools' of influence. But I find that its argument still makes an intelligible, if elliptical, conclusion to a critical book which at that time was mostly unwritten. In a sense, 'After Postmodernism' manages to articulate the goal to which this verbal fiction has been striving all along.

Part One

CONFESSIONS OF
A SELF-MADE MAN

2

The Mask of Dorian Gray
in the Novels of F.P. Grove

In his preface to the fourth edition (1939) of *A Search For America* Grove writes, 'Why ... did I choose a pseudonym for my hero? Well, while a pseudonym ostensibly dissociates the author from his creation, it gives him at the same time an opportunity to be even more personal than, in the conditions of our present-day civilization, it would be either safe or comfortable to be were he speaking in the first person, unmasked' (xviii).

Grove's need of a mask did not, of course, spring just from present-day social conditions. As everyone knows by now, Frederick Philip Grove was not the Swede he claimed to be, but the German writer Felix Paul Greve. In view of his past, he was not likely to feel safe or comfortable speaking to even his Canadian wife unmasked. But Greve, alias Grove, alias Phil Branden, was also articulating in his second American novel an aesthetic doctrine which was crucial to the larger relationship of life and art in his work. In Wilde's *Intentions* (1891) which Greve translated into German in 1902 (Spettigue 77), he found the decadent doctrine which he was to translate, a quarter century and a whole new continent removed from his crimes, into the fiction which had by then become a mode of life for him. But 'The Critic as Artist' only supplied the gist of his epigraph for the fourth edition of *A Search for America*: 'Man is least himself when he talks in his own person. Give him a mask, and he will tell you the truth' (*Intentions* 191). For his life afforded him better material yet in which to find the truth of masks.

Wilde, like his unknown follower, had also been inclined to use 'art as the medium for simultaneous self-revelation and concealment,' though, lacking Greve's obscure origins and a secret identity, he could only deny, as he would do in the 'Preface' to *Dorian Gray*, an explicitly 'autobio-graphical theory' of art (Cohen 130). But in critical essays such as 'The Decay of Lying,' he had already developed a strategy to free his persona from his historical person, and to free art 'from life so that it [could] be free from its attendant moral claims' (Cohen 149). This strategy involved 'a reversal of the mimetic theory' (Cohen 149) in order to make art into the supreme reality and to make life imitate art. The cultured liar could thus be himself the model for an art that was prior to nature, that could keep the upper hand on life without descending into the 'true decadence' (*Intentions* 22) of realism. 'We don't want to be harrowed and dis-gusted,' Wilde said, 'with an account of the doings of the lower orders' (14). Life itself had therefore to become its own mode of aesthetic creation. Says Wilde, '[W]hat is interesting about people in good society ... is the mask that each one of them wears, not the reality that lies behind the mask. It is a humiliating confession, but we are all of us made out of the same stuff' (15). Thus for Wilde, art redresses any failure of nature to complete itself; art offers life the highest models for its own expression and reinvention. In consequence, 'Life imitates Art far more than Art imitates Life' (*Intentions* 56).

Douglas Spettigue has shown just how much of Grove's 'life' imitated the art and life of diverse writers such as Wilde, Stefan George, and André Gide (190–4). The old image of Grove the realist has all but given way to a decadent or modernist portrait of the artist. More recently, Walter Pache offers a fascinating view of Grove as a dilettante out-Wildeing Wilde himself. Where the latter merely 'regarded life as an aesthetic experience ... Felix Paul Greve created "Frederick Philip Grove" to carry out an even more radical artistic experiment with real-ity. His struggle to create Canadian literature single-handedly has the makings of a decadent attempt to subordinate the real world to an artistic concept.' Yet neither Grove's work nor that of Wilde should allow us to conclude that 'in inventing a new identity for himself, Grove turns life into art, casting off all restrictions which his own past, the historical situation, and current literary conventions would have placed on his existence' (Pache 190). For Grove is careful to maintain the paradox that a mask allows him to speak more personally than he could do in the first person. He is not as free of the past as a postmodern critic would have him; the world, it seems, is not so easily invented.

Paradox informs Wilde's own concept of the mask: 'A Truth in art,' he wrote in 'The Truth of Masks,' 'is that whose contradictory is also true. And just as it is only in art-criticism, and through it, that we can apprehend the Platonic theory of ideas, so it is only in art-criticism, and through it, that we can realise Hegel's system of contraries. The truths of metaphysics are the truths of masks' (*Intentions* 269–70). In his essay 'Oscar Wilde und das Drama,' Felix Paul Greve observed a similar play of contraries in what André Gide also called the 'mask,' or what Greve called *Gestalt* (or form), more narrowly yet, the 'symbol' (Greve 18).[1] Greve's symbol neither exists in nature nor does it belong to a world of Platonic Ideas. It can only find expression in man's conception of the world, in 'the self-knowledge of *Gestalt*. ' And yet art 'gives us images neither of reality nor of ideas'; rather, it 'forms a bridge between both ... The element of movement in drama is in the struggle of an individual ... towards the discovery of the symbol hidden within himself' (Greve 25). As an expression of symbolist doctrine, this is close to Yeats who was also influenced by Wilde. But the truth of Greve's 'symbol' is particularly the truth of Wilde's 'mask': it realizes what is irreal by making it incarnate in the person. In more dialectical terms, the contraries of real and ideal converge in the truth of the mask.

Spettigue indicates that Greve still had some doubts about Wilde the *poseur* and saw 'supreme artistic excellence in *Reading Gaol* and the *Tales* because in these Wilde has dropped his mask' (88). More likely, however, Greve sensed in *The Picture of Dorian Gray*, which he also translated, the validity of his own aesthetic theory of incarnation. For all of *Dorian Gray*'s insistence that life must imitate art, it demonstrates the opposite: 'Life *is* more real than art. Contrary to the thesis of "The Decay of Lying," art *is* a reflection of life' (Cohen 136). What Dorian's picture imitates, in fact, is his moral corruption. The ageless face of the decadent is supposed to mask his evil to the world, but the real 'symbol hidden within himself,' the portrait which daily grows more hideous, threatens continually to unmask him. The painting, in other words, is the truth of the mask, his self-knowledge incarnate. It impels Dorian to confess to murder, until he tries to destroy it. But what he stabs is the

---

1 I am indebted to Doctor Martin Kuester of the University of Augsburg who supplied me with a first edition of Greve's introduction and translation. He also provided me with his own translation of 'Oscar Wilde und das Drama,' which I quote wherever Greve is cited.

image of his own conscience; he kills himself when he defaces the painter's work. The picture only recovers the painter's ideal image when Dorian's corpse reveals its actual disfigurement.

Philip Cohen shows very convincingly how Wilde came to feel 'that he had been led astray by Walter Pater's writings, especially by *Studies in the History of the Renaissance*' (128). And so *Dorian Gray* served as the crucible 'where he tested – and rejected – the theories put forth in *Intentions*' (13), much as Pater had tested his own aesthetic theories – and found them wanting – in *Marius the Epicurean*. For the 'structure of *The Picture of Dorian Gray* is unambiguously, rigorously moral. Through the portrait, Wilde monitors Dorian's steady, irreversible progress toward damnation' (Cohen 123), while the hypocrisy of a Paterian aesthete is revealed quite as fatally through the figure of Lord Henry Wotton. 'Poor Harry exists – and merely exists – at several removes from actuality. Selecting the stance recommended by Pater and championed by Wilde in "The Critic," Wotton views life, specifically Dorian's life, as though it were art' (Cohen 141). Yet Henry's vicarious enjoyment of the fruits of crime and of sexual indulgence could never extend to embracing, as his own crime, Dorian's murder of Basil Hallward, the portrait painter. Instead, Henry finds Dorian's confession to be out of character, an affectation that is more like an artistic miscalculation: 'I would say, my dear fellow, that you were posing for a character that doesn't suit you. All crime is vulgar, just as all vulgarity is crime' (*Dorian Gray* 344). Such a reduction of morals to mere paradox, while typical of Wilde himself, is calculated to expose 'the *real* "sterility" and corruption embodied in Pater's aesthetics' (Cohen 148). It is the final proof that an aesthete who views 'Dorian as an *objet d'art*' cannot escape the responsibility of action any more than Dorian can escape the truth of his artistic mask.

Greve himself notes that Wilde 'would probably have veiled the moral a bit more, although it was essentially the moral intended by the author himself, if the purpose of the novel had not first of all been to raise money' (52). Yet, beyond the mere projection of a cash-starved translator, this was a moral of which Greve approved, which proved the paradoxical truth of the mask. For the picture of Dorian Gray is another portrait of contraries, of that which is and that which could be, united in the same figure.

A Search for America offers a similar configuration of real and ideal selves, suggesting how much Grove had learned from *Dorian Gray* about the need, through displaced confession, to unite the two. But the form of the novel is also confessional in a more traditional sense; it follows the pattern of the *Confessions* of St Augustine in looking down from an enlightened prospect on the path leading to conversion: 'My view of life, if now, at the end,' says the masked narrator, 'I may use this word once more, had been, in Europe, historical, [sic] it had become, in America, ethical. We come indeed from Hell and climb to Heaven ... America is an ideal and as such has to be striven for; it has to be realized in partial victories' (*America* 382). And yet the realization of an ideal self can also be assisted by some skilful apologetics. The 'historical' self at the beginning of the novel is really a scrupulous judge of American morals who, again and again, is made the scapegoat for the sins of New World men. He is betrayed in Toronto by his friend Frank who lives by graft in a greasy diner. Crooked book-agents in New York send him off to be their fall guy in Connecticut, even though he is their only employee to 'square ... up the advances which I had received' (*America* 192). The worst that can be said of the Old World man is that he has been a dilettante and a snob; but democratic life turns out to be one long, crooked game in Lincoln's imagined land.

The narrator thus frames his account of his time in the republic with two gambling scenes which suggest a more subtle shift in his moral stance. In the first scene in New York, young Phil loses everything to a pair of confidence men who have paid him off in counterfeit money. He is hauled down to the police station for spending bad bills, but when the con game is explained to him, he waves off any concern for his lost savings: 'Oh,' he says, 'that part of it is nothing. So long as I don't need to reproach myself' (*America* 127). He does not even need to reproach himself for sitting in on the game, since he was only trying to shield a drunken gambler from real gaming sharks. In the final scene in a Dakota bunkhouse, Phil has learned to sit out the poker game, though he is helpless to save a foolish immigrant from losing a whole season's wages: 'Iniquity was being perpetrated, even though in a game; I heard the unspoken call for redress' (*America* 370). But now the call does not come in his own person, as before in New York, but in the medium of writing, behind the mask. The truth is not that he has been converted from the historical man to the ethical man, since he has played the missionary from the moment he got off the boat. Rather, his major conversion is from a use of direct to indirect discourse, from first person to masked, artistic speech.

In another sense, Grove, like Dorian Gray, has to keep some distance between his ideal and actual selves. Young Phil would have us believe that his only sin is a serious misunderstanding of democracy, although Grove hints obliquely at other sins as well: 'Howard and Hannan, Frank and this captain of waiterdom, they were all of a type – they were what I had very nearly come to accept on a level of equality! I had simply not been keeping myself at the proper distance' (*America* 133). Here, however, Grove has found a private bridge to his younger self, Felix Greve, who borrowed more than he bargained for from his friend Herman Kilian and had to pay with a year spent in Bonn's central prison (Spettigue 92–9). Hannan, the cultured New York counterfeiter, sends Phil Branden to jail for a crime committed in another time and another country. The reality is glimpsed behind the mask, even though Phil himself gets out of jail in hours, free of so much as the need for self-reproach. Similarly, Frank, the shady Toronto waiter, becomes a mask for the imposter who really did flee a wife in Kentucky to live and write under a pseudonym in Canada (Hjartarson, *Stranger* 269–84). 'Carrol's as little my real name as yours is Branden,' the mask speaks with authorial irony. 'I'm hiding. Buffalo's my home town. I'm hiding from my wife' (*America* 80–1). Perhaps we shall never know all the biographical details of Grove's American odyssey; but his narrative offers a fascinating glimpse of his use of displaced confession in the act of reinventing himself. He shows just enough of his secret portrait of Dorian Greve to avoid the necessity of full confession. The way things are and the way things ought to be show up in fitful glimpses from both sides of the mask.

This strategy of displaced confession is writ large in two other autobiographical works, *Settlers of the Marsh* and *In Search of Myself*. In general terms, *Settlers* becomes the displaced confession which then authorizes the self-invention of his Swedish autobiography. Grove makes the specific claim in *In Search of Myself* that *Settlers* grew out of his American odyssey: 'I thought of how it had worked itself out, slowly, inevitably; for the central figure, Niels Lindstedt, reached far back into the past, to a summer day when, in some little lake in Nebraska or South Dakota, I had had a swim with a young Swede who, for some reason or other, confided to me that, up to the day of his recent marriage, he had not known of the essential difference between male and female' (*Myself*

372). The young Swede, as Tom Saunders once remarked to me, is very likely Grove himself, though the portrait of a more innocent Dorian Grove might serve as well to mask the novelist's own development. The gradual corruption of Niels Lindstedt is a fairly obvious confession, for anyone who knows the facts, of Greve's own corruption in Bonn and Berlin. There are at least three such displacements, including Niels's obsessive work habits (read Felix's compulsive work as a translator), the fateful liaison with an older woman (Else, the Berlin architect's wife, who ran off with Greve to Italy and later followed him to Kentucky), and the commutation of Niels's ten-year sentence to six-and-one-half years (roughly the time from Greve's own imprisonment to his flight from Germany). (See Spettigue 202–3).

Yet the larger displacement which becomes the mainspring of the novel is Niels's tortured memory of his mother (a woman whose poverty-stricken labour clearly parallels that of Bertha Greve after her separation from young Felix's father). Niels's first glimpse of Ellen holding her bedridden mother's hand leaves him feeling ashamed: 'Somehow she reminded him of his own mother; and like his mother she aroused in him a feeling of resentment against something that seemed to be wrong with the world' (*Settlers* 24). His resentment is somewhat clarified by 'a scene which was profoundly distasteful to him' (*Settlers* 44): the flirtation of Mrs Lund with her useless husband. But what is generally wrong with the world is the seethe and surge of random sexuality which threaten to overwhelm him. At times, he has to find relief in the right psychological landscape: 'Once or twice, on moonlit nights, he went to the bridge and lost himself in the shadows of the road-chasm beyond' (*Settlers* 49). But after he is cornered by the merry widow at Nelson's wedding, he escapes to the bush, only to feel the aspens rearing all about him. Nelson warns him:

'Better be careful. She's set her cap for you. What do you intend to do next?'
'Fence,' Niels [responds with unwitting irony]. (*Settlers* 53)

At the end of this scene, he has a vision of his mother looking into his heart with reproach and pity: 'pity with him, not because of what assailed him from without; but pity with what he was in his heart' (*Settlers* 56). He is released from her paralysing vision only when he has yielded, suffered, killed, and finally atoned for his enslavement to passion. The narrator has insisted up until the murder itself on the inevitability of this 'grim tragedy,' and Niels insists on going to jail, as Grove had likewise done in imitation of Wilde. But the end of the novel confirms the comic structure which is implicit in the presence of the blocking figure: Niels has only to confront his mother's sexuality to accept the animal man in himself. The vision of his mother's face melting into old man Sigurdsen's is the sign that he contains them both, is free to father and mother himself.

The manuscript revisions of the novel further clarify the Oedipal nature of its conflict. Chapter 1, 'Mrs Lund,' which in two earlier drafts was entitled 'Nelson' (Grove Collection, box 10), focuses more sharply the composite image of the mater dolorosa – made up of Mrs Lund, Mrs Amundsen, and his dead mother – in the toils of a disgusting father. Niels's revulsion from the scene of parental sex-play at the Lunds makes the death of the fathers in the revised second chapter stand out as a wish-fulfilment dream, probably rooted in the circumstances of Bertha's marriage to Charles Edward Greve. Amundsen must fall through the ice and Lund disappear in the bush before Niels is able to sympathize with his surrogate father, old Sigurdsen, who raves in a fever of the sensual 'hussy' whom he bedded so long ago in Copenhagen.

It is Ellen's story about the father as beast which renews the problem in the third chapter of how the son can ever take his place. Clara is used by Neils (not to mention Grove) as a means of psychological purgation, though her presence is so melodramatic that even she must stop at times to wonder at her unreality: ' "If only I had a revolver, a knife ..." She stopped, realising that she was becoming theatrical' (*Settlers* 153); yet she soon forgets herself, adding that ' "When you married me, you committed a crime!" She paused. Once more her pose was theatrical' (154). Such narrative apologies aside, Grove needs Clara to confess what otherwise could not be said: Else, prison, the author's dereliction after his mother's death, and his growing isolation in Germany the more he tried to imitate his hero Wilde. And so, when Niels returns to the White Range-Line House, he finds 'the door to the east [bed]room was closed; that to the west room open; the reverse of what it had been in his time' (*Settlers* 198). It is our clearest indication that Grove is closing the door on his old life to the east in Europe, and is giving himself over to a new life and identity in the west of Canada. For the first time, Greve's dual self is united in one figure; Niels becomes the mask through which Grove disguises his own fall, by which he proves the folly of naïveté and the wisdom of worldly experience. Niels is at once a confession of what Felix Paul Greve had been and an inverse apologia for what Frederick Philip Grove was to become. The image of the settler is the author's first full discovery of the symbol hidden within himself.

The strength of *Settlers of the Marsh* is not to be found among the old strictures of prairie realism. Its allegorical representation of chastity and passion, its wholesale lapses from verisimilitude, its lack of dialogue through the chapter of the murder, and its authorial subjectivity in so much tragic commentary have forced critics to look for other sources of its unity. About the furthest we might go in claiming *Settlers* for realism is to say that art imitates the secret life of its author. Mrs Lund's struggle with debt and her dignified attempt to keep up appearances strike a deep chord in Grove, as well as Niels, and sound the keynote of his confessional aesthetics: 'He understood that this woman knew she was at the end of her life and that life had not kept faith with her. Her voice was only half that with which we tell of a marvellous dream; half it was a passionate protest against the squalour surrounding her: it reared a triumphant vision above the ruins of reality' (*Settlers* 33).

Twenty years later, the ruins of reality would stretch away on every hand in the 'Prologue' to *In Search of Myself*. At the end, the artist's vision seems unable to sustain him as he toots his horn to a Canadian audience who will not hear. Mrs Lund's consolation is further off than ever, although the imagined woman has somehow become the imagined homeland, herself 'the ancient city of Lund' reconstituted as the mother country.[2] Later in his autobiography, Grove describes his literary shock of recognition upon first sighting the bush country west of Lake Manitoba: 'Once more something clicked in my mind; this was the landscape in which Niels Lindstedt had lived; Len Sterner; Mrs Lund; and many other creatures of my brain' (*Myself* 299). But the reader of *In Search of Myself* experiences a similar shock on finding Niels to be the resident

---

2 K.P. Stich, 'Grove's New World Bluff,' *Canadian Literature* 90 (Autumn 1981), establishes 'patterns of landscape and of character that reveal the confessional nature of *Settlers of the Marsh*' (111), although his view of Niels as 'a surrogate of the new Grove' and Clara 'as a surrogate of Grove's former self' (120) is too simplistic. Mrs Lund must also be considered a complex surrogate of Bertha Greve, of Greve himself as debtor, and of the imagined mother country.

farm inspector at Castle Thurow, and Len Sterner of *The Yoke of Life* to be an old fisherman who comes to blackmail the squire's wife over a boat lost once before in a novel, not on the Sound but on Lake Manitoba. These curtain calls from the novelist's cast of characters are the ultimate instance of Grove's continuing need to find a homeland in his art. He does not give credit, in any conventional sense, to his originals in life since Niels and Mrs Lund and the rest are already masks of his former self. Rather, the quest journey of the autobiography is to people his beginnings with other versions of himself, to make his 'life' imitate his previous art in one grand, self-contained *Künstlerroman*. And so the search for self becomes a revision of all his other stories of origin, a final attempt to live purely and wholly in his art.

Grove's own apt metaphor reveals the scope of his 'autobiographical' revisions: 'The whole globe was a palimpsest: no doubt even the Americas would one day reveal older worlds to the archeologist' (*Myself* 86). Later, Grove explains his vagueness about the Siberian steppes in similar terms: 'Even if it were within the scope of this book to give detailed descriptions of what I saw, I could not do so; like the face of Europe my memory is a palimpsest on which writing has overlaid writing' (*Myself* 147). Grove's life, like the Siberian steppes, is the page written over with story after story. '[T]he steppe,' he claims, 'changed my whole view of life; the steppe got under my skin and into my blood ... and only when I struck my roots into the west of Canada did I feel at home again' (*Myself* 150). What seems more likely to have changed his view is so much blank space, the page of history rubbed over again. For the prairies offer him the erasure which allows him to write once more; his homecoming is completely writerly. Now the palimpsest holds all the versions of the truth; the self is replicated in ways that are faithful both to life and to art.

The central replication in the novels and the *Künstlerroman* continues to be the story of the son split between his parents. The father's injustice, which has all the fire of emotional truth, appears latterly in *In Search of Myself* to be Grove's self-conscious attempt to incorporate the experience of Niels Lindstedt. The narrator remarks of his mother's decision to leave the father how 'she inferred that a proud child's innermost feelings, his very spiritual chastity, as it were, had been outraged' (*Myself* 60). The same metaphor characterizes Niels when Nelson makes some careless comments about Ellen: 'His friend's remark was like the violation of a confidence, like an intrusion into the arcana of holy ground; for as yet Niels was chaste to the very core of his being' (*Settlers* 40). So, too, the advice the narrator gets from his mother just before her death is the same as Ellen heard from her mother in *Settlers*. 'Don't ever marry. Marriage makes weak' (109), Mrs Amundsen says in the earlier novel, whereas the mother in the artist-novel 'urged me, that I, for one, would never marry ... Women, she said one day, make a man weak' (*Myself* 94). Such repetition becomes the author's way of writing his life into his own art, of reclaiming the space cleared by his displaced confession.

The artist finally comments on this method of self-replication in his account of a gigantic farmer who supplied the figure for Abe Spalding in *Fruits of the Earth*. On second meeting, Grove writes, 'he had not seemed to me to be quite the sort of giant I had imagined when he had first topped the crest of the hill. Yet, somehow he had bodied forth for me the essence of the pioneering spirit.' It is not just that the real man could never embody the imagined ideal: 'if I had heard him speak as no doubt he had been used to speak, without relevance to my creation ... [a] perfectly irrelevant actuality would have been superimposed upon my conception of a man who, as I saw him, had perhaps never lived; for he lacked that infusion of myself which makes him what he has become' (*Myself* 260-1). This infusion of self is the very means of aesthetic incarnation, the bridge which unites the actual and conceptual in the fabricated mask, which joins much of Grove's work to the grand design of a totalizing artist-novel. Wilde had already given Grove his defence of such a method in 'The Decay of Lying': 'The justification of a character in a novel is not that other persons are what they are, but that the author is what he is. Otherwise the novel is not a work of art' (Wilde, *Intentions* 14).

We return to the concept of *Gestalt* which Greve had linked to Gide's and Wilde's theory of the mask. The play of contraries in the formed mask is not a concealment but a kind of revelation of self to the self such as Wilde had felt compelled to make in his life as well as in his art. Grove's own displaced confessions thus seek to unite contraries of real and ideal until, in his fictional autobiography, he fully manifests the symbol hidden within himself. The old realist demand that art should imitate life now finds an unexpected answer in his novels of confession. Yet, in ways which have long been hidden, the 'autobiography' fulfils obliquely Wilde's dictum that life imitates art more than art imitates life. *In Search of Myself* is finally the artist incarnate, his own bridge between history and the idea of himself, the final truth of the mask.

Grove's doctrine of aesthetic incarnation gives one further twist to the 'confession' of artistic failure in *In Search of Myself*, to what has been described as Grove's 'overwhelming need to defend his career as a writer, to explain that his failure was really a "foregone conclusion" ' (Hjartarson, 'Design' 87). For the story of the writer is in large part the story of the cost of bridging two worlds: 'I would rather do anything but write … But I also know that, unless I do as my inner needs dictate, I am letting myself in for serious trouble. For those figures of mine will not stay down; they won't let me rest or sleep; they want to be born into death' (*Myself* 387). It is an odd statement unless the artistic birth should also be a form of *kenosis*, the emptying out of one's prior existence. Then, as Grove says, the figures 'were born long ago; they have lived their lives almost in spite of myself; and now they want to die.' But the author who would be incarnate in his mask faces a whole new prospect of losing himself. 'In this record, I know,' he writes, 'I am dying to myself' (*Myself* 387). Such is the destined end of most incarnations.

3

Forms of Autobiography
in *Fifth Business*

Like his creator, Dunstan Ramsay is the author of a fictional autobiography in *Fifth Business*, a work which in some respects becomes a double of the one we read. He readily admits that 'The autobiography of Magnus Eisengrim was a great pleasure to write, for I was under no obligation to be historically correct or to weigh evidence. I let myself go and invented just such a book about a magician as I would have wanted to read if I had been a member of his public; it was full of romance and marvels, with a quiet but sufficient undertone of eroticism and sadism, and it sold like hot-cakes' (229). Though his portrait of the artist as a young magician is pure invention, Ramsay's fictional 'auto'-biography is also an extrapolation of his own persona, created in his teens. For even then, little Paul Dempster had showed that he 'had the hands and I had not, and although there were times when I considered killing him, just to rid the world of a precocious nuisance' (39), Ramsay must accept the budding magician as an alter ego who supplements his own magian persona. For the younger boy remains his ally in a lifelong quarrel with foes of the spirit. Though what the 'spirit' might prove to be is more doubtful. Especially when a card trick is every bit as good as a tale of saints to put to flight the leaden hours of a Presbyterian Sunday afternoon.

The ready-made definitions of the budding magician's father, an evangelical minister, do more than to express a usual 'puritan' hostility to the liberal imagination. Since the older boy dabbles with 'the Devil's picture-book' (42), he is clearly *persona non grata* among the Baptists; but even his more literary interest in *A Child's Book of Saints* is not likely to wash in a Protestant village which 'conspicuously lacked ... an aesthetic sense' (25). And yet, as Ramsay confesses, 'I did not feel I had done wrong, though I had been a fool to forget how dead set Baptists were against cards. As for the stories about saints, they were tales of wonders, like *Arabian Nights*, and when the Reverend Andrew Bowyer bade all us Presbyterians to prepare ourselves for the Marriage Feast of the Lamb, it seemed to me that *Arabian Nights* and the *Bible* were getting pretty close – and I did not mean this in any scoffing sense. I was most hurt that Dempster had dragged down my conjuring to mere cheating and gambling; it had seemed to me to be a splendid extension of life, a creation of a world of wonder, that hurt nobody' (43). A lad with the yearnings of a Paterian aesthete will thus seek all his life to answer the question, 'Why do people all over the world, and at all times, want marvels that defy all verifiable facts? And are the marvels brought into being by their desire, or is their desire an assurance rising from some deep knowledge, not to be directly experienced and questioned, that the marvellous is indeed an aspect of the real?' (199).

Ramsay's confident statement about the marvellous being an 'aspect of the real' seems intended, like 'the slogan of "art for its own sake" ... to indicate that it is not subservient to any overriding reality' (Iser, *Pater* 31). For the religious aesthete longs, quite as much as his secular counterpart, to be free of ordinary reality. And yet the art of hagiography, like the saintliness of art, can only set him free if natural and supernatural phenomena are made equivalent in a 'life' which is recreated as its own aesthetic object.

One of Davies's more astute recent critics outlines the problem most exactly: 'Ramsay's involvement with the Soirée of Illusions (the Arabian Nights) and with the Bollandists and their *Acta Sanctorum* (The Bible), equates the psychology of religion with the goals of theatrical representation ... Consider the magic show in *Fifth Business*: it still meets the same needs as the catalogues of sainthood that Ramsay compiles. He does encounter the Soirée in the course of his investigation of the miraculous shrine of Guadalupe, quitting Peter for Simon Magus without qualms. Truth resides in the play of imaginative forces unleashed alike by the endeavours of art and religion' (Duffy, 'Truth' 6–7). Ramsay is still cunning enough to protest, however, that 'I was not such a fool or an aesthete as to suppose that all this art was for art's sake alone. It was about something, and I wanted to know what that something was' (*Fifth* 124). But the charge of aestheticism can only be forestalled by his appeal to an apparently transcendent order of experience.

For this reason, Ramsay's autobiography is oddly schizophrenic, dependent as it is on mystical experience and yet deficient as it also is in a sense of any higher power beyond the individual. The magian world-view is, as Duffy suggests, reducible to the religious pragmatism of a William James for whom 'religion is emptied of its objective meaning but crammed with psychological value' ('Truth' 4). *Whatever turns your crank* – whatever works for you – this, for the unbedazzled critic, is Davies's latent 'message.' Here it might be noted that Ramsay is also guilty of confining the saint who saved his life to a madhouse, thus putting her 'to work' for him for the rest of her life.

But Ramsay, who never gives any hint to the Jesuit Blazon of what becomes of his 'fool saint,' proves to be far more devious in his 'use' of a man who is 'so obviously, indeed theatrically, a priest' (*Fifth* 170). For he needs the religious aesthete to authorize his secular quest to 'find [his] answer in psychological truth, not in objective truth' (177). He even puts the padre to work to confirm a view he has held since childhood, ever since the village atheist had parodied the Reverend Andrew Bowyer at prayer – 'O Lord, take Thou a live coal from off Thine altar and touch our lips' (54). At the time, young Ramsay had concluded instinctively: 'If he hoped to make an atheist of me, this was where he went wrong; I knew a metaphor when I heard one, and I liked metaphor better than reason. I have known many atheists since Sam, and they all fall down on metaphor' (54–5). Yet the child who prefers metaphor to reason does not always appreciate the metaphors of others: 'I had been worsted by moral bullying, by Dempster's conviction that he was right and I was wrong, and that gave him an authority over me based on feeling rather than reason: it was my first encounter with the emotional power of popular morality' (43). Curiously, 'the Devil's picture-book' is far more metaphoric than the magician's mechanical card-tricks. And so 'right reason,' it seems, must be made to outweigh feeling, and the liberal spirit to triumph over authority. Hence the critic's concern about the 'elitist, irrationalist ideology' of the novel (Duffy, 'Truth' 2), since Ramsay tries to usurp that emotional authority for himself while maintaining a façade of reason with his sympathetic reader.

The author of Eisengrim's fictional autobiography has already shown us, however, that the critic is mistaken to confuse the novelist with his creation. For Ramsay seems to be seeking, like George Moore's artistic alter ego, to be a self-made man, freed by his parents' deaths to 'create a complete and absolute self out of the partial self which was all that the restraint of home had permitted' (Moore 196). An extended pattern of dramatic irony in Davies's text will ultimately lay bare the egoist's 'worship' of the icon of the 'Little Madonna' (*Fifth* 251) as a specious justification for his 'life' as an autonomous work of art. His ultimate equation of saintliness with a magic show will also undercut his implicit proposition that the 'spirit' is manifested in a *trompe-l'oeil*. Instead, the reader can regard such moves as narrative sleights of hand, the narrator's version of a magic trick.

Ramsay finally betrays his real interest in the magian world-view during the concluding scene of the *Soirée of Illusions*, where, taking up his customary role as the hidden spectator, he admits that 'the faces I saw below me were the usual studies in pleasure, astonishment, and – always the most interesting – the eagerness to be deceived mingled with resentment of deception' (265). Such obvious delight in deception might be expected from the child who once confessed that 'I was tall and strong and a good liar' (64), much less from the man who confessed of his relationship with Diana Marfleet that 'I lied in every word I uttered' (82). But as a basis for 'spiritual' values in art, this self-styled aesthetics of lying has its foundation in Wilde's 'The Decay of Lying,' that most militant bible of the decadence, rather than in Pater's more 'orthodox' doctrine of the aesthetic moment. And once we see that the autobiographer writes to justify a murder, we might also consider how his portrait resembles the picture of Dorian Gray, that supreme Wildean liar, who also took consolation in a paradox that life imitates art.

As Davies describes it, *Fifth Business* began as the story of a parson, then the parson's son seeking revenge on 'the boy who "killed" his mother & caused his premature birth' ('Retrospect' 7). But when it had to be set aside for several years, 'the novel, when I began to write it, was about guilt, and not revenge, though revenge plays some part in it' (8). Such a change of focus is inherent in the decision to make the narrator the protagonist, since it is he, not the vengeful parson's son, who appears to wrestle with the burden of guilt. The thematic question of the novel, posed by the author after the fact, is whether 'the truly guilty [were] always as burdened as were those whose upbringing and moral training disposed them to feel guilt and perhaps also to assume guilt which was not truly theirs.' The act of writing is thus foregrounded as a type of self-scrutinizing confession, though if the narrator is not truly guilty, what does he confess? The formal question of the novel has therefore to be whether this tension between confession and some other mode of autobiography is resolved, or even addressed, in the narrative.

The hagiographer's model for autobiography, the *Confessions* of St Augustine, is formally significant for his writing since he uses some of the narrative strategies also adapted by Dante in *La vita nuova* and by Bunyan in *Grace Abounding*. Chief among these formal devices is what might be called the transcendent location of the narrator. As one theorist notes, 'In Books I through IX, the Augustine who has already received the gift of faith stands upon the fixed point of an immutable truth and looks back, or rather *down*, upon the sinful life he led between his birth and conversion ... The narrative mode of part one, with its firmly situated narrator and its wandering protagonist, posits conversion as the point where the agitated protagonist will come to rest in the enlightened narrator, and the action will stop' (Spengemann 1, 4).

The agitated protagonist of *Fifth Business* is enlightened rather late in his story by Liselotte Vitzlipützli who assures him that 'What I am saying is not for everybody, of course. Only for the twice-born' (226). After his 'conversion,' Ramsay rests in the new-found faith 'that I have been cast by Fate and by my own character for the vital though never glorious role of Fifth Business' (15). Ostensibly he is led to a point outside his life where he can see it as a completed moral design. As he looks back on his old life at the beginning of his memoir, he can also look down, literally, from 'this house among the mountains – a house that itself holds the truths behind many illusions.' He seems also to have removed himself from time by addressing his former Headmaster from beyond the grave: 'You will not see this memoir until after my own death' (254). Implicitly, then, his vantage point is not only retrospective but timeless; he no longer stands within the temporal span of the action he describes.

Ramsay's conversion does not prove, however, to be quite the end of his action or to offer a very secure resting place for the narrator. His arrival in Switzerland is precipitated by the unwanted revelation of the Brazen Head that he has been part of 'the usual cabal' which has 'killed' (266) Boy Staunton. The born-again narrator is so unnerved by this latent exposure that he nearly dies of fright. His continuing bad conscience suggests that his narrative location is hardly as 'transcendent' as he would like us to believe. His admission that 'I am driven to explain myself to you, Headmaster, because you stand at the top of that queer school world in which I seem to have cut such a meagre figure' (15) is also an indication of how deeply he is still enmeshed in time. The obsessional nature of his relation to his audience of one makes him sound more like some Ancient Mariner, doomed to expiate his guilt by extended retelling.

Of course, Augustine had also made this act of searching confession – long after the transcendent moment of conversion – part of the formal paradigm of the saint's life. The apparent climax of conversion in the ninth book of the *Confessions* inaugurates a new mode of narrative inquiry: 'the unconditioned ground of rest is displaced from the narrator to a point somewhere beyond him ... Once portrayed as an ending achieved prior to the writing of the autobiography, conversion is now portrayed as the beginning of a process whose end must be achieved by way of the autobiography itself' (Spengemann 4). If Dunstan Ramsay is constrained by a similar binary vision – his knowledge of the timeless pattern and his experience of temporal uncertainty – then the autobiographical act might well complete the process of his 'conversion,' allowing him to reconcile the tension in his experience between 'Fate and my own character' which has cast him in a unique role. The loop his narrative describes from 'eternity' back into time may be the creative act of repetition by which he is redeemed. But here the moral need of repetition seems oddly compromised by his structural use of repetition. The supposed climax of his second birth – his renaming as Fifth Business – has already happened as early as the second chapter, 'I Am Born Again,' when he is renamed for St Dunstan by Diana Marfleet. At this point, the pattern of rebirth not only looks premature; it appears to be deductive instead of experiential. One *a priori* scheme succeeds another without analysis of their likeness or difference.

A deductive method has some place in a 'transcendent' mode of confession, but in the mode of experience, confession must be 'a revelation of the self to the self, an act of self-knowledge, a process of discovering the true meaning of one's life' (Spengemann 5). Yet Ramsay's whole compulsion to 'explain' himself grows more and more deductive. For example, he wants to confine his responsibility for Mary Dempster to the single incident of the stone-in-the-snowball which he vaguely initiates. His written narrative employs Mr Mahaffey, the Deptford magistrate, to articulate what amounts to a domino theory of guilt: 'There was guilt, you know; undoubtedly there was guilt. I don't know quite what could have been done about it, but look at the consequences! McCausland says definitely she became a moral idiot – no sense at all of right and wrong – and the result was that terrible business in the pit. I remember that you were there. And the ruin of her husband's life. Then the lad running away when he was really no more than a baby. I've never seen such grief as hers when she finally realized he had gone. McCausland had to give her very heavy morphia before Miss Shanklin could remove her. Yes, there was guilt, whether any kind of charge could have been laid or not. Guilt, and somebody bears it to this day!' (136–7). If the magistrate has his grim suspicions about what the man is hiding, he still makes the boy no more than a necessary, not the sufficient, cause of a chain reaction. 'Were you the child who started it?' his summary implies.

Here, Ramsay must be silent about an admission he has made earlier in his narrative: 'In my bitterness I ill-wished Amasa Dempster. This was a terrible thing to do, and I knew it. In my parents' view of life, superstition was trash for ignorant people, but they had a few reservations, and one was that it was very unlucky to ill-wish anybody' (43). He knows, in other words, that the parson's ruin did not follow inevitably from the snowball; it took another shove of the dominoes. But he can use Mahaffey's summary to disguise the ripple of guilt which spreads out from the hidden stone of revenge. Confession shades into apology; autobiography takes the way of self-justification.

George Woodcock remarks that 'the heritage of St Augustine has given autobiography a ... misconception to live down: that it is necessarily either a confession, in the sense of letting all the skeletons out of the cupboards of one's memory, or an apologia, aimed at justifying what, despite the skeletons, one has become. Both of these ideal forms emerge from the more puritanical aspects of the postclassical Christian tradition, obsessed with guilt, longing for justification; St Augustine's book claims to be apologia as well as confession, but in the full sense is probably neither, for the shaping hand of the imagination is already at work on it' ('Autobiography' 16). His restatement of the central assumption of Roy Pascal's *Design and Truth in Autobiography* (1960) – that the genre is imaginative as well as historiographical – allows for a third option, neither confessional nor apologetic, in determining the form of any autobiography. Spengemann even catalogues the options: 'Historical self-explanation, philosophical self-scrutiny, poetic self-expression, and poetic self-invention – these are, so far as I know, the only procedures available to autobiography' (xvi–xvii). Yet Ramsay's 'poetic' attempt either to express or to invent himself is complicated by his very obsession with guilt and his longing for justification. The tension among these forms is what is hardly recognized by the many critics who tacitly assume that *Fifth Business* is self-inventive autobiography.

Socio-cultural critics such as Ronald Sutherland take Liesl at face value when she says that the narrator will become a new man by putting behind him his 'horrid village' and his 'hateful Scots family' (217). 'That dreadful Canada' is a region of the spirit to be eschewed for sunnier climes. Sutherland is only more political than most when he argues that Ramsay 'represents a remarkable and profound transition in Canadian values' since he gives up 'the guilt-ridden, self-effacing role of the typical Calvinist-Jansenist-conditioned character ... and starts on the path toward becoming the new type of Canadian hero, the self-reliant, individualistic, independent person' (77). This substitution of Ralph Waldo Emerson for John Knox is, however, less an act of imaginative recreation than a preliminary work of decreation. It is a way to get rid of the burden of history and the albatross of Calvinist dogma. 'Whence this worship of the past?' Emerson had railed in *Self-Reliance*. 'The centuries are conspirators against the sanity and authority of the soul' (Whicher 157). Ramsay proves his spiritual sanity, Sutherland suggests, by getting rid of his beginnings.

Emerson's 'authority of the soul' is not so easily established for other critics by an acceptance of a revolutionary cultural model. Many see Liesl as offering an educative program which leads to some form of *anamnesis* or recollection of the past. David Monaghan, for example, claims that Liesl enables Ramsay 'to resurrect his almost submerged childhood self,' that 'essential spiritual and imaginative self' (70, 66) of the authentic boy. Here, the cultural model of Wordsworth is closest to the psychological model of the Jungians who make self-creation or 'individuation' the end of a process of psychic integration in the novel. Gordon Roper first mapped out this fertile territory; Ramsay, who is unaware of 'how his own shadow projects its image onto Boy,' is led by Padre Blazon and ultimately by Liesl to integrate the more primitive side of his personality. 'His acceptance later of Liesl's invitation to join her and Paul in Switzerland suggests that he has come to know his shadow side and to live with it, as in his inner journey he has arrived at a harmony of forces' (Roper 38).[1] F.L. Radford, the subtlest of the Jungian critics, is more uncomfortably aware of how 'Davies brings back unacknowledged guilt on the last page of *Fifth Business*,' resulting in the heart seizure which 'allows Ramsay both to expiate his responsibility for Staunton's death and to evade direct acknowledgment' of it. But Radford sees the ending as leaving 'the reader room for creative speculation' and keeping 'the character of Ramsay humanly alive, with room for the growth and self-understanding that should only end with death' (79). Though Radford is sensitive to Ramsay's tendency to deduce mythic patterns in his life, he is content to see him 'in his true role as Jung's hero of the psyche' (78), and thus to make him the object, not the subject, of the psyche's underlying actions. Ramsay is ultimately representative of Davies's use of Jungian concepts.

The narrator's deductive use of myth none the less proves embarrassing for myth critics who see his 'individuation' as an example of the 'wholeness of the psyche' (Radford 80). Ramsay's use of one 'myth' in particular is exemplary in quite a negative way. As one version of the story has it, 'the Queen took a fancy to Gyges and together they pushed Candaules off his throne ... The other is that Gyges killed Candaules' (*Fifth* 157–8). Ominously, Ramsay will not want Leola when she does ask him to cuckold her husband. Instead, he fulfils his own prophecy in the final show-down by naming Boy and himself into the second version of the myth: 'My observation has been that we get the women we deserve, King Candaules ... and those who eat jam before breakfast are cloyed before bedtime' (264). Gyges is quite aware that he is using Eisengrim to get rid of Candaules. Revenge, in other words, is still very much what the work is about.

Davies's 'twice-born' revenger's tale turns out to be a rather sceptical advertisement for Jungian rebirth since Ramsay's narrative is layered over

1 Nancy E. Bjerring, 'Deep in the Old Man's Puzzle,' *Canadian Literature* 62 (Autumn 1974), though less explicitly concerned with Jung, makes 'Dunstan's rebirth' (56) depend upon Padre Blazon's Jungian metaphor of 'the totality of God in the totality of the self' (58) and the basic concept of psychic 'integration' (60). Marilyn Chapman, 'Female Archetypes in *Fifth Business*,' *Canadian Literature* 80 (Spring 1979), openly apotheosizes Liesl as 'the wise woman in Ramsay's psychic world' (136) who helps him to complete 'the process of individuation' (131).

with various forms of guilt, not least of which is the guilt of concealment. Ramsay's only excuse for betraying Boy to Eisengrim is that Fifth
Business made him do it. Asked by Eisengrim why he has kept Mary's
ashes all these years, he mentions his 'sense of guilt unexpiated' which
embroils him in further explanation: 'Here it was. Either I spoke now or
I kept silence forever. Dunstan Ramsay counselled against revelation, but
Fifth Business would not hear' (263). Ironically, he must split himself
into two people to spare his 'real' self any blame. In an extreme evasion
of responsibility, his apologia strains towards schizophrenia. The narrator's method of self-justification thus leads to schizophrenic tensions of
form in a 'confession' which is also an apologia for 'poetic self-invention.' But why that poetics requires defence is a question whose answer
can only take its shape from the narrator's methods of defence.

The self-justifying narrator of an autobiography who cannot shake his
guilt is advised to appear frank about his shortcomings but to avoid the
sort of overview which leads to final judgments. As Ramsay says at the
beginning of 'I Am Born Again,' 'Because I do not want to posture in
this account of myself as anything other than what I was at the time of
my narrative, I shall write here only of what I knew when it happened'
(67). He is none the less uneasy about what shows through the cracks of
his mask; as he warns his Headmaster and also reminds himself, 'You
will not see this memoir until after my own death, and you will surely
keep what you know to yourself. After all, you cannot prove anything
against anyone' (254). Clearly he is not interested, as the Jungians think,
in further self-knowledge, only with avoiding, as Liesl said he must,
cruelty to himself by telling someone what he knows. Yet even as he
confesses a little of his secret, he reminds his reader of 'the variability of
truth.' Or, as he prefaces his posthumous confession of the manner of
Boy's death, '[H]ow could I ... have written a life of Boy without telling
all that ... I know about the way he died? And even then,' he hedges,
'would it have been the truth?' (254). It is, of course, a question which
threatens to discredit him unless he can appeal, ambiguously, to the
'variability' of truth. But is truth variable in and of itself? Or only in the
eye of the beholder? Or is it best varied in the telling?
   This calculated ambiguity serves Ramsay well in other rhetorical techniques by which he takes the reader into his confidence, such as in his
account of Boy's engagement to Leola: 'I promised that this would be a

frank record, so far as I can write one, and God forbid that I should pretend that there is not a generous measure of spite in my nature. This encounter put us in one of those uneasy situations that are forced on people by fate' (101). Establishing his rhetorical *ethos* with his frankness (if pairing 'spite' with 'generous' can be termed ethical), he then slips back to fate as the true explanation of his conduct. His guilt thus recedes beyond his proper power; it is no sooner glanced at than it disappears.

Liesl, who also does magic with moral problems, supplies Ramsay with his alibi as Fifth Business. David Monaghan is so distressed by the apparent conflict between this new public identity and the private one in which Ramsay recovers the best of his childhood self that he senses 'a real confusion in Robertson Davies' mind about the subject of *Fifth Business*' (64). The two roles are in fact incompatible; one leads to love and 'an aftermath of healing tenderness' (*Fifth* 227), the other to betrayal and elaborate self-justification. Radford alone admits that this new identity 'enables him to rationalize his betrayal of Staunton' (75), though he foreshortens the pattern of individuation to allow for integration of Ramsay's anima, if not his shadow, into his self: 'It is only after he passes the test of "the loathly lady" in meeting, fighting and embracing Liesl that he is able to reconcile the demonic and angelic sides of the *Magna Mater* and accept woman as a whole being' (Radford 74). Liesl's schizophrenic influence in his use of Fifth Business reminds us, however, that Ramsay's rationalization runs very deep, and that his acceptance of the demonic with the angelic leads to a veiled sort of murder. His very refusal of self-knowledge suggests that Liesl, not the author, is the source of any confusion in the novel, and that the narrator who does not accept his own 'whole being' is not likely to be ready to accept the 'whole woman' either.

Liesl's rhetoric, not to mention her logic, serves as the definitive model for Ramsay's apologetic technique. Her tactic is to accuse before she excuses, even as Ramsay has learned to do in creating his *ethos*. But Liesl's accusation is more telling because it is offered in her own defence: 'If a temperamental secret-keeper like you cannot hold in what he knows about Eisengrim, how can you expect it of anyone you despise as you despise me? ... Oh yes, you do despise me. You despise almost everybody except Paul's mother. No wonder she seems like a saint to you; you have made her carry the affection you should have spread among fifty people' (217). Later, when the shoe is off the other foot and Liesl prepares to excuse her seduction of Ramsay, she directly contradicts herself: 'You make yourself responsible for other people's troubles. It is your hobby. You take on the care of a poor madwoman you knew as a boy. You put up with subtle insult and being taken for granted by a boyhood friend ... You are a decent chap to everybody, except one special somebody, and that is Dunstan Ramsay. How can you be really good to anybody if you are not good to yourself?' (225-6). Here, the comic incongruity of the lady who has been punched and kicked now protesting how the gentle-man has been good to everyone but himself is also very funny, though it serves to deepen the narrator's calculating ambiguity. Liesl's proposal to play his 'personal devil' also makes her Jungian advice more darkly incongruous when one recalls that Jung said the projected shadow side of the personality 'is always of the same sex as the subject' (Jung 10). Her lying devil may well prove to be the real thing, but Ramsay is blithely unconcerned; he needs the devil's own authority for better lies in the making.

Even Liesl's plainest truths offer fertile ground on which to cultivate new confusions. Her indictment of Calvinism, for instance, is quite transformed by the time Ramsay is done with it: 'It is a cruel way of life,' she says, 'even if you forget the religion and call it ethics or decent behaviour or something else that pushes God out of it. But even Calvin-ism can be endured, if you will make some compromise with yourself' (226). This 1960s gospel of 'I'm Okay, You're Okay' is clearly welcome to the 'Presbyterian child' who once insisted, 'I was of the damned' (23). But his relief is greater still when Fifth Business can be construed in the old Calvinist terms of election or predestination, the first of the 'Five Heads' of Calvinist doctrine (Danielson 71): 'Oh God! Packer, who cannot know and could not conceive that I have been cast by Fate and my own character for the vital though never glorious role of Fifth Business!' (15). His subtlest compromise of all, then, entails an adoption of the Calvinist faith in personal election without its corresponding belief in human depravity. The final responsibility for 'evil,' though it no longer has so harsh a name, is turned back on God or fate, as Calvin's own critics said it would be (Danielson 80-2).

Ramsay's 'fatalistic interpretation of his role' (Peterman 123) has made some readers uneasy, especially since fate is enlisted in the interest of apologetics. Michael Peterman is forced to the rather painful conclu-sion that 'In many ways Fifth Business is a justification of personality as received. If a man has a cruel or mean streak it is his duty not to eradicate it but to recognize it and to understand the part it must play in his life' (125). But Ramsay's deterministic outlook seems quite foreign to his Jesuit mentor, Padre Blazon, who says, 'You know that Jesuit training is based on a rigorous reform of the self and achievement of self-knowledge' (176). Blazon may be one of those teachers in the Deptford trilogy who 'are not criticized in essential matters; they are beyond criticism, like the wise men in fables and fairy tales' (Peterman 130). And yet the discrepancy between the teacher's doctrine and the pupil's use of it suggests that, for Davies, it is the narrator who is to be criticized in essential matters.

The most telling thing about the role Blazon is asked to play in Ramsay's defence is that he is made, as a sort of God-figure, to approve of the apologist's encounter with the devil. The devil has proved herself a very tricky fellow, and a long-standing prejudice against her role is not likely to be overcome by her own say-so. Ramsay's recourse to a Jungian-sounding Jesuit is clearly intended, then, to legitimize his faith in his own actions: 'Trust your own judgement,' Blazon tells him. 'That it [sic] what you Protestants made such a dreadful fuss to assert your right to do' (174). But Ramsay's attraction to authority figures exposes a latent contradiction in this individualism, which Liesl urges and Blazon allows: the self may well be its own judge in religious matters, but it still wants authority to excuse itself from judgment.

Peterman, who endeavours throughout his monograph on Davies to do justice to the 'egoism of the hero figure ... [which] dominates his work' ('Preface,' n.p.), finds 'something of a narrative model' (151) for Ramsay's egocentric individualism in John Henry Newman's *Apologia Pro Vita Sua*. Indeed, Ramsay's apologia bears several striking resemblances to the great Victorian's: both are occasioned by a detractor; both trace the history of minds given over to 'the world unseen'; both are stimulated by the *Arabian Nights*; and both seek evidence for faith in saints and miracles (Peterman 126-7). But the egoism which underlies both works is also their greatest difference, since Newman's authority does not finally reside in the self. In his youth, Newman was obviously capable of Ramsay's sort of egoism, resting 'in the thought of two and two only absolute and luminously self-evident beings, myself and my Creator; – for while I considered myself predestined to salvation, my mind did not dwell upon others, as fancying them simply passed over, not predestined to eternal death. I only thought of the mercy to myself' (Newman, *Apologia* 25).

But the more he 'was led to give up my remaining Calvinism' (29), the less Newman was inclined to rest in the thought of his own election or even in the power of his own reason, trusting more to 'the principle of dogma: my battle was with liberalism; by liberalism I mean the anti-dogmatic principle and its developments' (65–6).

By contrast, Ramsay's ambition 'to see what a saint was really like and perhaps make a study of one without all the apparatus of Rome' (*Fifth* 161) is an obvious attempt to appear both liberal and dogmatic; he wants to borrow the dogma of saintliness without accepting the competence of any external authority to limit his rational freedom. His 'compromise' with Catholicism, like his 'compromise' with Calvinism, is supposed to prove his special state of grace even as it prevents any chance to judge him.

The more likely presence of Newman behind Ramsay's story is to be found in Blazon himself, for whom Newman's *Grammar of Assent* offers a working definition of personal experience as the final evidence of religion. In Newman's words: 'I begin with expressing a sentiment, which is habitually in my thoughts, whenever they are turned to the subject of mental or moral science, and which I am willing to apply here to the Evidences of Religion as it properly applies to Metaphysics or Ethics, viz. that in these provinces of inquiry egotism is true modesty. In religious inquiry each of us can speak only for himself, but he cannot speak for others; he cannot lay down the law; he can only bring his own experiences to the common stock of psychological facts' (Newman, *Grammar* 300). Blazon, like Newman, speaks more for individual intuition than for relativism when he says, 'What good would it do you if I told you she is indeed a saint? I cannot make saints, nor can the Pope. We can only recognize saints when the plainest evidence shows them to be saintly. If you think her a saint, she is a saint to you. What more do you ask? That is what we call the reality of the soul; you are foolish to demand the agreement of the world as well' (174). The true modesty of egotism, for Newman and for Davies's priest, consists in this intuition of the self as a ground of apprehension of something beyond the self.

Ramsay, however, prefers to interpret Blazon's subjectivism in the light of a later, antithetical Victorian, Walter Pater, who had urged, 'Trust the eye: Strive to be right always in regard to the concrete experience: Beware of falsifying your impressions' (*Marius* I, 243). Such advice is heeded in a singular way when he finally does lay eyes again on the

Little Madonna, more than forty years removed as he is from that first 'concrete experience': '[W]as it truly the face of Mary Dempster? No, it was not, though the hair was very like; Mary Dempster, whose face my mother had described as being like a pan of milk, had never been so beautiful in feature, but the expression was undeniably hers – an expression of mercy and love, tempered with perception and penetration' (251). Ramsay's subjective impressions, in other words, are all that is required to confirm the inner likeness of his 'saint' to the plaster icon. Whatever works for him can also work for you.

Only at one point does Ramsay seem to adopt Blazon's more modest egoism in urging Boy to try 'to be a human being. Then maybe something bigger than yourself will come up on your horizon' (264). Ironically, this 'something bigger' turns out to be Ramsay himself; Boy's childish retort goads him instantly to play Gyges to Boy's Candaules. His subsequent appeal to Fifth Business is his last-ditch reliance on fate as the 'something bigger,' his only means now of easing the burden of a murderous egoism.

Ramsay's fatalistic interpretation of Boy's death is still strangely counterpointed by his insistence on free will in his temptation by the devil. While he is modern enough to hint at some sexual knowledge of his devil, he coyly structures the 'dirty bits,' at which Blazon sniggers, to climax in a description of how he 'had wrung Liesl's nose until the bone cracked' (250). The story evidently ends here, without any mention of Liesl's second visit to his bedroom, or of the moral compromise involved in accepting the role of Fifth Business. St Dunstan carries the day, as the old man – who, if he takes the part of Jung's Wise Old Man, is still vulnerable to deceit – clearly recognizes as the intent of the story: 'Oho, Ramezay, no wonder you write so well of myth and legend! It was St Dunstan seizing the Devil's snout in his tongs, a thousand years after his time. Well done, well done! You met the Devil as an equal, not cringing or frightened or begging for a trashy favour. That is the heroic life, Ramezay. You are fit to be the Devil's friend, without any fear of losing yourself to Him!' (250). This final benediction should confirm the power of the heroic will to determine its own destiny; but what it actually confirms is the mythic role the narrator assumes for himself. And what Ramsay further declines to say is that the devil has seen to it that the saint is superseded by the Fifth.

Blazon none the less asks about a 'sin' of omission which is quite as portentous. He chides Ramsay for making no mention of his fool-saint in his big book on saints, to which Ramsay responds with the advice given him thirty years before by Father Regan. But Ramsay adds nothing of the fool-saint's own view of her canonization. Elsewhere he had already confided to his memoir that 'She knew well enough who was her jailer. I was the man. Dunstan Ramsay, who pretended to be a friend, was a snake-in-the-grass, an enemy, an undoubted agent of those dark forces who had torn Paul from her' (232). In her final days, Mary 'spent some of her time in fits of rage against me as the evil genius of her life' (243). His prior admission could be taken as evidence that he faces his darker side, were he not so quick to dismiss Mary's raging as madness, brought on by his foolish, if well-intentioned, remark about her lost son (232). His bemusement could even be genuine, as it was that other time he could not accept the spectacle of Mary's copulation with a tramp: 'I decided that this unknown aspect must be called madness' (53). But his neglect of the facts in his final conversation with the priest is a case of selective memory, not unlike that of which he accuses Boy: '[H]e had so far edited his memory of his early days that the incident of the snowball had quite vanished from his mind' (261).

We are never told what Ramsay does say of Mary Dempster, only that Blazon asks him to 'remind him.' But once again the priest's commendation shows much of what has not been told: 'As for the miracles, you and I have looked too deeply into miracles to dogmatize; you believe in them, and your belief has coloured your life with beauty and goodness; too much scientizing will not help you. It seems far more important to me that her life was lived heroically; she endured a hard fate, did the best she could, and kept it up until at last her madness was too powerful for her. Heroism in God's cause is the mark of the saint, Ramezay, not conjuring tricks' (248–9). Since Mary's heroism is immediately transposed in Ramsay's autobiography into a confirmation of his own heroism, finally rewarded by his discovery of the Little Madonna, the priest's valediction gains the status of the last word on his spiritual development: '[H]e was laughing and pinching his copper nose with the tiny chocolate tongs. "God go with you, St Dunstan," he called' (250). Ironically, the gesture points to Ramsay's unconfessed failure with the devil. He pulls every nose but his own, ignoring the probability that the real devil one has to conquer is within. Ramsay's careful editing of his story is thus undone by body language he fails utterly to read. Through it, the author is able to restore the balance of acquaintance and resistance in the confrontation with the 'shadow.' But Ramsay's compromise makes it impossible for him to pull his own nose while he is wearing the mask of a saint.

The creation of a mask, of course, is another, very basic, form of 'self-invention.' But if the mask fits, it should be its own defence; whatever guilt its maker feels should be absorbed behind it. Ramsay's continuing guilt suggests a gap between his explanation and his conduct that even he does not understand. This gap and its cause are teasingly illustrated in his final discovery of the icon from Passchendaele. Padre Blazon's farewell sends him directly into the presence of his Little Madonna. The sequence of events, like the sequence of paragraphs, is meant to testify to his virtue: 'There she was, quite unmistakable, from the charming crown that she wore with such an air to her foot set on the crescent moon. Beneath this moon was what I had not seen in the harsh light of the flare – the globe of the earth itself, with a serpent encircling it, and an apple in the mouth of the serpent' (251). The new element is most revealing, for what he has edited from his memory of the first occasion is the fear, just before he sees the Virgin, that his injuries will give him tetanus and he will die of lockjaw: 'It was a Deptford belief that in this disease you bent backward until at last your head touched your heels and you had to be buried in a round coffin' (76). At the time, he had at least been able to guess what the icon signified: 'Not knowing what it was meant to be, I thought in a flash it must be the Crowned Woman in *Revelation* – she who had the moon beneath her feet and was menaced by the Red Dragon' (77).

The man who is nearing sixty years of age no longer recognizes himself in the tableau of the encircling serpent menacing the Virgin, 'that old serpent, called the Devil, and Satan, which deceiveth the whole world' (Rev. 12:9). As a boy-soldier, he had not yet been fully in the picture, had not been actualized as one of its elements. But as a man who has been cursed by the 'Virgin' on her deathbed, he dare not consider who he has become. His anticipation of '[t]he mysterious death of Boy Staunton' in the very next words of his ensuing chapter completes his ironic role as the 'Dragon' who in truth devours the 'Child.' The narrator who seeks his legitimacy in myth is finally unmasked by it; for in the icon of the Crowned Woman he is identified with the original rebellious figure who had proclaimed himself self-created.

Though never conceding Mary Dempster's identity as the Virgin, Padre
Blazon does ask Ramsay, 'What figure is she in your personal mythology?
... Lots of men have visions of their mothers in time of danger. Why not
you? Why was it this woman?' (177). The most obvious answer, the one
saved for his memoir, is that he has rejected his mother for what looks
like a good reason. And yet, while 'Mrs Ramsay may be a possessive
demon-mother to her own son. . . she is [also] a saintly life-giver to Paul
Dempster' (Radford 67). The Jungian explanation is that Ramsay projects his negative feminine side onto her: 'his own mother increasingly
assumes the aspect of the Terrible Mother, while he projects upon Mary
Dempster the image of the Pietà which Jung opposes to the former'
(Radford 68). The concept of projection presupposes that what is
glimpsed in the receiver is felt all the more powerfully because it is not
recognized in the sender. Put succinctly by Jung, 'Projections change the
world into the replica of one's own unknown face' (9). All Ramsay will
'see' in his mother's face is the domineering woman who 'had eaten my
father' (81). And yet his own refusal to be eaten is revealed as a contest of
wills for quite an unusual authority, as he hints soon after his defeat: 'It
was necessary for me to gain power in some realm into which my parents
– my mother particularly – could not follow me' (37).

The whipping he gets for a paltry stolen egg shows how far in fact his
mother has been able to follow him and just why she is so indignant. But
he will not explain himself to her or to us after he is caught in a lie: 'I
took refuge in mute insolence. She stormed. She demanded to know if I
thought she was made of eggs. Visited unhappily by a good one, I said
that that was something she would have to decide for herself' (35). One
critic, who calls Ramsay a 'transparently deceptive unreliable narrator,'
finds him using various eggs and stones throughout his narrative to create
a 'family of saints and parental archetypes' in order to 'transform his
past into a kind of mythical harmony in which he is not overshadowed by
Boy Staunton' (St Pierre 130, 128, 132). The primary contest for the
egg, however, is with the mother, and it goes to the very heart of his
mother's feeling of authority over him; he mocks her reproductive power.
Her Highland temper will not brook his insolence, much less such arrogance, though his declaration of absolute independence has unexpected
consequences: ' "Don't you dare touch me," I shouted, and that put her
into such a fury as I had never known' (35).

Ramsay's own outrage is not done away with many years later in his memory of their formal reconciliation: 'This I had to do on my knees, repeating a formula improvised by my father, which included a pledge that I would always love my mother, to whom I owed the great gift of life, and that I begged her – and secondarily God – to forgive me, knowing full well that I was unworthy of such clemency' (36). His indirect expression of the formula sounds faithful to the terms of the conflict ('owed the great gift of life'), though it may not justify his sneer about the pecking order in which first his mother must be placated 'and [then] secondarily God.' For his mother, he insists, is the one who is playing God, who really holds herself highest on the list of creators whom he has offended. But he will not repeat his mother's accusations against him, interpolating other phrases such as 'my increasing oddity and intellectual arrogance – not that she used these words, but I do not intend to put down what she actually said' (36). For she seems to have touched a nerve that Liesl (222) and Padre Blazon will later put their fingers on as well: '[S]top trying to be God' (177). The son is evidently guilty of projecting his own failings onto his mother.

An aesthete who wants to be free of nature should obviously hate his mother's natural power. But Ramsay overdoes it more than a little when he learns she has died: '[H]ow she would have paraded in mock-modesty as the mother of a hero, the very womb and matrix of bravery, in consequence of my three years of degradation in the Flanders mud!' (81–2). For his rebirth as the hero out of that mud is still threatened by the primacy of the womb, though his anxiety about the power of creation is not limited to gynophobia. He also sounds afraid that the doctor who brought him back to life might take some credit for his existence: 'I was one of his successes, though I rather think I cured myself, or the little Madonna cured me, or some agencies other than good nursing and medical observation' (79). He will even break off with Diana Marfleet out of his fear that 'she regarded me as her own creation' (88). His anxiety about mothers – '[W]hat was wrong between Diana and me was that she was too much a mother to me ... I had no intention of being anybody's own dear laddie, ever again' – is sharply defined in terms of his old struggle to be the master of the egg, the source of his own creation. Dunstan Ramsay will not be anybody's son (which is not the same thing as being a perpetual 'Boy').

Given the differing nature of their claims upon the narrator, it is hard to equate the two women as mothers. For Mrs Ramsay is a convention-

ally moral woman who sees Mary's adultery as an affront to virtue; her
son's association with such a woman is a personal insult. Diana, on the
other hand, is more liberal in her attitude to sex; and Ramsay appears to
accuse himself of being more than liberal, almost frivolous: 'I see that I
have been so muddle-headed as to put my sexual initiation in direct
conjunction with a visit to a musical show, which suggests some lack of
balance perhaps' (85). His defence of himself is none the less characteristic; he attempts to equate the two experiences as 'wonders, strange lands
revealed to me in circumstances of great excitement,' before excusing
himself on grounds of 'rather delicate health, mentally as well as physically' (86). Diana, who really does accuse him of frivolousness, is supposed to look as possessive as his mother, though her charge – 'I looked
on her simply as an amusement, a pastime' (90) – is actually borne out
by his remark about the musical show. Forced to give him up, Diana does
so graciously, going so far as to supply the name which might free him of
his mother's maiden name. And yet he says only that it is Diana who
shows a 'light-minded attitude' toward 'sacred things' such as christen-
ing (93). Instead of admitting her sacrifice, he dwells on her sacrilege,
salving his conscience with the thought that 'blasphemy in a good cause
(which usually means one's own cause) is not hard to stomach.' His easy
dismissal of her as being too much like his mother can only force a new
estimate of the supposed 'man-eater.'

Fiona and Diana are in fact directly comparable in their work as
nurses, and here the mother proves to be as selfless as the lover. While
Ramsay lies in hospital under Diana's care, his mother is giving her life
to save others in the influenza epidemic of 1918. Diana continues Fiona's
work of nursing a 'fighter' like Paul Dempster back to life by bringing
Ramsay himself back from the dead. Curiously, he will honour neither
woman for her devotion, though he is quick to credit Mary Dempster
with the resurrection of his 'dead' brother, Willie. Mary performs
instant 'miracles' where his mother has to slave away with more practical
and ordinary aids to maternity. Yet Fiona's story makes a better saint's
legend to Milo Papple than Mary Dempster's: 'And your Ma, Dunny –
God, she was a wonderful woman! Never let up on nursing and taking
soup and stuff around till your Dad went ... [Then] [y]our Ma lost heart
and she was gone herself before the week was out. Fine folks' (105–6).
Father Regan offers the same sort of judgment in words that second
Milo's: 'I'm trying to be kind, you know, for I admired your parents.

Fine people' (138). Fiona Ramsay, for all her faults, is not the domineering monster: her face shows instead the unacknowledged face of the child.

Ramsay's Virgin of the Immaculate Conception, the reverse face of the mother *imago*, mirrors him as well when he describes her as his own creation: 'I had made her what she was, and in such circumstances I must hate her or love her. In a mode that was far too demanding for my age or experience, I loved her' (31). His unreasonable guilt over the birth of little Paul – guilt which is never adequately explained – takes on an entirely new significance: '[E]ven now I hesitate to recall some of the nights when I feared to go to sleep and prayed till I sweated that God would forgive me for my mountainous crime. I was perfectly sure, you see, that the birth of Paul Dempster, so small, so feeble and troublesome, was my fault' (22). On the one hand, he wants us to see his rivalry for the mother in Freudian terms: 'The first six months of Paul Dempster's life were perhaps the most exciting and pleasurable period of my mother's life, and unquestionably the most miserable of mine' (19). On the other hand, he betrays a keen rivalry with the mother (Fiona as well as Mary) for the creation of the child: 'In the hot craziness of my thinking, I began to believe that I was more responsible for the birth of Paul Dempster than were his parents, and that if this were ever discovered, some dreadful fate would overtake me. Part of the dreadful fate would undoubtedly be rejection by my mother' (24). The rejection would come not from any sexual disloyalty to his mother but from his competition in creating a son and mother both.

Ramsay, who has read Freud, is prepared at this stage to make implicit use of the Oedipus complex to explain his relation to his mother. Later, however, Padre Blazon substitutes a more relevant myth of incest: 'Indeed, in the underworld hagiology of which I promised to tell you, it is whispered that the Virgin herself, who was born to Joachim and Anna through God's personal intervention, was a divine daughter as well as a divine mate; the Greeks could hardly improve on that, could they?' (172). This unorthodox version of the Annunciation comments ironically on Ramsay's relation to his saint: 'Did not God usurp Joseph's function, reputedly by impregnating his wife through her ear?' (172). For the snowball that hits Mary Dempster in the head is itself directed by a 'usurping' maker. 'Whoever it was, the Devil guided his hand,' Fiona says of the thrower. 'Yes, and the Devil shifted his mark,' confesses the adult narrator (25). But the confession is a throw-away line, the nearest he will come to admitting his demonic parody of the Creator. Later, the creature who would be his own creator improves upon the story of incest in his 'apparently mad mission' (143) to find another virgin saint, seemingly to support his decision not to marry. Wilgefortis, who is pictured as a hermaphrodite, none the less becomes an image of his need to be his own parent, the self-contained composite of the mother and father he rejects.

But why would a 'hermaphrodite' choose a child-bearing woman to be his patron saint? Padre Blazon, in asking him to consider who Mary is in his personal mythology, seems to think that she is simply a surrogate of the Holy Mother. Ramsay appears, instead, to look on her as his surro-gate self: 'I rather think I cured myself, or the little Madonna cured me' (79), he says smugly, as if there could be little to choose between them. The remarkable rising of his spirits, which he attributes to that 'relief of guilt' (160) which comes with his increased responsibility for Mary Dempster, underlies his equation of the saint with the self: 'If Mrs Dempster was a saint, henceforth she would be *my* saint' (160). Like-wise, his freedom from any dogmatic check upon her status shows that he intends, having made her once before, to make her something else again: 'Now I should be able to see what a saint was really like and perhaps make a study of one without all the apparatus of Rome, which I had no power to invoke' (161).

The making of a saint is a crucial step in legitimizing the self-made man. Such a patron would sanctify his work of self-creation since the saint herself would be of his making. We recall that Father Regan once warned him about trying to 'set up some kind of a bootleg saint' (138), which is exactly what he does, making her saintly authority depend on him. He is hard-pressed all the same to explain what a saint is doing locked up in a public madhouse. He goes to some length to explain the financial and emotional strain on him, but then rejects the most obvious solution – help from his partner in crime: 'Boy had a way of dominating anything with which he was associated; if I got help from him – which was not certain, for he always insisted that one of the first requirements for success was the ability to say "no" – he would have established himself as Mrs Dempster's patron and saviour and I would have been demoted to his agent' (180). The patron saint is evidently not the real patron in this arrangement, since Ramsay is concerned only for his own authority: 'My own motives were not clear or pure: I was determined that if I could not take care of Mrs Dempster, nobody else should do it.

She was mine.' The possessiveness he once projected upon his mother turns out to be his own. But the saint he creates as an *apologia pro vita sua* also becomes the image of his own unmaking: 'It was as though I were visiting a part of my own soul that was condemned to live in hell' (180).

Mary Dempster's dying words ask her jailer to think again about his identity:

'Are you Dunstable Ramsay?' she said. ֽ
I assured her. Another long silence.
'I thought he was a boy,' said she and closed her eyes again.   (244)

The boy she remembers was born to a mother; he even bore his mother's name. Such is the self she would have him recover. 'Forgive yourself for being a human creature' (178), Blazon had likewise cautioned him. But Ramsay does not see himself as he really is, though his saint finally strips the mask of his legitimacy. Even as he weeps at her death as he has not done 'since my mother had beaten me so many years before,' his belief that he was the victim brings his mother back in horribly inhuman shapes: 'When at last I fell asleep I dreamed frightening dreams, in some of which my mother figured in terrible forms' (244). In the absence of his first, best mask – the icon of his self-creation – he cannot face the fury of truth. Now he is plagued with a 'wretchedness so awful that I might as well not have been sixty years old ... [but] the feeblest of children.' Forced to be his 'mother's' child again, he regresses to a point where he would lose entirely his self-possession were it not for another female guarantor of his faith in self-creation.

Liesl helps, as much as Mary Dempster ever did, to free the man from the troublesome limits of his first birth: 'What I am saying is not for everybody, of course. Only for the twice-born. One always knows the twice-born. They often go so far as to take new names. Did you not say that English girl renamed you?' (226–7). The man who refuses to be anybody's 'laddie' makes no further comment on his dependence on women for his second birth; nor does he remark to Liesl that the latest renaming makes him 'thrice-born.' His 'conversion' is the assumption, rather, of a new mask he can wear to the world, if not to himself. Fifth Business is public in yet another sense, since it allows him to include Eisengrim and

Staunton in his secret ambition: 'Had you thought that we are all three of the company of the twice-born? We have all rejected our beginnings and become something our parents could not have foreseen' (262). The difference, however, between his public mask and the private one of saint-maker is that he no longer even tries to deceive himself. He does not mean at all to let Staunton, for example, off the hook of the past, urging him 'to recover something of the totality of your life. Don't you want to possess it as a whole – the bad with the good?' (264). He is really justifying his betrayal of Boy to Eisengrim even as he rids himself of his most dangerous link to that past. But the obvious discrepancy between himself and this persona makes some recovery of his old self imperative. What he does at last in writing his autobiography is to transform the saint-maker into the saint.

His choice of a narrative beginning now looms larger as the hidden image of his desire to be a self-made man. For he omits any account of his parents or his birth in his first chapter to focus instead on the fateful snowball. Paul's birth, which causes Dunny so much grief at the time, is delayed until the third chapter. His opening sentence none the less makes another kind of 'birth' announcement: 'My lifelong involvement with Mrs Dempster began at 5.58 o'clock p.m. on 27 December 1908, at which time I was ten years and seven months old' (9). Now Mary replaces his mother as he dates to the minute the paradigm of all his subsequent rebirths. The unusual precision of the date has been noticed before, if only as an 'astrological witness' to the character of events. Since it is Paul Dempster who is born under the sign of Saturn, the 'natal horoscope' is said to predict his 'need to create what Jung has called a persona' (Murray 117–18). Yet it is the autobiographer who really needs a 'mother' to conceal his self-created persona.

Susan Sontag, in *Under the Sign of Saturn*, supplies the 'horoscope' which more likely explains the complex relation of the autobiographer to his writing: 'The mark of the Saturnine temperament is the self-conscious and unforgiving relation to the self, which can never be taken for granted. The self is a text – it has to be deciphered ... The self is a project, something to be built' (117). Ramsay's own melancholy is related to several forms of guilt, although the thing for which he can never forgive himself – the need to be self-existent – is inherent in his project of making a text of the self. 'Recent theoreticians of autobiography argue that the very project of writing, the act of signification itself, alienates the writing self from his subject.' In part, that is because 'language forces the subject to objectify himself as though he were a third person. At the same time, through the pronoun "I," language masks the dubious enterprise of self-objectification the subject is engaged in, suggesting to the listener that he is finding out something about the subject of the statement' (Martens 40). This primary split between grammatical subject and object, then, leads to public deception, or to a secondary split between the autobiographer and his audience.

Ramsay's problematical insistence on the first person none the less goes beyond the usual problem of autobiography. For his greatest dilemma has little to do with his reliance 'on a referential model of language, where the "self" is elided into preexisting rhetorical structures' (Martens 40), since he refuses any prior 'author,' whether it be a mother or any other 'language' of begetting. His novel solution to the supposedly 'natural' problem of autobiography thus suggests a hidden Oedipal dimension to the crisis of self-consciousness: it is as if the 'I' which is writing could only forgive the 'I' which is written by making up a substitute Nativity story. The Christmas season and a mother named Mary offer a saving illusion that the self-made man is born of woman. In such fashion, he can almost live with the paradox that he must fabricate himself, yet cannot forgive himself, must confess yet somehow beatify himself.

Ramsay's confession of overwhelming guilt is hereafter controlled through largely witting emphasis. We recall that he has proposed to make his narrative 'as brief as I can, for it is not by piling up detail that I hope to achieve my picture, but by putting the emphasis where I think it belongs' (16). Yet he will later admit of his relationship with Diana that 'I lied in every word I uttered – lied not in fact but in emphasis, in colour, and in intention' (82). His very emphasis on the snowball is a far-reaching example of his uneasy sense that he continues to lie in colour and in intention: 'If I had not been so clever, so sly, so spiteful in hopping in front of the Dempsters just as Percy Boyd Staunton threw that snowball at me from behind, Mrs Dempster would not have been struck. Did I never think that Percy was guilty? Indeed I did' (22). The facts do not deny Percy's guilt; much less do they deny that Dunny's slyness was first directed at Percy. But the narrative act is also a chance to rewrite history as, ideally, it should have been. Through a subtle shift of emphasis, Ramsay converts his later spite of his mother into the story of his new 'beginnings.' The flight of the snowball changes direction slightly; now it serves to 'impregnate' the Virgin and to install him as the father of his Holy Family. The boy who 'pelted home' (11) – the verb defines his secret action – also establishes his characteristic use of myth: 'I gave my story a slight historical bias, leaning firmly but not absurdly on my own role as the Good Samaritan. I suppressed any information or guesswork about where the snowball had come from, and to my relief my mother did not pursue that aspect of it' (11).

It has been argued that monologue in *Fifth Business* – of this very sort which invites no question or any form of dialogue – helps to 'establish an absolute and rigid hierarchy of spiritual wisdom, which is very powerful and never seriously challenged' (Bonnycastle 30). Monologue is a very deceptive tool, however, for any narrator who expresses delight in the magician's 'subtle technique of misdirecting the attention of his audience, which is the beginning and end of the conjurer's art' (*Fifth* 211). Like Eisengrim who 'began his show by appearing in the middle of the stage out of nowhere' (201), so too Ramsay appears in his writing out of nowhere, dodging the guilt not of some unlucky snowball but of the act of self-creation. Narrative, in other words, is his final work of conjuring a saintly new persona, and he does it much better than he could ever '[s]ecure and palm six half-crowns' (39).

The magician complements Ramsay's chosen image of himself because he shows him how to dominate an audience without having to seem domineering. Ramsay remarks of Eisengrim's performance in the Teatro Chueca that 'I have seen displays of hypnotism in which people were made to look foolish, to show the dominance of the hypnotist; there was nothing of that here, and all of the twenty left the stage with dignity unimpaired, and indeed with a heightened sense of importance' (203). It is all a performance, of course, as Ramsay is well aware. For behind the scenes he observes Liesl holding a keen intelligence in check 'so that Eisengrim might dominate the conversation' (207). 'Further,' Ramsay says, 'it was clear enough to me that his compelling love affair was with himself' (220). But here, at least, he fails to notice himself in the hypnotist's mirror. If the monologist should now feel no rivalry with the magician, no conscious threat to his own need to dominate, it is because Paul is already twice his creature – first in the manner of his birth, and second in the matter of his 'autobiography.' The memoirist helps in more ways than one to invent his own *alter ego*.

Boy, on the other hand, is one of those who 'seemed to have made himself out of nothing' (111) with no credit to Ramsay. He is thus destined to be a bitter rival to the man who sees other people as his creatures. Ramsay is forced to repudiate him – 'spite' him as he puts it – because Boy insists on being self-made like himself. At one point, he even sneers at Boy for being 'the quintessence of the Jazz Age, a Scott Fitzgerald character' (114). He would seem to be thinking of Jay Gatsby who 'sprang from his Platonic conception of himself' (Fitzgerald 99); and yet Ramsay shares nothing of Nick Carraway's transcendentalism which offers up Gatsby as a tragic sacrifice to the incorruptible ideal. Instead, he portrays a darker side to New World romanticism by making Boy the scapegoat of his own pretension to divinity. Unwittingly, he accuses Boy of what he does himself: 'You created a God in your own image, and when you found out he was no good you abolished him. It's a quite common form of psychological suicide' (241). His reprimand turns back on him in the ensuing chapter, however, when he has to abolish a 'saint' who cannot ward off his vengeful mother. But he avoids suicide because he makes a new 'God' in his own image – this time in the form of a wise old hagiographer – and has him conduct the canonization: 'God go with you, St Dunstan' (250).

Ramsay's story, as it is projected onto Boy, becomes at last the history of a man who would rather not know himself: 'Aside from my teaching, my observation of Boy's unwitting destruction of Leola, and my new and complete responsibility for Mrs Dempster,' writes Mary's unwitting destroyer, 'this was the most demanding period of my life' (164). Demanding, indeed, must be the life of a man who uses his rival as proxy for begetting another son, as on the night Boy showed Ramsay pictures of the naked Leola: 'I think I stirred some uxorious fire in Boy, for nine months later I did some careful counting, and I am virtually certain that it was on that night little David was begotten' (158). Of course, Boy was his proxy once before in inseminating the 'Virgin.'

Evidently the stone-in-the-snowball, which is supposed to be the image of Boy's character, is more like an image of his own unknown self. 'Boy,' he chides, 'for God's sake, get to know something about yourself. The stone-in-the-snowball has been characteristic of too much you've done for you to forget it forever' (264). He protests his best intentions at the very moment he draws fire from Eisengrim on Boy's unsuspecting head. Now the memoir closes as it opened, with a proxy who throws his snowballs for him. In circular fashion, the autobiographer thus 'writes' in flesh and blood before he justifies himself on paper.

The stages in Ramsay's defence of himself disclose at last how such a self-conscious narrator can be caught in this authorial circle of irony. Because his mother threatens his independence, he is driven in daily life to 'confess' his need of a more saintly mother figure. But because the saint refuses to serve as an icon of his self-creation, he turns to his devil to help put off his forebodings with another mask. Yet Boy's death makes him feel the falsity of Fifth Business, even while he does his utmost to shore up his front with a formal apologia. The act of writing thus lets him gather up his earlier forms of justification into an autonomous text where the self becomes synonymous with the thing it creates.

Henceforth, the self Ramsay projects to the world appears, like the face of Dorian Gray, to be the picture of innocence, if not of immortal youth. But when Ramsay contrives to get rid of Boy – who has taken over Dorian's role of eternal Youth – it is clear that Boy is for him his self-knowledge incarnate, just as the picture was the embodiment of Dorian's truest self. And so Ramsay's elimination of his shadowy *alter ego* is likely to unmask him too, just as it did his literary ancestor. Still, the most revealing difference between the two now consists in their differing modes of presentation. In the third-person novel, the man himself is judged while his portrait recovers the ideal image of the man; but in the confessional novel, the man's self-representation has to be framed inside a more 'objective' picture. That picture is to be found in the icon of the Crowned Woman. Ramsay, who has rid himself of two mothers and one 'Child' in his efforts to be self-made, is finally revealed as the missing 'Dragon.' But his life imitates art in yet another way, since it also turns out to be circular in form. Because the self-made man can offer no real ground of his own being, he retreats from the new mode of poetic self-invention back through apologia to inadvertent confession. In this way, the memoirist appears in his own icon as the serpent encircling the globe who is put, firmly and finally, under the mother's heel.

Finally, the reader's role in this process of unmasking the autobiographer is projected in Ramsay's baleful response to one would-be biographer, 'that ineffable jackass Lorne Packer.' The grammatical illiteracy of the tribute published in the *College Chronicle* is a mere laughing matter beside its religious illiteracy – 'Packer, who pushes me towards oblivion with tags of Biblical quotation, the gross impertinence of which he is unable to appreciate' (15). For the man who wants to live in myth is not likely to appreciate the biblical commendation, 'Well done, thou good and faithful servant.' Not when the speaker in Christ's parable is God himself: 'Thou hast been faithful over a few things, I will make thee ruler over many things: enter into the joy of thy Lord' (Matt. 25: 21). The poor fool has presumed unwittingly to be Ramsay's God.

In his survey of the changing modes of autobiography since Augustine, Spengemann concludes that the nineteenth century gives rise to an unprecedented form of self-portraiture (though he ignores the overt aestheticism of Moore and Wilde for an 'American' ideology discovered rather obliquely in Hawthorne). Here, at last, 'The autobiography becomes, not a history or a philosophical analysis of a life lived elsewhere, but a series of actions performed in the composition of it' (150). Henceforth, it is no longer possible to accept without qualification

> the assumption that a substantial self or soul precedes and governs individual experience and may be discerned through that experience. This assumption had enabled historical autobiographers to explain, philosophical autobiographers to search for, and poetic autobiographers to express, the absolute self behind their conditioned actions. Those autobiographers who have managed to maintain Augustine's belief in unconditioned selfhood have continued to write about themselves in the three forms he erected upon that belief. But, for those who have anticipated Hawthorne's conclusion, that the self is continually reshaped by efforts to explain, discover, or express it, autobiography in the Augustinian sense is no longer possible.
>
> In this situation, every individual action is artistic ... 'Our actions write our autobiography, which is, of course a fiction.' The corollary of this proposition is that every fiction is, willy-nilly, a self portrait. (Spengemann 167)

In these terms, Dunstan Ramsay's self-portrait is obviously a fiction, as the etymology of the word alone would suggest (a 'made thing'). But if autobiography is inherently fictional, it is also fictive in another sense in *Fifth Business*, inasmuch as it allows the creature to deny that he is anything but his own creation. He proclaims his unconditioned selfhood in the very act of denying the world (or parents) from which he springs. Though Spengemann concludes that a substantial self may not precede its own becoming in the act of writing, Ramsay's life story exposes the true intent of such 'self-creation' – the desire, in the words of George Moore's *Confessions*, 'to create a complete and absolute self out of the partial self which was all that the restraint of home had permitted' (54). Later in *The Manticore*, the heraldist Pledger-Brown will write to Boy Staunton's son, David, objecting to this very tendency: 'You talk about individualism; what you truly want is to be links in a long unbroken chain' (259). But Ramsay himself wants nothing of the sort; the self which is supposed to be partial – or at best provisional – appears substantially as the author of himself. He is his own best work of art, made to survive his own death, as he hints in various written asides to his Headmaster.

On the other hand, Ramsay's cult of the marvellous offers him another chance to be free of reality while he is still alive. Yet he must needs be more magician than artist who can yoke William James's pragmatism to the mysticism of Carl Jung, thereby producing 'a dynamic that at once releases its initiates from the constraints of moral absolutes. At the same time, it provides them with an encompassing symbology that condones much, even as it adds greatly to the characters' sense of self-importance' (Duffy, 'Truth' 17–18). Though Duffy concludes: 'Who could resist canonizing a text of such appeal? We get the saints we deserve,' Robertson Davies proves just as doubtful as the critic is of an aesthete who, like Dorian Gray, 'takes' other lives to immortalize his own. And so the devil in *Fifth Business* comes back to remind us that the saint is not what he seems, and has not, and never could, survive his belated role as the 'Fifth.' For, in spite of Ramsay's claim, like Milton's Satan, to be 'self-begot, self-rais'd/By our own quick'ning power' (*Paradise Lost*: v, 860), or even to 'know none before him,' the Devil clearly knows her own, inviting him in a public post card to come live with her and 'the Basso ... before The Five make an end of us all' (*Fifth* 266). Most unexpectedly, the aesthete who frees himself from origins is 'born again' of a woman, if in a fashion he cannot understand. And so his portrait which records his every sin and disfigurement can finally look back at the world with an expression that almost passes for innocence.

4

The Self-Created Story-Teller in *The Stone Angel*

Every discoloration of the stone,
Every accidental crack or dent,
Seems a water-course or an avalanche,
Or lofty slope where it still snows
Though doubtless plum or cherry-branch
Sweetens the little half-way house
Those Chinamen climb towards, and I
Delight to imagine them seated there;
There, on the mountain and the sky,
On all the tragic scene they stare.

                              W.B. Yeats, 'Lapis Lazuli'

A stone figure would appear to transcend the very life it represents in one of Yeats's last poems, its Paterian moment frozen into a 'consummate extract' of life. The old poet concludes none the less that art is neither an intuition of eternity – an ideal form – nor a 'supreme reality' transcending the 'fiction' of life; rather, it is a natural part of that life. For form itself can not fix 'the transient into a permanent image' (Iser, *Pater* 37); 'urns' – whether of Chinese or Grecian design – crumble, and their stone faces, like our human ones, return ultimately to dust. And so the Romantic's anguish at the separation between art and life is finally beside the point. Though Keats had lamented his own mortality in unforgettable terms – 'For ever wilt thou love, and she be fair' – the 'tragic scene' on which Yeats stares at the close urges no agonized sense of loss or alienation, but only 'Gaiety transfiguring all that dread.' Just as surely, however, the young poet who had once defended 'Wilde against the charge of being a poseur,' saying that 'it was merely living artistically' (Ellmann, *Yeats* 77), comes to see at the end of his life that nothing, not even art, is superior to nature. Art imitates life both in its rise and its fall.

'Above the town, on the hill brow, the stone angel used to stand' (*Angel* 3), an unwitting disciple of Yeats (much less of Wilde) begins her own meditation on approaching death. At first the ninety-year-old curmudgeon of Laurence's novel lacks the quiet gaiety of Yeats's persona, founding much of her story, as Wilde 'founded much of his art[,] upon the tension between the pose and the real self' (Ellmann, *Yeats* 75). Thus Hagar would have us think she is really as hard as stone when, in fact, she is terrified of being humanly vulnerable, of being open, like everybody else, to a 'black sea sucking everything into itself, the spent gull, the trivial garbage from boats, and men protected from eternity only by their soft and fearful flesh and their seeing eyes' (*Angel* 225). Hagar's story, in other words, is a monumental pose, told to *herself* to free her from the threat of nature, until she learns to rejoice in the nature of being. 'The truths of masks,' to turn a phrase from Wilde, become 'the truths of metaphysics.' For art itself is the stony mask which has to become flesh in *The Stone Angel*.

This very excess of artifice in Hagar's story has bedevilled critics from the first reviews of the novel: 'It is, for one thing, more consciously *written*: one is aware of the stylist without being sufficiently unaware of the style. I have said the flashbacks were neat and predictable' (Robertson 54). A more revealing approach ignores the author's self-conscious artifice to focus instead on Hagar's resistance to the nature of the place she inhabits: 'Just as her father's stiff stout house stands "antimacassared in the wilderness," so she learns to wrap herself in her sanitary *persona* and to scorn the dark Métis from "the wrong side of the tracks"' (Cooley 33). What is 'distinctively "Canadian"' about this view is that Hagar represents 'the "garrison mentality" in its need for rigid conformity and its fear of spontaneity and sensuality' (Hehner 41).

What proponents of the 'garrison mentality' have none the less failed to see in their look-out from the nineteenth-century Canadian fortress is that other Victorian residents of more civilized landscapes – Vivian in 'The Decay of Lying,' for example – were just as eager to shut nature outside the pale of civility. Nature, Vivian said in Wilde's dialogue, was unfinished, anyway; art offered people much better models for their own reinvention and completion: '[W]hat is interesting about people in good society ... is the mask that each one of them wears, not the reality that lies behind the mask. It is a humiliating confession, but we are all of us made out of the same stuff' (*Intentions* 15).

That humiliating confession must be made by the old woman in *The Stone Angel*, all the same: 'In shaking off her fabricated masks and tenacious stranglehold on life, Hagar finally moves toward personal wholeness' (Cooley 46). But 'the specious version of herself [which] she has received from her society' (Cooley 46) is not, in fact, received from her society at all, not even though Hagar will continue to insist on her place in such 'good society.' For Hagar's more 'humiliating confession,' like Wilde's, is the truth that nature itself is finally levelling. And social levelling is nothing, in Hagar's view, compared to the deeper levelling of the grave: 'The both of them. Both the same. Nothing to pick and choose between them now. That was as it should be. But all the same, I didn't want to stay any longer. I turned and walked back to the car. Marvin stood talking to the man for a while, and then he came back, too, and we drove on' (*Angel* 306). And so her 'demon' of fear (292), which quite naturally 'rage[s] against the dying of the light' (*Angel* ii), leads her into a confessed wilderness of pride. But having realized so much, the stone angel cracks completely and shows her true nature. Now what she reveals is that narrative itself might be a pose, her last, best refuge against the fear of death. What she confesses in the end is that art has not and can not save her life; probably it has even kept her from life. But by the time she reaches her moment of truth, the story is nearly over. Truth is thus equated with closure, with the end of Hagar's life and of *The Stone Angel*.

The Diviners more obviously fits decadent assumptions about writing, particularly Wilde's idea that art is 'the supreme reality and life ... a mere mode of fiction.' As Morag observes, writing can be 'A daft profession. Wordsmith. Liar, more likely. Weaving fabrications. Yet, with typical ambiguity, convinced that fiction was more true than fact. Or that fact was in fact fiction' (*Diviners* 25). In other ways, as well, this female artist-as-liar recalls Wilde: 'Morag is fascinated. Does fiction prophesy life? Is she looking at Lilac Stonehouse from *Spear of Innocence*?' (309). Conversely, the title of her first novel might really be taken from the emblem on the 'crest badge' of Christie's Clan Logan: 'A passion nail piercing a human heart, proper' (48). But life, in the form of an undesigning book designer, seems to mirror art when the novel itself enters the world: 'The dust jacket for *Spear of Innocence* shows a spear, proper, piercing a human heart, valentine' (261). In other ways, as well, Morag's life unexpectedly imitates art. The Shipley plaid pin which she gets from Jules Tonnerre turns out to be from the Clanranald Macdonald, of whom Archie Macdonald is the real-life prototype for her mythic ancestor, Piper Gunn: 'Clann Gunn, according to this book, as she recalls from years back, did not have a crest or a coat-of-arms. But adoption, as who should know better than Morag, is possible' (432).

The aesthetics of the decadence merge fully with the aesthetics of postmodernism in *The Diviners'* preference for story about story, about process instead of the created product. For the mythmaker, Christie, is hardly the only one to insist on the fictionality of fiction, on its provisional status: 'It's all true and not true. Isn't that a bugger, now?' (88). Morag will also draw attention to the fictional quality of history itself, whether personal or public: '*A popular misconception is that we can't change the past – everyone is constantly changing their own past, recalling it, revising it. What really happened? A meaningless question*' (60). In fact, history, as much as memory, is a created artefact; they're all '*totally invented memories*' (10). Without consciously acknowledging it, Morag in her writing thus follows Wilde's advice to 'Create yourself. Be yourself your poem.' She is her own aesthetic creation.

In such ways, Morag's past is open to change. But what about her present? 'Morag grows and learns, particularly in her relationship with Christie, throughout the second narrative level [the past], but does not move toward a significant character development on the first level; she has, in a way ... already "arrived" when the novel begins ... Nor can the reader see her change because of what she learns from her memories. This latter condition is true because Morag not only understands herself, she understands the memory process' (Gom 56). Thus the end of this 'story about story' is already realized in its beginning.

We are told that 'Something about Pique's going ... was unresolved in Morag's mind' (*Diviners* 5). But memory returns to the loss of her own parents to show what is really unresolved in Morag's mind. Colin Gunn's going, and his wife Louisa's, is the root of Morag's problem. Morag being left. The lost child is the mother, not the daughter. And so the 'child' has all the answers before the end of the first chapter. '*Perhaps I only want their forgiveness for having forgotten them. I remember their*

deaths, but not their lives. Yet they're inside me, flowing unknown in my
blood and moving unrecognized in my skull' (19). It doesn't take much
to realize that Pique will continue Morag's life on similar terms. 'As for
Morag, it is interesting that the reader takes leave of her ... where he had
first met her: watching the river that flows both ways and looking "ahead
into the past, and back into the future, until the silence" ' (Gom 57).

So artifice threatens closure in *The Diviners* as surely as it ever did in
The Stone Angel. Blood, it seems, will out with books as much as it will
with people: ' "You take after me," he said, as though that made everything clear. "You've got backbone, I'll give you that" ' (*Angel* 10). 'I
tried to shut my ears to it, and thought I had, yet years later, when I was
rearing my two boys, I found myself saying the same words to them'
(*Angel* 13). For no one really escapes the past, as Hagar is forced to
admit. She runs away to a weathered grey fish cannery only to find herself
in Bram's house, John and Arlene's vacated home. Now Morag, she had
the sense to quit running a long time ago. She's already come full circle.
There she sits like Janus, looking both ways. But she knows that history
is only repeating itself, so the past might not be as open to revision as she
claims: Jules *wants to see [Pique], but not for her to see him*. The aeons
ago memory. The child saying *I'll just go up and see my mother and
father, now, for a minute*' (447). Children in Laurence evidently inherit
their parents' lives; it follows, then, that the problem of each novel must
be what to make of that inheritance.

At least a *writer* watching history repeat itself can help to improve the
inherited technique of the earlier novel. 'It is the form of *The Stone
Angel*, with its two parallel plot lines and two Hagars, that *The Diviners*
uses most as its model ... [Here] Laurence has preserved the technique of
The Stone Angel and legitimized it' (Gom 50, 52). Of course, Morag has
an excuse that the old woman can't have, in stringing memories together
like beads on a string. Morag writes her memories in a notebook. Even
the most ardent supporters of *The Stone Angel* are prone to confess that
memory doesn't work like a novel unfolding. Hagar, they assume, can
tell her own story, but she can't be a novelist.

Writing a novel is Morag's declaration of independence. She breaks
away from the husband who refuses children by writing herself into her
blind protagonist: 'Lilac has aborted herself in a way that Morag recalls
from long ago. And yet it is not Eva for whom Morag experiences pain
now – it is Lilac only, at this moment' (*Diviners* 229). Morag's husband

'cannot ever say to her, finally, once and for all, that he cannot bear for her to bear a child' (246). The most he dares to ask is whether 'the main character – Lilac – expresses anything which we haven't known before?' The question is totally unfair to the younger writer: Morag learns in writing *Spear of Innocence* that Lilac's aborted child is her own. But the older writer has little to learn in writing *about* her first novel that she didn't discover at the time. Her primary doubling of herself as Eva had led initially to self-knowledge; but the secondary doubling of the text is now for the benefit of the reader, not the writer. Morag, in other words, can only pose in her last novel as a novelist; there is no real tension left between her art and her life.

Morag writes to her friend Ella, 'That incredibly moving statement – "What strength I have's mine own, which is most faint – " If only he can hang onto that knowledge, that would be true strength' (*Diviners* 330). But Morag has been hanging onto 'knowledge' which Prospero never had: a self which is doubled in the 'third person' and so made durable in language. She is not likely to lose such *knowledge* of her previous self as she is to lose that future power of *making*. The figure of Prospero only announces her terrible concern with lost doing; Morag must be up and doing, like her pioneering 'ancestor,' Catharine Parr Traill, to stave off her fear of helplessness. And so she redoubles her prior acts of making, though not to remake herself. To readers, it is all new; we are taken through the stages of her growing strength. But to Morag, it is ritual repetition, a kind of mythic gesture designed to take her back to her beginnings, not to further the knowledge of her strength. In other words, she knows the whole story before she ever begins to repeat it. And so it isn't 'natural.' No wonder she can't grow any more in the telling.

Hagar, at the end of her life, still intends to tell away the threat of endings. But how? When death itself proves to be the end of her story? Or when she insists on being even more deterministic than Morag, never free to make what she will of herself, but rather obsessed, almost beside herself? 'Now I light one of my cigarettes and stump around my room, remembering furiously, for no reason except that I am caught up in it' (*Angel* 6). Hagar is caught up by her author, it would seem, who spirits her through time like the Ghost of Christmas Past. Rubbing her nose in it. Until she cries uncle. 'Pride was my wilderness, and the demon that led me there was fear' (*Angel* 292).

Pride goeth before a fall. All the critics defer to the proverb. ' "Pride was my wilderness" – strength was my weakness – is Hagar's moment of truth' (Thomas 68–9). 'Hagar's life represents a progress from one displaced garden to another until the realization comes to her that her pride has kept her from joy and live [sic], has created the wilderness which has been her life' (Thompson 96). 'Although Hagar's pride is a wilderness because it isolates her from human contact, it also proves a basis for moral awareness' (Kertzer 504). Hagar insists all the same how it was a demon that left her in a wilderness of pride, that Fear was his name, and that his numbers are legion. But demons are a hell of a thing to face in criticism. Proverbs offer refuge.

Pride, not a proverb, is Hagar's refuge. Pride keeps the demon at bay. 'Above the town, on the hill brow, the stone angel used to stand. I wonder if she stands there yet, in memory of her who relinquished her feeble ghost as I gained my stubborn one, my mother's angel that my father bought in pride to mark her bones and proclaim his dynasty, as he fancied, forever and a day' (*Angel* 3). Pride saves Hagar, as it saves her father, from the taint of the dead mother. Weakness, she sees, is fatal. No wonder she cannot put on her mother's shawl to comfort her dying brother: ' "Hagar – put it on and hold him for a while." I stiffened and drew away my hands. "I can't. Oh Matt, I'm sorry, but I can't, I can't. I'm not a bit like her" ' (*Angel* 25). Identification, she learns, may be just as fatal as weakness.

In memory of her. Though Hagar never stoops to her father's hypocrisy, her own 'memorial' can hardly recall a mother she never knew. She can only hold to a marble surrogate who is blankly reassuring. The stone angel abides where her mother does not. It is her own proud front against the fear of death, against the fear that she has taken that life: 'It seemed to me then that Matt was almost apologetic, as though he felt he ought to tell me he didn't blame me for her dying, when in his heart he really did' (*Angel* 24–5). Nor can she let her guard down now; the feeble mother has to be changed into something strong. Into a woman more like Hagar's father. The stone angel – the masculinized woman – is all a pose, an artificial construction of herself. Though he would not approve of Wilde, her father might at least approve of his manly little daughter: 'Father didn't hold it against me that it had happened so. I know, because he told me. Perhaps he thought it was a fair exchange, her life for mine' (*Angel* 59). The child naturally blames the victim, being powerless herself. Her only hope is to exchange her identity. Since her father has fashioned this enduring image of his lost wife, Hagar makes herself over in the same pattern. The helpless daughter becomes the invincible wife.

The 'wife' isn't merely playing, either, at being Electra. The attraction to Daddy is the nature of his strength. 'Auntie Doll was always telling us that Father was a God-fearing man. I never for a moment believed it, of course. I couldn't imagine Father fearing anyone, God included, especially when he didn't even owe his existence to the Almighty. God might have created heaven and earth and the majority of people, but Father was a self-made man, as he himself had told us often enough' (*Angel* 16–17). To be self-made is to be subject to no power outside the self, not even death. 'Tis a consummation devoutly to be wished.

So 'Hagar flees death in various ways. By retreating to the past she is, of course, attempting to escape her future, her impending death. In memory, at least, she can be a young girl, a new bride, a mother' (Davidson 65). But memory is more than a safe retreat. It is a means of inventing a new history. Otherwise the dead mother taints everything with her mortality. 'But all I could think of was that meek woman I'd never seen, the woman Dan was said to resemble so much and from whom he'd inherited a frailty I could not help but detest, however much a part of me wanted to sympathize. To play at being her – it was beyond me' (*Angel* 25). Instead, she plays at being the self-made man: her father, who dies like everybody else.

In retrospect, Jason Currie's death should justify Hagar's war of independence. 'Within a year, Currie Memorial Park was started beside the Wachakwa River. The scrub oak was uprooted and the couchgrass mown, and nearly circular beds of petunias proclaimed my father's immortality in mauve and pink frilled petals. Even now, I detest petunias' (*Angel* 63–4). For the self-made man hasn't made himself to last. And petunias are a very poor substitute for immortality. Yet Hagar's problem at the end of her life is the same as it was at the beginning – how to create an enduring image of herself. The paternal, 'artificial' image is powerless to save her; and the maternal, 'natural' one proves to be deadly. What she needs is nothing less than a metamorphosis. 'The night my son died I was transformed to stone and never wept at all' (*Angel* 243).

As in life, so in story. She represses the painful truth of human mortality and starts her story over with the image of a woman 'transformed to stone.' The weeping mother, Niobe who was changed to stone out of pity for her grief, is here transformed because she will not weep.

Stone outlives the cause of tears. By telling her story to herself, Hagar thus tries to create the indestructible self that she yearns to be. But 'Hagar's vaunted strength is a sham' (Davidson 65). The tension between her pose and her real self is what makes her story so compelling. For she herself is driven to deconstruct it. And then to recreate it in terms of her newly confessed weakness.

'I'd be about six, surely,' Hagar says, finding a ground in what looks like simple chronology for the memoir she tells to herself: 'There was I ... haughty, hoity-toity, Jason Currie's black-haired daughter ... [My father] never believed in wasting a word or a minute. He was a self-made man' (*Angel* 6–7). 'I'd be about eight' (15), the self-made woman wastes few words in confirming the point of the lesson: 'Auntie Doll was always telling us that Father was a God-fearing man ... God might have created heaven and earth and the majority of people, but Father was a self-made man' (*Angel* 16–17). What the neat chronology conceals is this unacknowledged imitation of her father. Memory shapes a model to free her of her mother's ghost.

The self-made man still contradicts, at points, his own theology. 'I'd been named, hopefully, for a well-to-do spinster great-aunt in Scotland, who, to my father's chagrin, had left her money to the Humane Society' (*Angel* 14). Heritage is not to be denied where there's a dollar to be made. But family history repeats the lesson Father learned the hard way: 'You were named after him, Dan. Sir Daniel Currie – the title died with him, for it wasn't a baronetcy ... . His partner cheated him – oh, it was a bad affair all around, I can tell you, and there was I, without a hope or a ha'penny' (*Angel* 14–15). *There was I.* The passive expletive construction is the same one Hagar uses. Seemingly one is left at the mercy of one's inheritance. Better to take it all back, then, to start from scratch. 'He called me "miss" when he was displeased, and "daughter" when he felt kindly disposed toward me. Never Hagar' (*Angel* 14). The name itself is too painful to be borne. The outcast Hagar must be unnamed.

The daughter, however, has learned her father's lesson too well. She must reject him to be truly like him. Her husband is the one who shows her how to be free of a relational identity: 'I was Hagar to him, and if he were alive, I'd be Hagar to him yet. And now I think he was the only person close to me who ever thought of me by my name, not daughter, nor sister, nor mother, nor even wife, but Hagar, always' (*Angel* 80). And

Hagar she remains, unique and unattached, almost to the end of her days: 'Stupid old baggage, who do you think you are? *Hagar*. There's no one like me in this world' (*Angel* 250).

The trouble is, she marries a man named Bram. There's no one like him, either. But Abram and Hagar together are an old story. And the story ends badly, with Hagar outcast again. What's a girl to do? It's almost as if there *is* a God, at any rate an author, imposing a pattern from above. Hagar, suspecting the former, quarrels with the Father, resisting her creator. She has to unmake the old story. 'As we can see from the uncompromising portrait of Hagar's husband Bram ("Abram"), [Laurence's] use of the Genesis story is not simply as an allegory of the Genesis text' (Jeffrey 92). Hagar, in fact, is quite prepared to forget all about Genesis. Abram's first wife is dead. So there is no Sara for her to mock and jeer at in her barrenness, but there is also no Sara to drive her out into the wilderness. The child could be a problem, though, wanting to be born. 'What could I say? That I'd not wanted children? That I believed I was going to die, and wished I would, and prayed I wouldn't? That the child he wanted would be his, and none of mine?' (*Angel* 100). Mothers are supposed to die. Or at least be exiled. Yet what if they live? There's still that old threat of endings. Rewrite the story, then. Have Hagar, not Abram, drive the child into exile. Marvin, be Ishmael.

The second son is obviously Isaac, God's promised child to Sara. Henceforth, Hagar, be Sara. Not as the type of God's promised covenant, Abram's wife, but as the antitype, the virgin mother: 'I wasn't frightened at all when John was born. I knew I wouldn't die that time. Bram had gone to fix a fence down by the slough. Such mercies aren't often afforded us. I hitched up and drove the buggy into town myself ... Calm as a stout madonna' (*Angel* 121-2). There's the ultimate proof you're self-made. Even your husband can't make you. The invincible wife becomes the inviolable mother. By such means the bondswoman Hagar might achieve her own allegory. She will live happily ever after, without her husband. Death, be not proud.

Death still has dominion, though. The husband goes swiftly downhill and nearly takes his wife with him: 'I stood for a long time, looking, wondering how a person could change so much and never see it ... The face – a brown and leathery face that wasn't mine. Only the eyes were mine, staring as though to pierce the lying glass and get beneath to some truer image, infinitely distant' (*Angel* 133). She has to leave her old man in order to recover her true self: 'When I reached Bram, I saw how old he'd grown. His mouth opened when he saw me, and all I remember noticing was that his teeth had developed brown ridges at the front. We walked out of the store together, down the steps, past wrinkled Charlie Bean, gaping and shivering in his vigil, and that was the last time we ever walked anywhere together, Brampton Shipley and myself' (*Angel* 135). Hagar's not going to be anybody's old lady. She exiles Abram to the wilderness.

The wife is drawn back all the same to her husband's deathbed. She can't explain it. She goes. When she finds out that Bram had loved her after all, she rages as usual against fate: 'I could not speak for the salt that filled my throat, and for anger – not at anyone, at God, perhaps, for giving us eyes but almost never sight' (*Angel* 173). She sees none the less with blinding sight that sexual love is a coupling with death: 'He lay curled up and fragile in the big bed where we'd coupled and it made me sick to think I'd lain with him, for now he looked like an ancient child' (*Angel* 183). She can only deny the act, as she did before: 'Didn't I betray myself in rising sap, like a heedless and compelled maple after a winter? But no. He never expected any such a thing, and so he never perceived it. I prided myself upon keeping my pride intact, like some maidenhead' (*Angel* 81). Pride saves her from a sexual fall. The virgin can have no carnal knowledge of death.

When Hagar leaves Bram behind in the final wilderness, she seems to run right out of the Old Testament story. But the threat of determinism has crept up on her again by the time she runs away from Marvin's house. At the fish cannery, she finds 'an old brass scale, the kind they used to use for weighing letters or pepper. It tips and tilts to my finger, but the brass weights are lost. Nothing can be weighed here and found wanting' (*Angel* 154). MENE, MENE, TEKEL, UPHARSIN. Thou art weighed in the balances, and art found wanting. Nothing to do with me, she shrugs like her father. That's the book of Daniel. The judgment of Belshazzar is another story.

The irony of Hagar's memoir, of course, is that she's determined to forget what matters most. Though who could forget a dead son? She has to substitute Marvin for the son who dies: 'I had two [sons]. One was killed – in the last war' (*Angel* 104). She also has to substitute a secular story for the biblical one which threatened her freedom: 'I recalled part of a poem today – can I recall the rest? I search, but it evades me, and then all at once the last part returns and I repeat the lines. They give me courage, more than if I'd recited the Twenty-third Psalm, but why this should be so, I cannot tell' (*Angel* 162–3). Telling might expose the whole charade. For the good book does not lead a woman named Hagar to lie down beside still waters; it leaves her in a desert. If she happens to find herself in the wilderness anyway, she'd be happier with a folk-tale. Henceforth be Meg Merrilies.

Keats's homeless gypsy offers a saving image to the friendless woman. 'In choosing to recall the disreputable gipsy instead of the psalmist, Hagar seems to be following a romantic side of her nature, often repressed but as intrinsic to it as her stony pride' (Coldwell 94). Hagar's 'romantic side' continues, however, to exalt respectability over instinct. In modelling herself after Meg Merrilies, she is both preserving appearance and repressing truth. The source of her comfort is most evident in lines she neglects to quote:

> Her brothers were the craggy hills,
> Her sisters larchen trees;
> Alone with her great family
> She lived as she did please.
>
> (Keats 158)

The woman who has rejected family creates a fiction of her retreat to it. But Hagar is not the sister of all nature, nor is the stone angel a benefactor (as is the Amazon) of poor cottagers. The image of the gypsy is simply her excuse to 'live as she did please.'

Only when Hagar is forced to remember John's death does the biblical story overcome her repression: 'I was not thinking at all, not at all, and yet I recall some words that must have spun, unspoken, through me at that moment. *If he should die, let me not see it*' (*Angel* 241).

And she went, and sat her down over against him a good way off, as it were a bowshot: for she said, Let me not see the death of the child. And she sat over against him, and lifted up her voice, and wept.

And God heard the voice of the lad; and the angel of God called to Hagar out of heaven, and said unto her, What aileth thee, Hagar? fear not; for God hath heard the voice of the lad where he is.

Arise, lift up the lad, and hold him in thine hand; for I will make him a great nation.

And God opened her eyes, and she saw a well of water; and she went, and filled the bottle with water, and gave the lad drink.

(Gen. 21: 16–19)

'It's all true and not true. Isn't that a bugger, now?'

Of course there are no voices calling down from heaven any more. Just Murray Ferney Lees standing in for the good-hearted Meg Merrilies. So there's no one to save his lad, either. But Hagar's eyes are opened all the same. Murray shows her a well of forgiveness in her wilderness of pride. Memory serves at last to confront her demon Fear. But the truth is that she has hastened her fatal identity with the biblical Hagar. Only when she sees it does she find that she's misread the whole story of Abraham. For there's another side to the family history that she hasn't even begun to learn to tell.

> *Ich weiss nicht was soll es bedeuten …*
> *Dass ich so traurig bin …*
> *Ein Märchen aus uralten Zeiten …*
> *Das geht mir nicht aus dem Sinn –*   (Angel 256–7)

The song of Heine's boatman sounds alien, yet somehow familiar, in the chorus of voices which pleads away the night in Hagar's hospital ward. Alien to Hagar, because there is no evidence in the novel that she understands a word of German. Familiar to the reader, perhaps, who wants to hear in this song and Reverend Troy's hymn, 'a binary structure to make clearer the hermeneutic of the whole' (Jeffrey 96):

> I don't know what it means
> That I have been so saddened;
> A tale out of olden times
> That I cannot fully understand.

(Jeffrey's translation)

Still, the boatman perplexed by the song of the sirens is not a very good gloss on Hagar's predicament. Heine's only relevance for the reader who hears more than she does is the part about being bewildered by an old tale: 'I wish he could have looked like Jacob then, wrestling with the angel and besting it, wringing a blessing from it with his might. But no. He sweated and grunted angrily' (*Angel* 179). For Jacob's story, like his father Isaac's, overturns the usual law of primogeniture. The younger son wrests the birthright from the elder son, Isaac from Ishmael, Jacob from Esau, Joseph from Reuben. 'The firstborn very often seem to be losers in Genesis by the very condition of their birth ... while an inscrutable, unpredictable principle of election other than the "natural" one works itself out' (Alter 6). Hagar, like the God of Abraham (or Oscar Wilde!), would reverse the order of nature. In fact, the whole story of the covenant celebrates such a Wildean reversal. Hagar can't understand it. John is the younger son. He should be chosen. She herself has done her best to reject nature, the mother, mortality. But her awful strength achieves nothing. She cannot change fate or nature. Hagar is Hagar, her second son Ishmael. The story of the covenant remains an enigma to her, a tale told in a foreign language.

Yet in the very moment she stops willing it, the story is given to her. Her first son reveals himself as Jacob, the child of the promise. When she lets down her stony mask and gives in to nature, she is no longer blinded by fear:

'I'm – frightened. Marvin, I'm so frightened ...'
What possessed me? I think it's the first time in my life I've ever said such a thing. Shameful ...
I stare at him. Then, quite unexpectedly, he reaches for my hand and holds it tightly.
Now it seems to me he is truly Jacob, gripping with all his strength, and bargaining. *I will not let thee go, except thou bless me.* And I see I am thus strangely cast, and perhaps have been so from the beginning, and can only release myself by releasing him.
(*Angel* 303–4)

The story inherited from her ancestors does not constrain her after all. It prompts her to tell a lie to Marvin. But her new story may not be 'a lie, for it was spoken at least and at last with what may perhaps be a kind of love' (*Angel* 307). It is one of only two moments in her life when she is 'truly free.' The other is when she can laugh at appearance – most of all her own – with Sandra Wong, the 'celestial, as we used to call them' (*Angel* 286). '*Come ye before Him and rejoice*' (*Angel* 292), her minister had sung for her in a language she *could* understand. The joyous Hagar has become her own angel.

'Can angels faint?' she prefaces her final struggle with the Father. '*Our Father* – no. I want no part of that. All I can think is – *Bless me or not, Lord, just as You please, for I'll not beg*' (*Angel* 307). 'The special triumph of will wrought by Laurence in Hagar's characterization is thus a guarantee that readers will remember Hagar not only for what she chose, but for what she rejected' (Jeffrey 97). Unless, of course, Hagar rejects nothing in her role as a wrestler. Angels as well as men have been known to do as much in the biblical story. Still, the dogmatic reader can rightly complain that her story inverts the biblical one. For it was her father, not her husband, who sent her into exile. And her son seemed able to live without his father's blessing, though not without his mother's. Ultimately, of course, Hagar wants a God who will replace the lost mother, not just represent one more version of a self-made father. So the final problem of the 'angel' is to find her place in a story which has ceased to be patriarchal.

'I wrest from her the glass, full of water to be had for the taking. I hold it in my own hands. There. There' (*Angel* 308). It is a breath-taking moment in a lifelong struggle. For the angel herself is transformed into Jacob. Her desperate quest for metamorphosis is rewarded at last. But only when she has faced up fully to her past, like Jacob wrestling with the angel the night before he confronts his brother Esau:

> And he said, I will not let thee go, except thou bless me.
> And he said unto him, What is thy name? And he said, Jacob.
> And he said, Thy name shall be called no more Jacob, but Israel: for as a prince hast thou power with God and with men, and hast prevailed ...
> And Jacob called the name of the place Peniel: for I have seen God face to face, and my life is preserved.   (Gen. 32: 26–8, 30)

'Jacob is a man who sleeps on stones, speaks in stones, wrestles with stones, contending with the hard unyielding nature of things' (Alter 55). Hagar likewise never stops struggling against the unyielding nature of things. But the angel with whom 'Jacob' wrestles is the nurse, the nurturer, the rejected mother; the angel does not come from the Father's heaven but from the depths of the heroine's maternal nature. In consequence, the covenant must be rewritten; old names must be changed to express the new meaning.

'Jacob, *Ya 'aquov*, whose name ... could be construed as "he will deceive"' (Alter 43), is the better name for the woman who, like Wilde, discovers her truth in 'a lie.' The truth is that her first-born is her true child, as the second son knows: '"You always bet on the wrong horse," John said gently. "Marv was your boy, but you never saw that, did you?"' (*Angel* 237). The moment she acknowledges as much, the rest of the old tale is given to her. Quite naturally. For the mysterious principle of election gives way to nature itself. Hagar's story naturally subverts Genesis. But only when she quits trying.

'*There. There.*' At the end, the 'female Jacob' speaks the language she has learned from her daughter-in-law Doris: 'She only repeats over and over the mother-word. "There, there. There, there"' (*Angel* 66). After she accepts her own maternity, 'Jacob' blesses herself. Quite rightfully. For, finally, she needs to mother herself. To accept her identity with the dead mother. The stone angel is made flesh.

'And then – ' (*Angel* 308). The novel ends. Open-endedly. In a way that *The Diviners* does not. Though both are stories about story and story-telling, the family likeness gives way to individual difference. For *The Diviners* rests in conclusions that Hagar has learned to reject. Morag's '*totally invented memories*' (*Diviners* 10) belong to a species of art which wants its independence from nature. Like the decadent, and like Abraham's God, Morag seeks to make herself the pattern of an artificial order, above nature. She invents herself out of the junk-yard of memory, willing herself to be a new creature. Yet, paradoxically, she is the one who fails to transform herself in the telling.

On the other hand, Hagar has had enough of the patriarchal story of self-invention. To the end, she will not say *Our Father*. To do so would deny the logic of her whole story. But she does say yes at last to something beyond her own making. She consents to death. And gives up her niggling fear of dying like her mother. Hagar is finally naturalized by the story of her beginnings. For the end is not, and never was, an end in and of itself.

And so the conclusion to Hagar's tale renews what the decadents rejected in nature as a model for art: 'the concept of *tragic* feeling ...

Saying Yes to life even in its strangest and hardest problems, the will to life rejoicing over its own inexhaustibility even in the very sacrifice of its highest types ... *Not* in order to be liberated from terror and pity, not in order to purge oneself of a dangerous affect by its vehement discharge – Aristotle understood it that way – but in order to be *oneself* the eternal joy of becoming, beyond all terror and pity – that which included even joy in destroying' (Nietzsche 562–3).

Gaiety transfiguring all that dread.

The stone angel cracks. Crumbles. And art itself gives way to seasonal process. But in the midst of ruin, the story-teller embraces her demon Fear. And finds the same release as those serene figures in 'Lapis Lazuli':

> One asks for mournful melodies;
> Accomplished fingers being to play.
> Their eyes mid many wrinkles, their eyes,
> Their ancient, glittering eyes, are gay.
>
> (Yeats 160)

Part Two

PORTRAITS OF THE
MODERNIST

5

As For Me and My House
as a Diary Novel

Since the time of the Puritans, diary-keeping has been associated with habits of self-analysis and sincere self-expression. In the nineteenth century, 'the diary became a major confessional genre' through the vogue of the *journal intime* which both popularized and secularized a form synonymous with 'vigilant self-observation, designed to protect the Christian from falling into sin' (Martens 38, 55). Even today, readers' expectations are conditioned by these old habits of soul-searching which appear intrinsic to the form: 'The assumption is that because the diarist writes secretly he writes sincerely, and that the self in the diary is the "true" self and stands in contrast to the outward facade presented to the public' (Martens 38).

The narrator of English Canada's pre-eminent diary novel, *As For Me and My House* (1941), turns the issue of sincerity into something resembling a critical black hole because, in Paul Denham's words, she is 'an unreliable narrator whose unreliability we cannot verify' (124). The author's use of the diary form bears the brunt of the blame for making the question of reliability virtually undecidable: 'because of the interior monologue/diary form of the novel, we get Mrs Bentley's comments on events as they occur, but we never get a mature Mrs Bentley's account of her own past self, or of Philip' (122). And yet Denham does not insist that the diary form itself precludes retrospective writing; rather, it is the narrator's lack of soul-searching which makes it hard to explain her motive in writing. Sinclair Ross, in other words, has not really lived up to the requirements of his form; so another form, such as interior monologue, is required to explain the existence of the narrator's thoughts on paper.

The purpose of diary-writing is not the only convention which seems to have been violated in *As For Me and My House*; several more technical violations are just as serious. For instance: 'there is never any mention of pens, paper, or of time spent writing (which must be extensive, since some of the entries are several pages long) ... Furthermore, the diary form means that a lot of necessary information is conveyed in a rather awkward manner. Is Mrs Bentley really likely to write a summary of Philip's past life in her diary entry for the day they go for a walk in a spring snowstorm and watch a train pass? Not after twelve years of marriage, surely; in causing her to do it, Ross is straining at the limits of the convention' (Denham 119). In a word, it is easier to convict the artist of formal 'insincerity' than it is to gauge the insincerity of the narrator. And so, Denham concludes, 'Were it not for the dates at the head of each entry, it might be more satisfactory to think of the novel as an interrupted interior monologue' (120).

To salvage the integrity of Ross's art, Evelyn J. Hinz and John J. Teunissen do find it satisfactory, and even necessary, to think of the novel as a dramatic monologue, since this form at least presumes the convention of a guilty narrator. Here, 'an audience is assumed/implied, with the narrative consequently taking the form of the narrator's attempt convincingly to present a case' (Hinz 101). The critics' own attempt to present a convincing case is not helped, however, by ninety dated entries in pages which offer a day-by-day account of the narrator's life; this diary format is all the more damaging since the critical presumption of narrative unreliability begins and ends with a deduction about form. Fortunately, however, the narrator is every bit as conventional as the form they choose for her; she is convicted of having trapped Philip into marriage because her first suitor, Percy Glenn, skipped town after she got pregnant. Since form evidently follows function, the musician now opens up a whole new contrapuntal structure in the narrative whereby 'Mrs Bentley's "discovery" of Philip's infidelity is predicated by her own guilt' (Hinz 107) about Percy. And yet Percy's considerable talent in music has to pale, in this reading, beside another imputed ability; for the lover would be a virtuoso performer indeed who 'went to England shortly afterwards, played for a year or two in a string quartet, then made a concert tour of South America. That was the last I heard of him. From Buenos Aires he answered a letter I'd written months before to tell him I was married to a preacher' (Ross 77). Such is the hopeful stuff, it would seem, that romantic dreams are made of.

If there is justification for a critical gambit of this sort, it can only be the satisfaction of having come 'responsibly to terms with earlier criticism of the work as repetitive and discursive, with such flaws being the inevitable consequences of the use of the diary form. For we now see that Mrs Bentley is not *writing*, but *presenting*, her case to an implied audience, just as we now have a concrete explanation for her paranoia' (Hinz 113). Still, one asks, if the diary which is not a diary never gets written, how is a reader granted access to it? Dramatic monologues are invariably addressed; that's what makes them dramatic. So where do we see an addressee in a recognizably dramatic situation in *As For Me and My House*, such as we find, say, in Browning's 'Andrea del Sarto' or 'My Last Duchess'? Even J. Alfred Prufrock begins, 'Let us go then, you and I,' before we catch him quarrelling with his id in an interior monologue. Safe to say, then, that if the *language* of the speaker does not contain the implied audience, the critic has supplied the implication.

There is still the possible objection that these day-accounts are 'too structured and restrospective to create the sense of introspective and immediate personal jottings' (Hinz 102). 'Jottings' is unecessarily disparaging, however, of the diary novel, if not of its model in daily life. In the decades immediately preceding Ross's writing, the diary had informed major novels such as André Gide's *La Symphonie pastorale* (1919) and Jean-Paul Sartre's *La Nausée* (1938). This is not to say that a banker writing in Winnipeg at the end of the 1930s needed to know French literature in order to grasp new possibilities in the form: 'Especially after World War I, the publication statistics for literature of all kinds written in the form of diaries, from pseudointimate journals to collections of travel and war impressions and factual reports on every subject, shot upward ... Furthermore, whereas it is not clear whether before the war the authors of diary fiction were aware that they were writing in a tradition, there are abundant indications, from subtitles to the mention of the form in works of literary criticism, that the diary novel had become a consciously accepted genre by the 1920s' (Martens 185).

There were earlier and more authoritative precedents, as well, for Ross's highly structured use of the form. No end of historical diaries, including Pepys's *Diary* or Boswell's *London Journal*, reveal a structural imagination at work. And the first novel in English to include the mimetic form of a diary, *Robinson Crusoe* (1719), offers a journal organized on the pattern of the Puritan story of conversion and self-improvement. 'Unlike modern journals, it is not a day-to-day record. It is rather a journal in the contemporary eighteenth-century sense of the term, a record of daily events. Although Crusoe uses dated entries, he does not [even] describe the events of a given day on that day' (Martens 69). By contrast, Ross's Mrs Bentley writes, for the most part, out of an immediate present: 'So today I let him be the man about the house' (3); 'True to his promise Philip took Steve to the country with him this afternoon' (45); 'Philip and Steve went off to the country again this afternoon and left me at home' (63). The structural rhythm of *As For Me and My House* depends upon both this sequence of daily events and the sequence of dated headings, upon the implicit idea that the narrator is *writing* to fill a gap in her life.

On the other hand, the day-to-day process of keeping a diary is inherently incomplete. The gap, in other words, is present in the form before the diarist ever begins to write. So this sense of temporal incompletion *inside* the form should help to redefine the sense of emptiness or incompletion in the narrator's life. For the fictional diarist wants to 'tell time' in more than just the present or past tense. Like the real diarist, of course, she 'cannot foresee what will happen or what [she] will think on any future date, and if [she] keeps [her] diary as a genuine record, [she] cannot predict what [she] will write in the future. The diary is thus a form that eludes the [imputed] author's full control' (Martens 33). All the same, the diarist is not quite helpless, not even if 'diaries are defined by a periodic and forward-marching time of writing. It is a psychological truism that it is easy to superimpose a fiction on the past in accordance with some present interest, but the hold of the past over the present, or of the present over the future, is less certain, and its mechanisms are less clearly predictable' (Martens 34).

Mrs Bentley confesses a good deal of her purpose in writing her diary when she says, 'But somehow, with a man like Philip, you don't predict the future from the past' (Ross 10). As early as her second daily entry, she none the less reveals her customary way of structuring time: 'The rain has kept on all day ... The leak in the roof is worse' (7). Turning from the moment to the immediate past, she recounts a series of impressions from 'ten o'clock this morning' which show an urgent (if jealous) need to predict the future. In the course of these predictions, she says with unwitting dramatic irony, 'I think I'm going to like Judith' (11). Of course, this switch to the future tense includes some other people whom she thinks she might not like, such as 'Mrs Finley and her kind ... the proverbial stone walls against which unimportant heads like mine are knocked in vain. We'll see' (12). Much of her diary is thus made up of a need to 'see' beyond the moment, to gain the advantage on her enemies, or even to cope with impending change in her marriage: 'We're getting on – thirty-six and thirty-four. Getting to the place, I'm afraid, where it's not enough to put a false front up and live our own lives out behind it. At least where it's not enough for him' (16).

Later, when she has come to believe that Judith is her enemy, that her own future is totally uncertain, and that even her husband now puts up a false front to hide from her, the diarist writes, 'If I can just hold myself controlled and quiet like this a few weeks longer – I know it will be all right then' (126). But a narrative which ends in the birth of a child always has a way of reaching further toward the future. And so her daily writing becomes a way of planning obsessively for that future, particularly when the impending birth of the baby threatens to exclude her: 'I've fought it out with myself and won at last. We're going to adopt Judith's baby' (154). Here, at last, Philip's own words echo the whole concern of her diary: 'Do you really think we could make a living in this store you talk about? It sounds like starvation – but another Horizon every three or four years – that's not much of a prospect to look forward to either' (156). Even at the end of the novel, with 'her' baby in hand, Mrs Bentley is focused as ever on her future prospects, 'trying to grasp how much the change is going to mean' (164). In a town named Horizon, of course, *prospects* become a vital motive for narrative. Perhaps the diarist in this novel has both natural and symbolic reasons to write her way toward the future.

Still there is that technical 'awkwardness,' noted by Denham, of the fictional diarist having to convey information about her husband's past in writing. But is this rehearsal really unmotivated? Or is it a diarist's only means 'of reimposing his control on the diary[?] He can – although the idea is farfetched – decide what he will write in advance. He may structure his perception of the present, and his account of it, according to insights conceived in the past. His past writing may [even] influence his present writing, so that a kind of plot is superimposed on the diary' (Martens 33). It would seem that Mrs Bentley has good reason to tell herself the story of her husband's birth, since it superimposes a long-standing 'plot' on their married life, explaining what the present means in terms of his past and offering her direction for where they might be headed in the future. And yet, as she herself is driven to confess, she doesn't even know the story of his past in detail: 'I know it only in fragments, pieced together through the fifteen years I've known him. Before we were married he told me who he was and what he came from, his head set defiant, his voice quick and hard, warning me, asking nothing. Once he tried to write, the second year we were married, and all through his clumsy manuscript I read himself. That was what spoiled it, himself, the painful, sometimes bitter, reality. Even I might have done it better ...' (29). And yet isn't that what she does, writing it all down for herself, if not for him, in a *secret* diary? The virtual opening of her narrative is thus a deceptively simple sentence: 'His mother was a waitress in a little Main Street restaurant.' Out of this fragment of history, she can build a satisfactory 'plot' upon the daily fragments of her own experience.

At this point, however, we must recognize a crucial difference between the keeping of a diary and the writing of a memoir. For the diarist ignores her own past, except as it bears on her relationship to Philip, and so avoids having to bridge the gap between her writing self and the younger self who is her ostensible subject. The diary's very first sentence announces this crucial shift in subject – 'Philip has thrown himself across the bed and fallen asleep, his clothes on still, one of his long legs dangling to the floor' (3) – and thereby establishes the 'subject's' necessary ignorance of her writing. The diarist's plot, in other words, is not intended to link her to her past self, but to predict a more assured future self. Contrary to the autobiographer, she is not at all content with her present self. But, unlike the heroine of the fairy-tale who awaits her future prince in sleep, this 'princess' has to awaken a male Sleeping Beauty to ensure the happy ever-after. In the diary novel, the 'future that awaits the hero, as evidenced by the pages of the book that await the reader, is a future the narrator himself cannot predict. These forms are thus especially well suited to the presentation of unreliable narrators' (Martens 138).

The diary novel, then, no less than the dramatic monologue, can be ironic, though its lack of an implied audience requires new forms of authorial control by which we might gauge that irony. Still, these two narrative situations do have one important parallel: the diarist is just as subject as the monologist to momentary pressures of selection. Both lack the hindsight or opportunity for revision which might be called the basic contract of autobiography, the fundamental protection without which most autobiographers would not set pen to paper. But a 'dramatic' witness to a monologue, no less than a memoirist's impending readership, forces him to worry what his audience might think; he inclines toward *apologia*. A retrospective plot thus becomes a narrator's saving grace, however open it may be to internal contradiction or to other voices within the text which can, at most, be only partially suppressed.

The diarist, by contrast, has no audience but herself, so she must worry about nothing beyond the 'second person' of her own conscience. Her greater disadvantage appears in time, more precisely in her narrative sense of an ending, since she has only a prospective plot to work with. And so a form which can only second-guess the future is all the more open to dramatic irony or to counter-control by the author. For the changing times and perspectives of the diarist's writing create their own sort of 'play between two time levels. The reader is freed from the perpetual level of the diarist's present tense and given a glimpse into his future. Two kinds of time exist simultaneously and jar on each other: "real" but unwritten time that has its certain telos (i.e., the time in which the reader's superior consciousness moves), and the deluded, narrated time of the diarist's consciousness, which projects a false telos onto the future' (Martens 139).

Mrs Bentley's 'plot' of her husband's past life reveals one such continuing attempt to project a borrowed telos onto the future: 'His mother was a waitress in a little Main Street restaurant. His father, a young student preacher, died without marrying her before Philip was born' (29). Like father, like son. But if the son should get an illegitimate child and die, the diarist's future is more uncertain than ever, precisely because this preacher is already married. Given the shift in paradigm, the unwed mother, who is not a waitress but at least a 'hired girl,' is going to have to be the odd one out. Now if only she would do everyone a favour and die in childbirth? And, true to form, the diarist confesses to exactly this wish-fulfilment after the event: 'For me it's easier this way. It's what I've secretly been hoping for all along. I'm glad she's gone – glad – for her sake as much as ours. What was there ahead of her now anyway? If I lost

Philip what would there be ahead of me?' (161–2). A closer examination of her governing 'plot' thus opens the way to defining Mrs Bentley's false telos throughout the novel. But what if Philip should prove not to be the father of Judith's child? Then we would have to reformulate several larger questions in the novel about the artist's relation to his (or her) materials, and about the fundamental relation of art (and religion) to life. In other words, the confessional mode of the diary, with all of its built-in questions about the narrator's sincerity and morality, would turn into a version of the *Künstlerroman* with a whole new set of questions about the morality and sincerity of the artist.

Looked at retrospectively, the plot of *As For Me and My House* turns very narrowly, even harrowingly, upon a moment of adultery. But looked at prospectively, the diarist's 'plot' predicts that adultery is welcome, even necessary. Three weeks before Mrs Bentley 'discovers' her husband's infidelity, she takes a certain amount of pleasure (not to mention pride) in the unrequited love of the 'other woman': 'She still doesn't know. If she did she wouldn't have come here today and sat looking at him so admiringly right in front of me ... she demurely sat down again when we left the table and did her best to talk to him. He stood it for about ten minutes, then said he had to go out and get the car ready for tomorrow. His expression as he passed me in the kitchen made me realize what a good job I once did' (108). The following week, she is still sure enough of herself to invite Judith to supper again: 'I think that was maybe why I asked her – to watch her eyes follow him, her breathing quicken a little – to look then at him, and know how completely it was wasted' (109). In the hands of a lesser artist, the conventions of dramatic irony would be exceedingly heavy-handed. But there is a much larger dramatic irony in the diarist's misreading of the situation, especially if Judith's agony should in fact be 'wasted.'

Her confessed stage-management of Judith's pain now introduces two new issues in the narrator's quest for control of her future. The first, dramatic issue has to do with her 'control' of her husband. When they have been forced within several days to give up Steve, their foster-child, Mrs Bentley is not particularly unhappy. Not at first, at least: 'I see an unflaring, leaden look in his eyes. It was recklessness at first – the best anyway he could do – now it's resignation. And I don't know whether to regret it or be glad. It will be easier if it's really resignation, if the dreams have run themselves out, if he submits at last to the inevitable, to me; only now, queerly, I start wondering is resignation what I want. It will be easier if he gives in, stops straining away – but am I going to care much, then, whether he strains away or not?' (120). Her doubt, of course, has everything to do with what sort of future she hopes to have. Most of all, she wants control of her life. But if Philip *is* her life, then control becomes almost a hopeless paradox.

The very next day, the diarist comes down with a curious case of morbidity, almost as if she must give up her old project: 'El Greco's tail is like a rat's again. With his wet coat plastered down and clinging to his ribs he looks so gaunt and angular that today when Mrs Bird dropped in I said a stranger dog might take him for an angel of destruction from the canine lower world. "You *are* ill to think such morbid things," she said triumphantly. "Much more ill, my dear, than you've any idea. I'm going this minute to fetch the doctor"' (121). The connection between the narrator's 'illness' and her ambivalence about 'control' is further illustrated in a quickening of dramatic events by which she now feels swept along: 'Judith came over after the doctor was here, and swept and dusted and got supper ready ... She knows now, and I'm afraid of her.'

Apparently the only way Mrs Bentley can regain control of her life is to exert an imaginative – that is to say, narrative – control over events. How, otherwise, might she gain control over Philip by *surrendering* all control of him? Or how, for that matter, is such an unwilling fish as Philip to be landed by such a timid angler as Judith? Writes Mrs Bentley: 'I keep shivering, imagining, dreading. It will take a worse ache in my shoulder than this one to keep me in the bedroom while she sits out here alone with him. I suppose it's every woman's lot, dread of what she knows can't be true, of what she knows won't happen' (122).

So what 'really' happens?[1] A dream wakens Mrs Bentley on the night of August 13 and sends her looking for her husband who is not in bed beside her. She tiptoes to the door of the lean-to bedroom where she hears a 'frightened, soft, half-smothered little laugh, that I've laughed often with him too' (123). She creeps back to bed directly, 'a queer, doomed ache inside me,' without looking to see whether Philip is still in the study

---

1 Portions of what follows have been revised from my article, 'The "Scarlet" Rompers: Toward a New Perspective in *As For Me and My House*,' *Canadian Literature* 103 (Winter 1984): 156–66.

where he went after supper, 'the familiar stealthy click of the door' (122) evidently shutting out Judith too, just as it had her. Narratively, of course, she has inured us to Philip's habit of staying late in his study, as if to avoid the conjugal bed, though a scant week before he is 'caught' with Judith, the diarist has described him coming to bed to find her awake: 'He didn't mind, but he wasn't eager either. Kind still, far off, as if he were sorry, understood now, felt it was the least he could do … He seemed trying to tell me that I must be resigned too' (120). Though who could have foretold the sort of abnegation that might find adultery in a 'half-smothered little laugh'? The husband following her almost immediately to bed, the self-sacrificing narrator still says nothing. She no longer even wonders what it was he had understood before in their moment of intimacy and to which he must now be resigned. And yet, because he had acted as 'if he were sorry' and 'felt it was the least he could do,' what might she have failed herself to understand?

Laughter in dreams, for one thing. Once before, her narrative had recorded an incident in which she woke up to hear Philip 'muttering in his sleep.' But she seems to have been greatly mistaken in the dream she herself was having: 'It seemed hours that he kept on, searching vainly for his text; and then with a laugh he seized the Bible suddenly, and hurled it crashing down among the pews' (15). But this dreamed Philip proves to share almost nothing of the rebellion of the iconoclast when he professes in daylight that 'Religion and art … are almost the same thing anyway. Just different ways of taking a man out of himself, bringing him to the emotional pitch that we call ecstasy or rapture' (112). Judith's laugh – or her ecstasy – might just as easily be explained in the context of delusive dreams.

Here, the dream which leads Mrs Bentley to catch her husband in the 'act' is more directly misleading: 'It was a kind of nightmare. My hands were tied, and someone was stealing Minnie's hay. I could see El Greco sitting on his haunches in the garden, but when I called him he didn't hear me. He seemed a long way off, as if I were looking at him through the wrong end of a telescope. Paul was telling me he was a wolfhound, and wouldn't know how to chase burglars anyway' (123). Her 'tied hands' sum up much of her habitual concern about control. And stolen 'hay,' especially from the poor old mare, is obviously symbolic. Only Paul's presence is unexpected, as is his apparent knowledge of watch-dogs that fail to bark. But the dreamer's view of the dog 'through the wrong end of a telescope' suggests that she looks at things only to diminish them, which doesn't augur well for the husband when she starts out of bed to look for him. If, as she worries at the end of this day's entry, she 'can't see life for illusions' (125), she might have good reason to feel 'uneasy, afraid, as if I were the guilty one' (124).

Another wife in Horizon has no such illusions about the guilt of her husband, not even in the face of townspeople's suspicions. 'Yesterday,' Mrs Bird reports some months later, '[Mrs Wenderby] slammed the door almost in Mrs. Finley's face' (147). Yet Mrs Wenderby, it would appear, is doing much more than holding her head high in the face of public scandal. At the 'Ladies Aid' bazaar of 16 March, she sells Paul 'a dozen doughnuts, a pair of rompers, and a cushion top' (156). Paul, who has been sitting there 'with a hangdog, guilty, miserable look,' helplessly hands the rompers to Mrs Bentley in front of Mrs Finley. That good worthy was sniffing 'so nastily I stumped right over to Mr. Finley and sold them to him again for a dollar twenty-five.' Mrs Bentley is more than a little aware of the social code at play in this scene, as evidenced by her use of the adverb 'nastily' to mask her own bit of nastiness. For she is quite as eager to pin the scarlet letter on her arch-foe's husband as she is to protect an old friend.

Paul, of course, has been blamed before by Mrs Wenderby, though Mrs Bentley has never stooped to question the morality of this other accuser's husband. She has always been too busy blaming her own husband and finding solace in Paul. The previous May, when she let herself imagine that Philip 'didn't want me along' (45) on a trip with Steve to Partridge Hill, she had been too troubled to worry about Paul's silence as they waited in the study for Philip to return. 'It's like being a child in the presence of grown-ups who have troubles that can't be explained to you,' she reports of the feeling which the study always gives her. 'The books understand, but you don't' (46). Paul then mentions a particularly illuminating book: 'Faust, too, the early Faust, before they made a tenor of him, it was for knowledge, not a mere comely Marguerite, that he made a compact with the devil and let himself be carried off alive to Hell.' If Paul is worried about Marlowe's Dr Faustus turning into Goethe's Faust, it is because he is evidently tempted himself to debauch a comely Marguerite. But whom? Mrs Bentley will not let herself think for almost another year that she is Faust's Marguerite, and so by then, her ignorance of 'the books' will let her assume the place of Goethe's virgin.

Near the end of May, when Mrs Bentley notices at last that 'Paul has his troubles too,' she is pointedly unaware of their significance. Paul seems to be just another victim of the god Propriety, a humanist hero who dares to teach little bigots that, vulgarly speaking as the vulgar should speak, they have bellies. But the town euphemist has her reasons, it would seem, for objecting to his particular use of 'bellies': ' "Cows may have them," says Mrs Wenderby, "and you, Mr. Kirby, but not my daughter Isobel or I" ' (70). Her omission of the hired girl, the only other female quartered under her roof, suggests that Judith is the one most liable to get a belly.

On the facing page Judith also faces another brand of criticism, which reminds us that we are reading a diary novel, not a diary, since the novelist quickly brings in another voice to comment on the narrator's perspective. Judith has come to visit Mrs Bentley and Philip emerges from his study to stare at her 'with such a direct, searching look that she flushed again and got up to go' (71). Whatever Mrs Bentley thinks, Mrs Wenderby's concern for euphemism is repeated 26 June the day Paul receives 'another note from Mrs Wenderby ... warning him that if he insists on saying *sweat* in the classroom instead of *perspiration* she'll use her influence to have the school board ask him to resign' (91). Before Judith gets in trouble, then, the diarist finds grist for her mill in this grim, almost preposterous, small-town euphemist. But once Judith's secret is out, the beadle of town morality proves she is capable of a higher order of euphemism. For rompers, not scarlet letters, are the real fashion of prairie towns, though Mrs Bentley is quick herself to pin the letter on her husband without ever mentioning it to him. She even makes a point of her own martyred silences (134), certain as always that 'This is the best way' (126). In fact it is the only way of keeping her narrative control of Philip.

Faced with Paul and his own sort of euphemism, the narrator is much less canny in the dramatic moment. He remarks to her on 7 June that 'while words socially come up in the world, most of them morally go down.' 'You learn a lot from a philologist,' Mrs Bentley says with unwitting irony. 'Cupid, he says, has given us *cupidity*, Eros, *erotic*, Venus, *venereal*, and Aphrodite, *aphrodisiac* ' (76). Now Paul may be oversexed and even unfocused in his affections, but he tries all the same to confess something to her. And Ross's narrative design suggests that Paul is not alone in his need of Mrs Bentley's understanding. In one of a series of paired chapters, Judith follows Paul to the Bentley house, apparently to confess something of her own about an impending or continuing liaison. 'But busy with my retrospects, looking at Horizon and drawing up a balance sheet, I wasn't much company for Judith' (77). The older woman doesn't ask the younger one about her restlessness even after they have lain down by the railroad tracks to make angels in the dirt: 'Judith used to do it with the neighbour boy who keeps asking her to marry him,' she says with an almost conscious pun. This subliminal perception hastens her sudden sizing up of the competition. Now, for the first time, she notices that Judith has breasts: 'It surprised me a little. Somehow, so white and silent and shy, she had never occurred to me as a woman before. I left off my balancing and sat watching her, with a vague uneasy feeling of regret. For I've never got along with women very well' (77).

Her sudden self-revelation speaks volumes. For she has warned us time and again that she is temperamentally jealous, as, for example, when the young Mrs Holly with 'fawnish' freckles comes to call on the minister: 'I kept staring at [those pale yellow freckles], thinking how lovely they would be if she weren't a woman' (26). The visit triggers a terrible fight between the Bentleys, after which she hates the furniture because 'It has taken sides against me with the house' (25). Never thorough in her self-analysis, Mrs Bentley at least has the honesty to admit that 'There's something lurking in the shadows, something that doesn't approve of me.' None the less she flees up the tracks toward the outside world, running away from Philip 'while his hand was still warm and insistent' (23). She excuses herself, though she will later blame him for avoiding her, by insisting in her turn, 'I had to. The house was too small, too oppressive with its faint old smell of other lives. And the little town outside was somehow too much like a mirror' (23).

By the end of their first service in Horizon, Mrs Bentley had already sized up the women and concluded that 'it would have taken an imagination livelier even than mine to find much to be afraid of there' (10). But at the first hint of Judith's sexual restlessness, the wife's imagination comes to life. Still 'sure' of her husband's rectitude, she now begins to assert her power by teasing the girl with Philip. Of course, she believes she knows the reason why Judith avoids her after 13 August; it is beyond her comprehension to see that the 'two oranges' over which Judith weeps so piteously are not coals of fire heaped upon the 'harlot's' head, but counters for a lost ideal of friendship. Judith grieves because she has removed herself from decency, not because she has become her friend's rival.

While Mrs Bentley's jealousy may give her licence to interpret this single friend's laspse from 'company,' she is more puzzled, after the beginning of the school year, by the absence of the schoolteacher. 'What's wrong with Paul these days, he never comes round,' she says to Philip. She is shocked and hurt by her husband's guilt, as she sees it, now projected onto her: 'I'd say that's one for you to answer' (132). Self-absorbed as she is, she cannot see Paul for what he has become, even though he has ridden by the house that day on Harlequin, 'and when he saw me watching at the window [he] gave a nod and then bent over quickly, pretending to try the saddle girths.' For Paul has returned to town strangely depressed after the summer. 'He finds himself skeptical even of his theories that a boy ought to grow up alone with a horse. "Unless he intends staying among horses. He's not much good afterwards for getting along with people" ' (127). Mrs Bentley has never shared his faith in horses anyway, not since the day Paul first 'let me see his skewbald bronco Harlequin. A temperamental, knowing little beast, that plunged hysterically halfway across the street at sight of me' (40). But Paul's abrupt heresy is hardly so concerned with the kind of fear Mrs Bentley has that an animal might see through her. Rather, he sees in the dog El Greco a reflected truth about himself: 'He's ashamed inside – knows this isn't where he ought to be' (137). Although Mrs Bentley feels a rebuke to Philip in these words, her husband might have the better reason to rebuke her: 'Why not get your mind off Paul, and remember you're a married woman?' (134). If she has any claim left to our sympathy as a martyred innocent, it is only because she has transferred her own jealousy onto a 'faithless' mate.

All the same, the innocent is hardly as pure as she thinks. From her second day in Horizon, she has been self-consciously cultivating a potential admirer (though definitely not a lover) in the schoolteacher whose 'slow steady eyes ... stay right with you till they're satisfied' (7). Later, she will not remember that those eyes have suddenly lost their moral authority. But for now, she is quietly vain about Paul's admiration for her music: 'I liked him for that. The musician in me dies hard, and a word of praise still sends my blood *accelerando*. "Come then and spend an evening with us soon," I invited recklessly. It was dangerous, but with my vanity up that way I didn't care' (8). That evening, by contrast,

Judith is curiously lacking in vanity when Mrs Bentley compliments her on her voice. But then it appears that Judith cannot afford to be vain, not in view of the town: 'Miss Twill and the matrons ... don't quite approve of her, and there was a tight-lipped silence for a minute when I remarked after service how well she had sung her solo. She herself broke it at last, saying awkwardly and nicely that she'd rather be like me and play an instrument' (11). And well she might, tired as she is of her solo life; she has already been noticed walking out along 'the railroad track as late as ten o'clock at night. Naturally people talk' (12).

The pestered morality of the town, as it turns out, is not nearly so cruel as the woman who walks out along the track with Judith, only to send her a little gift at Christmas, 'deliberately to hurt her' (147), once she thinks her own ox is gored. Not even Mrs Wenderby has been as self-concerned as this in her public crusade against impropriety. But Mrs Bentley's concern for the proprieties begins and ends with herself. When she dares Judith, the day after Paul has confessed his interest in venereal matters, to join her on a ride back to town with the railway section hands, her fear of public scandal is more than offset by her complacency: 'It was dangerous, but if I asked them to let us off before we reached town they would think we didn't want to be seen with them. I hadn't the heart for that, they looked so appreciative of our company' (78). In a more damaging way three weeks later, she makes Judith's evident romantic disquiet refer to her own marital situation, even though Mrs Wenderby has just been fulminating against the apostle of 'bawdy' language: 'There was a strange wariness in [Judith's] eyes. I asked her to sing, and her voice was the same, not strong and full as usual, but constrained, lifeless. We tried a while, but couldn't find much to talk about. I admitted to myself at last that the trouble is Philip' (91).

So long as Mrs Bentley's 'admissions' are to her diary, they need never be denied by life. But if we find in Judith's lifeless behaviour a hint of some climax to the liaison, especially with Paul leaving town for the summer, we might not be remiss in counting forward forty weeks (the full gestatory term) to 8 April, the date Judith's baby is born. Mrs Bentley is not alone in thinking the baby arrives 'a month before its time' (161), since 'The doctor says the baby should be born sometime in May' (146). If Philip were in fact the father, the birth should take place after the middle of the month. But Mrs Bentley herself writes on 25 March, 'It's just six weeks away' (158). Old-time country doctors are evidently not the only ones who have to make rough estimates of such matters. At any rate, Mrs Bentley also describes the 'sudden' onset of Judith's labour in the following way: 'In the afternoon she went for a walk, refusing to let her sister go with her, and promising to be back within an hour. But the fields were soft and sticky, and the hard walking exhausted her. About dusk a neighbour boy out hunting cattle found her resting on a stone pile, cold and ill already, and wandering in her mind' (161). The survival of a new-born infant, in such conditions, without acute medical care, makes it quite unlikely that the baby is five weeks premature.

Most conclusive, however, is Paul's oblique confession of his grief after the girl's death. On the windy day he runs an errand for Mrs Bentley and her adopted infant, he confesses more than is his wont: 'It was a bad wind, he said dryly. Most of the false fronts were blown down, and Mrs Ellingson had lost her chicken coop and nearly all her hens. There was a slow, deliberate quietness in his voice, and he took pains not to look at me.' Still he does not feel constrained to avoid her eyes after she ignores the implication that at least one false front has been left standing. '[T]he expression in his eyes,' she remarks of the moment she presents him with the baby, 'was so wondering and incredulous that I realized he knew what all along I was certain I was keeping secret' (162).

Wise in her own conceit, Mrs Bentley doesn't doubt that Paul should wonder at her martyred silence, just as the prior week she had not questioned his silence before her matronly virtue. On that occasion too, 'there was such a strained, helpless look in his eyes that suddenly I felt the windows all accusing me ... It seemed strange that I now should make another suffer who had suffered so much that way myself' (158). No sooner has this reflexive thought occurred to her than 'Paul asked brusquely, "Why is a raven like a writing-desk?" ' (159). The riddle, as Mrs Bentley observes, comes from *Alice in Wonderland*. While she says, 'There isn't an answer,' she forgets to note the context of the Hatter's 'nonsense.' He is replying to Alice who has just remarked with some severity, 'You shouldn't make personal remarks ... it's very rude' (Carroll 67). Mrs Bentley has evidently been guilty of some personal 'remarks' of her own concerning Paul's affections. But she also cannot understand, as she next admits in the adverb 'cryptically,' just what else he is trying to tell her in all these allusions to ravens. Poe's poem 'The Raven' ought to suggest something, especially if she were mindful of the poet's 'intention of making [the speaker] emblematical of *Mournful and Never-Ending Remembrance*' (Poe 463).

Paul continues to speak in riddles only so long as he feels guilt at mere abandonment of his 'Lenore.' But once the girl has died, his 'never-ending remembrance' makes it impossible for him to keep secret such enormous guilt. Presented to the baby without a hint of reproach, he can only interpret Mrs Bentley's silence as consummate tact. He is even confident that he can confide in her more directly, if still emblematically: 'Did I know, he asked gravely, that in the early ages of our race it was imitation of just such a little wail as this that had given us some of our noblest words, like father, and patriarch, and paternity' (163). Out of the truth of grief the philologist coins a false etymology for the word 'paternity'; it actually comes from the Sanskrit *pitrí*, pl. *pitaras*, through the Latin *pater* (Monier-Williams 626).[2] And so his proper name as the father is most fittingly expressed in the sound of his own sorrow: 'And I shook my head,' Mrs Bentley says, 'and let him explain.' Paul even goes so far as to tell her that she has named the child aright: ' "It means a lover of horses," he said. "You couldn't get a better one" ' (162). But the requirements of her plot do not allow such explanations from anyone.

At the end, she doesn't even await explanation from the 'guilty' husband: ' "Your baby!" I cried. "Yours – " and he stopped white a moment, and said in a slow hollow voice, "You were with her then – and she told you – " I steeled myself, afraid to admit what I had done, then shouted no, she hadn't told me, that I had always known; that I had wanted the baby so that in time his son would be my son too' (163). Philip's one incomplete sentence confesses nothing, asking only an implicit question about the witness. His wife, on the other hand, has just made him privy to her whole plot since he alone can fulfil it. She is evidently still bent on possessing her husband through 'his' child (165), in spite of her knowledge of the folk-wisdom that love 'won't survive possession' (65). Even her final words assert this controlling 'plot' when

2 Archbishop Trench, *On the Study of Words* (1851; London: Everyman 1926), which Mrs Bentley presents to Paul at Christmas (149), is significantly silent on the word 'father,' though it comments on Paul's other etymologies such as *pagan: country-dweller*. Paul's etymology is not far from Sanskrit *pida*, 'pain, suffering, annoyance' (Monier-Williams 629). Conceptually in error for once, the philologist is at least morally right.

her husband worries about the baby having the same name as he: 'Sometimes you won't know which of us is which.' To which she replies,
'That's right, Philip. I want it so' (165).

Because the author of a diary has no audience, 'the diary novel presents
the possibility of something approaching the collapse of the communicative triangle as it is found in fiction ... In the extreme case, instead of a
narrator who creates a narrated world and addresses himself to a fictive
reader, we have a narrator who takes himself as subject and is his own
reader' (Martens 5). But at the end of Mrs Bentley's diary, the narrative
'plot' is finally revealed to an audience who seems to read the narrator
very well. Philip, in other words, finds a way to keep the communicative
triangle from breaking down without ever violating the basic secrecy of
the diary. For, in sharing his wife's 'plot,' he actually enters the text as a
'reader.' But now his possession of the narrative secret means that he can
no longer be 'controlled' in the same narrative way. He even abolishes the
motive for diary-keeping by giving the narrator the future she 'wants.'
And so the diary ends in a new, more public, communicative triangle,
with the child taking the place of *narrated* world.

  This quest for a fit audience that we find in the diary is more obviously
Mrs Bentley's ambition for her husband's kind of art. She is actually
convinced that he has failed as an artist because he never found the
audience who was worthy of his talent: 'That's Philip, though, what I
must recognize and acknowledge as the artist in him. Sermon and drawing together, they're a kind of symbol, a summing up. The small-town
preacher and the artist – what he is and what he nearly was – the failure,
the compromise, the going-on – it's all there – the discrepancy between
the man and the little niche that holds him' (4). As far as she's concerned,
it's 'These little towns [which] threaten to be the scaffolding of his life,
and at last he seems to know' (17). Yet if she hadn't tied him down, he
might have 'gone off to fight it out alone' (103), learned how to solve the
technical problems with which he still wrestles

> till what he's doing turns out right. It doesn't mean that he just has
> a skill with a pencil. Even though the drawings are only torn up or
> put away to fill more boxes when we move, even though no one ever
> gets a glimpse of them but me, still they're for him the only part of
> life that's real or genuine.

That's why I believe he's an artist, why I can't deceive myself, or escape the hurt of it.   (25)

Still, the hurt of it, as she admits at other times, might have something to do with their differing views of his potential audience: 'I turned over the top sheet, and sure enough on the back of it there was a little Main Street sketched. It's like all the rest, a single row of smug, false-fronted stores, a loiterer or two, in the distance the prairie again. And like all the rest there's something about it that hurts. False fronts ought to be laughed at, never understood or pitied. They're such outlandish things, the front of a store built up to look like a second storey. They ought always to be seen that way, pretentious, ridiculous, never as Philip sees them, stricken with a look of self-awareness and futility' (4). Because she cannot admit to herself that Philip understands and pities what she finds ridiculous, she must at once reword her statement to fit the general proposition that Philip is a talented, but failed artist, portraying little more than his own 'self-awareness and futility.'

Elsewhere, however, Mrs Bentley discovers anything but a sense of futility in Philip's drawings. In one, she notes a broken 'old horse, legs set stolid, head down dull and spent. But still you feel it belongs to the earth … What the tired old hulk suggests is less approaching decay or dissolution than return. You sense a flow, a rhythm, a cycle.' By contrast, the town in the same picture 'stands up so insolent and smug and self-assertive that your fingers itch to smudge it out and let the underlying rhythms complete themselves. Philip himself could feel that there was something wrong, but he didn't know what' (69). Ironically, the broken old horse does not seem futile to her, set within the natural cycle. For it stands opposed, like her version of the rebel artist, to society itself. Philip's refusal to erase the town must then point up her Gulliver-like preference for 'horses' over people. And so she can only appeal to the reader, in the second person, to share her urge to rub out the town. Yet even her sympathy for the image of the horse creates a problem for us in trying to evaluate drawings we cannot see. For if she, and not Philip, is the true impressionist, then how can we be certain that he accepts these 'natural rhythms' or asserts that 'the town in contrast has an upstart, mean complacency'? After all, he is the one still trying to improve upon his town, 'giving last little touches here and there, as if it were just a matter of perspective, or a rounder buggy wheel.' Conversely, if the town should prove to be represented sympathetically, what does that do to Mrs Bentley's impression, recorded two days earlier, that 'He hates Horizon, all the Horizons, and he's clinging to the incident today as a justification for his hatred' (67)?

The problem of what to make of Philip's drawings is partially resolved by comparing his response to the presence of an audience with their own responses to particular drawings, and then with their implied presence as the *subject* of his art. Mrs Bentley would have us believe that Philip doesn't want any audience at all. For example, on the day she felt 'a sudden impulse to defend him, to prove he really was an artist,' she rejoices in the way the doctor's wife 'was excited and amazed and astounded to my heart's content. I drank it in deeply' (88). Philip, by contrast, is secretive and almost costive in his dismissal of both of them: 'I know all right what came over you,' he later says to his wife. 'I don't speak well enough for myself. That's it, isn't it? You have to put in a word for me – impress them – let them see that your small-town preacher husband has more to him than they can see on the surface' (88–9). She does not want to admit, however, that this instance of her churlishness recalls her 'speaking' so manipulatively for him at the church board meeting. She is even less inclined to see in him a genuine artistic modesty. He is simply antisocial and so a failed artist.

Other voices creep into the narrative all the same to contradict Mrs Bentley. Three weeks earlier, when, in 'a departure from all precedent,' she had already dared to show his work to Judith, 'He straightened his tie, fidgeted, looked out the window. But I could tell, just the same, that her admiration pleased him' (71). Once again, when Philip has 'stooped to copy' the cowgirl Laura's horse in a farewell gift of painting, 'Laura took it from him with a strange, soft look in her eyes, and said it was the nicest thing that anybody had ever given her' (104). Laura's response is the more surprising not only because she and Philip have sharply contrasting wills, but because a former lover gave her the horse, right under her husband's nose (95). 'It was something of a revelation to me, too,' Mrs Bentley has to confess. 'He's always been so disillusioned and unexpectant about his drawings – it never occurred to me that underneath such a front of resignation there might be a little pride in what he could do, and a secret little hankering for recognition' (104).

Of course, it is always possible that sexual attraction governs Philip's condescension to an audience. By that token, however, he would have to be dallying with Paul as well as with the mannish Laura and the shy, retiring Judith, if not the admiring Mrs Bird. For Paul is the one who most often defines the terms of Philip's artistic success: 'He had been drawing again, and under his papers I found a sketch of a little country schoolhouse ... It stands up lonely and defiant on a landscape like a desert. Almost a lunar desert, with queer, fantastic pits and drifts of sand encroaching right to the doorstep. You see it the way Paul sees it. The distorted, barren landscape makes you feel the meaning of its persistence there. As Paul put it last Sunday when we drove up, it's *Humanity in microcosm*' (80). Given her need, however, to see Philip's 'failure,' Mrs Bentley is forced to think that Paul's verbal response (most likely to the drawing, though she refuses to distinguish between the schoolhouse and the work of art) is what really succeeds: 'Faith, ideals, reason – all the things that really are humanity – like Paul you feel them there, their stand against the implacable blunderings of Nature – and suddenly like Paul you begin to think poetry, and strive to utter eloquence.' Now this very description of the artist's sympathy for his subject becomes an occasion for the narrator to usurp the subject with 'poetry' of her own.

Philip is not so indifferent to Paul, either, as Mrs Bentley would have us think, though here she must argue, paradoxically, that Philip only suffers him because of a need of recognition she later claims was unknown to her: 'He did a little prairie scene in oils this afternoon – on cardboard, because he wants to save the canvases till he's found himself in paints again – and when I called Paul in after school to look at it he screwed his face up hard to keep me from suspecting he was pleased. He was pleased even more though when Paul stood quite still in front of it a minute; so pleased that relaxing a little he asked him to stay for supper with us, and was nicer to him than he's ever been' (91). And so her later remark at the Kirby ranch that 'He's not entirely disillusioned yet. I've taken him too literally' (104) proves how she must forget what she already knows. For she is not entirely unconscious of Philip's real relationship to his audience, even though she refuses to see it represented sympathetically in his art.

Her resistance to the appeal of sympathy in his work recalls that more abstract denial of the kinetic power of art made by Joyce's Stephen Dedalus. Stephen says, 'The feelings excited by improper art are kinetic, desire or loathing ... The arts which excite them, pornographical or didactic, are therefore improper arts. The esthetic emotion (I use the general term) is therefore static. The mind is arrested and raised above desire and loathing' (*Portrait* 205). Of course, Stephen, who has argued for the 'impersonality' of the 'dramatic form' as the ultimate goal of literature (215), is unaware that the diary in which he records his angry desire for a girl and his loathing for his mother's teaching ends a third-person narrative about him. It turns out that Stephen's preference for 'static' art emotions has a lot to do with his refusal to feel sympathy for 'the sufferings of women' (*Portrait* 245) or to return his mother's love (248). Mrs Bentley, who presumes that her own love for her husband is unrequited, will insist that his art also lacks emotion because of such artistic 'impersonality': 'According to Philip it's form that's important in a picture, not the subject or the associations that the subject calls to mind; the pattern you see, not the literary emotion you feel' (Ross 80). Never mind that Philip also argues for religion and art as 'different ways of taking a man out of himself, bringing him to the emotional pitch that we call ecstasy or rapture' (112). For she has reasons as good as those of Stephen Dedalus to want to resist kinetic emotions in art.

Examining the latest of Philip's many pictures of Main Street, Mrs Bentley says, 'You feel the wind, its drive and bluster, the way it sets itself against the town. The false fronts that other times stand up so flat and vacant are buckled down in desperation for their lives' (43). Yet she refuses any claim the subject might have on her will: 'And yet you feel no sympathy, somehow can't be on their side. Instead, you wait in impatience for the wind to work its will.' Of course, she does express her *secret* will, masking it as the will of the wind itself, or else as the will of 'you,' the reader. This same refusal to pity appears to be based on a Dedalean safety in stasis represented by the picture; the town on the page isn't going to blow down around her ears. But outside the aesthetic frame (and outside her own house) her will is supposedly one with nature. To her, the artist's sympathetic vision actually opposes 'nature' in holding all these desperate false fronts 'buckled down' in time as well as in space.

Both the words and actions of the minister would seem to confirm the diarist's image of the cold formalist the day they pray for rain at the schoolhouse church on Partridge Hill: 'Through the long prayers for rain he sat with his eyes fixed straight in front of him. My own went out again to the still expanse of prairie, the deadly sun glare over it; and for the first time I wished that Philip could mean his prayers, reach out and comfort a little' (83). And yet it is apparent that she has not been listening to what he says in the pulpit when, a month later at Partridge Hill, a desperate woman tells her that '[t]hey won't have potatoes even, or feed for their chickens and pigs. It's going to be a chance, she says, for the Lord to show some of the compassion that Philip's forever talking about in his sermons' (113). Here, even more poignantly, Philip's refusal to blame the woman for her lack of faith elicits the kind of compassion and forgiveness from her that he implicitly demonstrates himself: 'He couldn't answer her. He just stood wetting his lips till she saw how it was with him and said, "You never mind – I'd no right saying such things anyway." Then she put her hand on his sleeve as if he were a boy in trouble, and without looking up again hurried off to her democrat.'

The compassion of the preacher is easily rivalled by the pity of the artist in his portrait of Joe Lawson, one of the farm parishioners at Partridge Hill. Even Mrs Bentley recognizes in the drawing what she seems to have missed in the man's 'big, disillusioned, steadfast hands, so faithful to the earth and seasons that betray them. I didn't know before what drought was really like, watching a crop dry up, going on again. I didn't know that Philip knew either' (139). But from the second page of the novel we have seen how the artist pities and understands his people. So we might conclude that he fits, more than Mrs Bentley will ever admit, into the 'little niche that holds him.'

Now it seems she has the best (and worst) of reasons for jeering at the town; for Horizon 'takes sides' with her husband against her, making her see herself almost the way she views false fronts in one of his drawings, staring 'at each other across the street as into mirrors of themselves, absorbed in their own reflections' (69). Because she is so absorbed in her own reflection, she never admits that Philip isn't the hypocrite she makes him out to be, whether in the pulpit or in the studio. Rather, as she confesses ambiguously, 'I resigned myself to sanctimony years ago. Today I was only putting our false front up again, enlarged this time for three. Philip, Steve and I. It's such a trim, efficient little sign; it's such a tough, deep-rooted tangle that it hides. And none of them knows ... They can only read our shingle, all its letters freshened up this afternoon, *As For Me and My House – The House of Bentley – We Will Serve the Lord*' (61). She does not recognize the allusion to the Book of Joshua which identifies her as one of those who hates the 'land for which ye did not labour,' or which makes Philip speak with the prophet's voice, saying 'Choose you this day whom ye will serve ... but as for me and my house, we will serve the Lord' (Josh. 24: 13, 15). For Philip, it seems, means his religion in much the same way as he means his art.

If Philip's pity for his audience is more than a matter of his medium, Mrs Bentley's hatred of Main Street is hardly confined to just her diary. In a revealing conversation with Paul one night at the supper table, she fails to see that her scorn for the town is the real cause of Philip's apparent 'spasm of hatred for me' (36). But his resentment is not at all as personal as she thinks, since it is linked to Paul's own hypocritical criticism of the town. Philip has already shown his impatience with hypocrites, complaining about hypocrisy when, after a report of Mrs Bird's visit, he 'asked wasn't it bad enough to put up with such people when we had to – did we have to have them every mealtime, too?' (22). So, at mealtime, Philip is unlikely to display a 'combative kind of bitterness' (36) in sympathy with Paul's fighting words; for the moment, at least, he feels more combative toward the critic. But Mrs Bentley insists, against either the logic of association or of dramatic sequence, that he 'flares' at her because he is thinking of 'the boy of his own I haven't given him.' In fact, the minister has good reason to be angry with her for having opened a door, within the privacy of their own home, to backbiting against the townsfolk. After all, she was the one who first introduced the topic: 'I explained that Horizon might not approve' (36). After this arch statement, why shouldn't Paul follow suit, thinking the minister must approve of such double standards?

Paul's hypocrisy is the more plausible explanation of Philip's initial, grudging tolerance of him. Though Paul has been hurt in the past by some small-town sophisticates, his deeper hurt is that he is really like them, without being able to join their communion or even to forgive himself in them. And yet he is the most sympathetic witness of Philip's art, causing Mrs Bentley to remark of the paintings of the hills with 'eternity in them' that they showed 'the same strength and fatalism, the same unflinching insight. Anyway they were words something like that that Paul used' (102). Finally, Mrs Bentley's response is true to all that is best in her: 'There was no hard thinking to do, nothing tangled to get straight. He's an artist, that's all, and he's going to waste.'

The artist himself, however, hardly seems to think that he is going to waste. Nor does he see any discrepancy between his sermons and his drawings, between the small-town preacher and the artist. 'Religion and art,' he will soon tell her, 'are almost the same thing anyway.' Yet she refuses to see any of it. Finally, she will not even consider how it might be his 'strength and fatalism' which can ensure the success of her narrative 'plot.' For he is fatalistic enough as a man to surrender his claim to innocence even as he proves strong enough, as an artist, to give 'life and form' to her yearning illusion. By becoming her sole audience, by helping her to realize her story, he thus converts his own art into life, much as he had done before by uniting his ministry with his painting.

Two forms of art thus come together in *As For Me and My House*, one which shows life seeking the clarity and design of art, and another which offers the best means of converting that art into life. The narrator/artist, the narrated/represented world, and the audience-as-subject are finally, if privately, united in the public birth of the child. Now Mrs Bentley's 'secret' is out at last; her 'text' is published. And so the man who, refusing hypocrisy, had once refused to smoke a pipe, can finally accept both pipe and tobacco from a wife who, though unable to create a fellow hypocrite, has done something better – created a narrative 'partner in conspiracy' (14):

> He turned the pipe over a few times, filled it, struck a match, then looked up dubiously and said, 'You're sure it's all right? The smoke won't hurt the boy?'
> He's a very small boy yet, mostly lungs and diapers, but we like him. Philip just stands and looks and looks at him, and puts his cheek down close to the little hands, and tells me that way how much I must forget. It takes twelve years without a boy to let you know how much one's worth. He doesn't look like Philip yet, but Philip I'll swear is starting to look like him. It's in the eyes, a stillness, a freshness, a vacancy of beginning.   (164–5)

The old family romance, so often hidden from the world, has now become an open 'book,' born out of an artistic collaboration of both 'parents.' And, contrary to the concluded diary, it shows signs of remaining truly open to the future.

6

The Clash of Realism
and Modernism in
As For Me and My House

There's a remarkable change in the weather of *As For Me and My House* when the preacher and his wife leave for the Kirby ranch on the Red Deer River. The wind drops; the dust clouds disappear; the light breaks over distant hills. All those Dust Bowl facts of life which have been called 'the most traumatic in our nation's history, the most debilitating, the most devastating, the most horrendous' (Broadfoot iv) seem to vanish in the space of a half-day's drive. While Mrs Bentley is relieved to be out of Horizon, she doesn't seem to notice the change; her former obsession with climatic conditions turns out to have been anything but objective, which fact alone should weaken the usual cliché about the novel's realism. But in a larger sense, the vacation describes an aesthetic shift of scene – something of a holiday from realism itself – from a repetitive and grinding report of small-town life to a new expanse of artistic form and vision. For the claustrophobic tensions of a failing marriage begin to open out upon aesthetic differences which help to qualify the supposed aesthetic ambivalence of the novel (New 26–32), asking us to witness a shift in Canadian fiction from realism to modernism.[1]

'Life,' Mrs Bentley writes in her first diary entry of the holidays, 'has proved bitter and deceptive to Philip because of the artist in him, because he has kept seeking a beauty and significance that isn't life's to give; but Steve is a shrewd little realist, who, given opportunity to meet life on its

---

1 Barbara Godard, 'El Greco in Canada: Sinclair Ross's *As For Me and My House*,' *Mosaic* 14 (Spring 1981): 54–75, opposes Philip's 'Modernist formalism' to the narrator's 'Romantic realism.' While her terms help to define the musical and visual preoccupations of the characters, they are less useful in describing the conflicting narrative tendencies in the novel.

own terms, ought to make a fair success of it' (Ross 94). That she considers herself a shrewd realist as well is implied in her report of the boy's first night in their home: Philip 'hasn't seen him with his eyes yet, just his pity and imagination ... That's what's been wrong with him. He hasn't been able to get above reality ... So instead of resenting Steve I ought really to be sorry for him. When their ride's over and they're back on earth he'll have scant pasturage from Philip. After a while the pity and imagination are going to run out; and there's going to be left just an ordinary, uninspiring boy' (53). Such indulgence of the artist's flight of imagination has to be qualified by her resentment of Steve, whom Philip has taken 'for Pegasus, and gone off to the clouds again.' But we do not find her condescending, since her appeal, here and elsewhere, is to a commonplace need 'to meet life on its own terms' (94).

By implication, Mrs Bentley's narrative is not likely to shrink from the realist's task of showing life as it is, rather than as it ought to be. Her gritty report of life reduced to the minimum and yet capable of sustaining hope expresses some of the courage of the realist temper which 'does not allow us to escape, since its basic strategy is to implicate the reader almost beyond endurance' (Becker 30). Still, one is surprised to hear the narrator suddenly blame Philip for being 'wary of life because he's expected too much of it, and now to spare Steve his own disappointments he encourages him to stand aloof and distrustful of it to [sic]' (94); for the artist was supposed to be occupied with the search for an impossible beauty, leaving such wariness and scepticism to the 'realist' herself.

The dramatic situation helps to discover the real reason why the narrator can't decide whether her husband is an idealist or a realist: Laura, the brassy cowgirl, has just expressed contempt for a man who would have his son ' "go round drawing little pictures too" ... I must admit,' Mrs Bentley says, 'that Philip isn't showing up to advantage here' (93). But a few days before, back in town, it had been entirely to her advantage to show off her husband, the artist, to the doctor's wife: 'I kept bringing out more and more drawings. I boasted a little, said she should have seen the things he used to do' (88). If the narrator is at all sensitive to the way the wind is blowing, it appears to be in dramatic, more than meteorological, terms. For, even as she admits to 'a hint of the benediction' in her voice and confesses, 'My heresy, perhaps, is less than I sometimes think' (93), we hear her preparing for another sort of heresy against the artist himself. Self-mockery, in other words, helps her to justify her sudden doubt of the sort of imagination which still has not lost its appeal for her.

Even so, the romantic view of imagination which she has tried to deny is oddly renewed after a week at the ranch: 'It's been one of Philip's hard days, when the artist in him gets the upper hand. Reality as the rest of us know it, [sic] disappears from him. It isn't that he sits daydreaming or lost in the clouds – at such times there's actually a vitality about him that you're relieved to get away from – but rather as if he pierces this worka-day reality of ours, half scales it off, sees hidden behind it another' (101). She is not so disparaging, away from Laura, of a vision which has as much in common with Wordsworth as it does with Kant's transcendental idealism.[2] Her interest in another version of reality beyond 'this worka-day reality of ours' is given cogency, even urgency, by her experience of the dark and open land:

We've all lived in a little town too long. The wilderness here makes us uneasy. I felt it first the night I walked alone along the river bank – a queer sense of something cold and fearful, something inanimate, yet aware of us. A Main Street is such a self-sufficient little pocket of existence, so smug, compact, that here we feel abashed somehow before the hills, their passiveness, the unheeding way they sleep. We climb them, but they withstand us, remain as serene and unrevealed as ever. The river slips past, unperturbed by our coming and going, stealthily confident. We shrink from our insignificance. The stillness and solitude – we think a force or presence into it – even a hostile presence, deliberate, aligned against us – for we dare not admit an indifferent wilderness, where we may have no meaning at all.

(99–100)

Again, her honest analysis of her feelings might suggest the true spirit of realism: the refusal of any doctrine 'which prescribes what one ought to think and feel' (McDowall 577); the courageous doubt 'of that whole cluster of things which are associated with traditional theistic belief,

---

2 I have drawn upon discussion of Kant and the Romantics in Graham Nicol Forst, 'Into Silent Seas: Ideas and Images of Intellect in Kant and the English Romantics,' *Mosaic* 14 (Fall 1981): 31–44.

such as the soul, telic motion, the power of divine grace'; and the 'absolute denial of the principle of idealism' (Becker 34–5). But Mrs Bentley, in concluding that 'we dare not admit an indifferent wilderness,' gives us reason to doubt her convictions, much less her courage. What is more, her use of the first person plural makes us wonder what she projects into the landscape, as opposed to what her husband 'sees' in his painting.

'As always with his drawings it's what you feel, not what you see,' Mrs Bentley says of Philip's work after the bleak day she has spent with Paul trying to imagine the vastness of geological time. 'Eternity, though, was too big for me,' she says with a shudder, before implicating her husband in her despair: 'Philip meanwhile had been going through it too. At least so his sketches said tonight ... Just the hills, the driftwood logs, and stunted trees – but brooding over and pervading everything the same conviction of approaching dissolution that made it cold sometimes this morning out in the blazing sun' (100–1). Her despair is none the less offset the next day by her sudden hope that reality might indeed be left behind, if only the artist could see 'hidden behind it another. More important, more significant than ours, but that he understood only vaguely. He tries to solve it, give it expression, and doesn't quite succeed. His nerves wear thin, let fly if you happen to intrude' (101).

This final insistence upon Philip's failure is harder yet to understand, given her immediate confession that 'The really hard part is the picture he turned out. The hills and river and driftwood logs again – not so deft or finished as the pencil sketches yesterday; you can see he's a little clumsy still in oils – but with the same strength and fatalism, the same unflinching insight. Anyway they were words something like that that Paul used. He went into the tent after supper and found Philip asleep, then came for me to see it too' (102). What she evidently feels in the painting, as she had felt before in the pencil sketches, is the 'conviction of approaching dissolution' (100) which she can only interpret personally: 'I've always contrived to think that at least we had each other, that what was between us was strong and genuine enough to compensate for all the rest. But tonight I'm doubtful. All I see is the futility of it. It destroyed him; it leaves me alone outside his study door' (103).

Futility, as the philologist would undoubtedly tell us, is hardly the same thing as fatalism: *futilis*, poured out, useless, has little in common with Paul's equation of 'strength and fatalism.' 'It seems,' Mrs Bentley concludes sadly, 'that tonight for the first time in my life I'm really mature' (103); but it should now be clear that 'futility' is a misreading of something which Paul, at least, finds 'strong' in the work. Later in the novel, Philip offers his own assessment of this failing in her aesthetic response: 'These things all mean something to you because you've lived in these little Main Streets – with me while I was doing them. You're looking at them, but you're not really seeing them. You're only remembering something that happened to you there. But in art, memories and associations don't count. A good way to test a picture is to turn it upside down. That knocks all the sentiment out of it, leaves you with just the design and form' (154).

The Bentleys' differing responses to art have often been explained in terms of the romantic division between head and heart, or, to use the articons of the novel, between El Greco and Franz Liszt (Cude 469–70). Recently, Barbara Godard has argued for the same division in Philip himself – a 'tragic' conflict of romantic theories of *ecstasis* and modernist formalism – which leads Philip to doubt the human value of his work (67–8). There is little doubt in Laura's mind, however, of the value of Philip's sketch of her stallion. She 'took it from him with a strange, soft look in her eyes, and said it was the nicest thing that anybody had ever given her' (Ross 104). While Mrs Bentley belittles the mere 'realism' of this painting – 'for once, he had stooped to copy' – she confesses surprise at his hunger for an audience. 'I've taken him too literally,' she notes lamely.

The danger of taking Philip too literally is not done away with, a week after their return from the ranch, when he tries to define for her his sense of vocation. But Mrs Bentley does not heed the metaphor which explains how fatalism can be the source of his strength: ' "Religion and art," he says, "are almost the same thing anyway. Just different ways of taking a man out of himself, bringing him to the emotional pitch that we call ecstasy or rapture. They're both a rejection of the material, common-sense world for one that's illusory, yet somehow more important. Now it's always when a man turns away from this common-sense world around him that he begins to create, when he looks into a void, and has to give it life and form. Steve, you see – if he can lose himself in religion, he can lose himself just as easily in art" ' (112). Instead, Mrs Bentley seizes upon Steve as her proof that Philip seeks merely to create in his own image. But the metaphor of creating *ex nihilo* takes its strength from the creator looking into the void, confronting the emptiness, and still giving it 'life and form.' Philip's fatalism is an acceptance of illusion – a modernist faith, perhaps, that art alone can redeem the world of contingency – and, as such, it is quite unlike his wife's dread of the void.

Mrs Bentley's 'sickness unto death,' her overwhelming fear of the void, thus becomes her ultimate test as a realist. And yet the only responsibility she takes for her despair is the admission that she thinks 'a hostile presence' into the emptiness – 'for we dare not admit an indifferent wilderness, where we may have no meaning at all' (100). '*We*,' she says somewhat mysteriously, since Philip, it is now clear, does not share her view. It is rather her last pretence of objectivity, of accepting the 'independence of things' (McDowall 571). For her utter subjectivity is exposed by her loneliness in nature: 'The close black hills, the stealthy slipping sound the river made – it was as if I were entering dead, forbidden country, approaching the lair of the terror that destroyed the hills, that was lurking there still among the skulls. For like draws to like, they say, which makes it reasonable to suppose that, when you've just walked away from a man because you feel he doesn't want to be bothered with you, you're capable of attracting a few ghouls and demons anyway' (95).

'The temper of realism,' as S. Alexander says in *The Basis of Realism*, 'is to deanthropomorphize; to order man and mind to their proper place among the world of finite things; on the one hand, to divest physical things of the colouring which they have received from the vanity or arrogance of mind; and on the other to assign them along with minds their due measure of self-existence' (279). The colouring which Mrs Bentley's mind gives to the hills is finally a measure of her concern for her own existence, to the extent that we must now doubt Philip's supposed 'conviction of a supreme being interested in him, opposed to him, arranging with tireless concern the details of his life to make certain it will be spent in a wind-swept, sun-burned little Horizon' (Ross 17). The anthropomorphic foe is really the narrator's creation, while the artist's will to give the void 'life and form' associates him with the figure of a creator-god.

If this conflation of religion and art recalls Joyce's 'priest of eternal imagination' (*Portrait* 221), Philip's view of the importance of art places him directly in the symbolist-modernist tradition of seeing 'the universe as contingent, poverty-stricken, denuded until it has been reimagined' (Bradbury 51). The failure of Mrs Bentley's realism has important implications for subsequent prairie fiction, as does Philip's apparent faith in the creation of 'pattern and wholeness which makes art into an order standing outside and beyond the human muddle, a transcendent object, a luminous whole' (Fletcher 407). But the balance of this study deals with the implications for form and matter in Ross's novel itself.

'This novel, Mr. Ross's first,' writes E.K. Brown in 1941, 'owes nothing to any other work of Canadian fiction; indeed the tone and method suggest some young Puritan artist in the novel living in Maupassant's time' (Brown 124). This recollection of Flaubert's immediate successor not only puts *As For Me and My House* squarely in the tradition of nineteenth-century realism; it recalls the old joke that here is the nineteenth-century novel we never had. But Edward McCourt and Roy Daniells need no recourse to the nineteenth century to further the realist consensus; admitting elements of melodrama, Daniells sees but one failing in the artistic method – the formulaic repetitions of act and gesture which restrict characterization of anyone but the narrator herself, unless she and her husband can be said to 'make up a single more complex character' (vii).[3]

Two decades of sustained criticism have done much to waive these reservations (see Cude 486–7), although the old standards of realism are occasionally invoked to suggest a serious failure of representation in the novel: 'In certain respects [the book] deserves the praise it has received for its virtues as a regionalist work – its evocation of the drought, poverty, and hopelessness of the 1930's on the prairies – yet in other respects it is conspicuously lacking in a sense of the complex texture of everyday life. Ross notes that the Bentleys do not have a radio (pp. 132–33), but readers may wonder why they never, unlike most rural people in the thirties, get invited to listen to anyone else's radio either' (Denham 120). By realist standards, the novel is surely lacking in other signs of verisimilitude; a native wonders why no one shops at the Co-op store, or why the men never gather at the Wheat Pool office or the curling rink, not to mention the beer parlour. But these omissions are for Denham merely a symptom of conflicting modes of art: 'Horizon's isolation,

3 Morton L. Ross, 'The Canonization of *As For Me and My House*: A Case Study,' in Diane Bessai and David Jackel, eds., *Figures in A Ground* (Saskatoon: Western Producer Prairie Books 1978) 189–205, offers a wonderfully acerb survey of the shifts in critical attitude and strategy which have attended various attempts to deregionalize the novel.

which is insisted on throughout the book, is almost total, but it is also highly artificial, more like that of a ship at sea before Marconi than that of a town on the prairies. This is one point at which the novel departs from regional accuracy and moves toward symbolism' (120).

The lack of humour in the novel also suggests its limited representation, giving a postmodernist like Kroetsch a better claim to 'regional accuracy.' I think, for instance, of a 1930s joke from Alsask (near Abbey and Lancer, Saskatchewan, where Ross worked in the 1920s, and in an area of the Dust Bowl where population had declined from one family per quarter section to one in almost a township). The joke has the farmer saying, 'I wish it would rain. You know, it would not mean much to me. I've seen rain before. But my kids are growing up now and I'd like them to see what rain is like before they get married and move away' (Saskatoon *Star-Phoenix* 9 July 1937). The wry self-deprecation, the amused endurance of the voice, the inflation into tall tale, are all authentic signatures for the insider, and yet they must sound utterly foreign to the outlander, Mrs Bentley. It is this very foreignness of the narrator which leads Dick Harrison to defend the novel as a species of pyschological realism in which the perceiving consciousness is at odds with its external surroundings (131 ff). But the psychology of the narrator, and the cultural issues it raises, have yet to be explored in terms of the author's selectivity, not just the narrator's.

One of the hallmarks of the practice of realism is the avoidance of two lives shown in contrast. The shifting triangle of *Madame Bovary*, the three young men in *War and Peace*, the three *Brothers Karamazov* suggest that what the realist seeks 'is a kind of spectrum, made up of three lives or more, in which there is no single protagonist and in which no outcome of a life is necessarily more important or better than another' (Becker 30). Ross's choice of two characters, one of whom as narrator is remarkable for her intense subjectivity, the other of whom as ostensible subject is rational, and supposedly formal, in his response to life, points rather to modernism's obsession with 'the interpenetration, the reconciliation, the coalescence, the fusion – perhaps an appallingly explosive fusion – of reason and unreason, intellect and emotion, subjective and objective' (Bradbury 48). What might be called the resulting binary form of the novel is itself reminiscent of structuralism, which one recent theorist has identified as the ruling philosophy of the modernist era (Johnsen 543–4).

When we look again at Mrs Bentley's portrait of the artist embittered by reality 'because he has kept seeking a beauty and significance that isn't life's to give' (94), we recognize an unflattering version of Marcel in the passage which sounds the artistic coda of Proust's *Le Temps retrouvé*: 'How many times in the course of my life had I been disappointed by reality because, at the time I was observing it, my imagination, the only organ with which I could enjoy beauty, was not able to function, by virtue of the inexorable law which decrees that only that which is absent can be imagined' (Proust 905). Mrs Bentley's insistence upon the actual failure of imagination is, as we have seen, counterpointed by Paul and Philip's definition of its substantial success. What has not yet been noted is Mrs Bentley's motive for ensuring the miscarriage of her husband's art.

'He's a failure now,' Mrs Bentley writes at the end of her first week in Horizon, 'a preacher instead of a painter, and every minute of the day he's mindful of it. I'm a failure too, a small-town preacher's wife instead of what I so faithfully set out to be – but I have to stop deliberately like this to remember' (16). Her pause is neither as self-conscious nor as self-critical as it might seem, for it comes the same night as her story of the pipe shows her need to have Philip share her hypocrisy: 'The pipe belonged to both of us. We were partners in conspiracy' (14). When Philip flared at her insistence, 'I flared in turn, and said that so far as hypocrisy went the pipe didn't make much difference one way or another. It was no worse smoking on the sly than taking out his spleen and temper on his wife' (15). This unconscious habit of projecting her 'plot' onto other lives is stressed in the very first entry she makes in her diary. Mrs Finley, she assures us after just one meeting, is 'an alert, thin-voiced, thin-featured little woman, up to her eyes in the task of managing the town and making it over in her own image' (5). Philip, too, as she observes the same night, 'likes boys – often, I think, plans the bringing-up and education of *his* boy. A fine, well-tempered lad by now, strung just a little on the fine side, responsive to too many overtones. For I know Philip, and he has a way of building in his own image, too' (6). What is anticipated in her belated memory that she's 'a failure too' is the probability that Philip is made over in her image; for he seems to bear the burden not of his failure but of hers; she is thereby secure from failure unless she stops to think about it.

The source of her discontent with Philip's drawing, as already noted, is its failed romanticism, what might now be termed his inability to pierce through the phenomenal world of Kant's *Verstand* to the numinous

vision of *Vernunft*, that state of perception which Coleridge names the
' "Condition of conditions," that "knowledge of necessary and universal
conclusion – of that which is because it must be, and not because it had
been seen" ' (Forst 38). At the same time, her prescription for the artist
partakes of another strain of romanticism, its 'cult of personality and
denial of external authority' (Murdoch, 'Sublime' 261). She has, for
example, a very revealing dream of the preacher 'searching vainly for his
text; and then with a laugh he seized the Bible suddenly, and hurled it
crashing down among the pews' (Ross 15). Frightened by the prospect of
his open rebellion, she none the less yearns for this spirit of defiance to
shine through his art. But instead he draws in caricature, with the result
that 'everything is distorted, intensified, alive with thin, cold, bitter life
... Something has happened to his drawing, and something has happened
to him. There have always been Horizons – he was born and grew up in
one – but once they were a challenge. Their pettiness and cramp stung
him to defiance, made him reach farther. Now in his attitude there's still
defiance, but it's a sullen, hopeless kind' (17). Her own defiance has
already shown up in her mockery of false fronts which 'ought to be
laughed at, never understood or pitied' (4), though this first description
of one of Philip's drawings suggests something quite out of keeping with
the artist's supposed bitter, but merely sullen, rebellion. As Mrs Bentley
has to admit, '[L]ike all the rest there's something about it that hurts.'

What seems to hurt Mrs Bentley most in these drawings is not the pain
and suffering of their human subjects, but her husband's insistence on
pitying what she hates. Two versions of the same picture, however, show
dramatic swings in the obvious subjectivity of her response. On 2 May,
she concedes, through her use of affective verbs, Philip's pity for the false
fronts he draws – for hypocrites of all kinds – before she closes a door
against any such feelings in herself: 'Some of them cower before the flail
of dust and sand. Some of them wince as if the strain were torture. And
yet you feel no sympathy, somehow can't be on their side. Instead you
wait in impatience for the wind to work its will' (43). On this particular
night, the Bentleys have just met Steve, and, as Mrs Bentley has to admit,
'Steve was on my mind. There was something rankling in me that my
reason couldn't justify' (42). Her rational faculty is not aware, either, of
the way that circumstances – her husband's desire for a son and her own
resentment – are suddenly projected into Philip's portrait of desperate
endurance. But on 6 June, we get a second account of this same drawing

which underscores the narrator's compulsion to make things over in her own image: 'Last night again he drew a Main Street, and this morning I looked at it and then went through his drawers to find another that he did a month ago. In the first one the little false fronts on the stores are buckled low against the wind. They're tilted forward, grim, snarling. The doors and windows are crooked and pinched, like little eyes screwed up against the sand' (74).

The repetition of verbs (buckled, lean, tilted) and the dating ('a month') leave no doubt that we are hearing Mrs Bentley's second thoughts on the subject. The only real change occurs in her affective diction: now 'cower' and 'wince' turn into 'grim' and 'snarling.' Once again, we have to look to the dramatic context to explain the changed aspect of the drawing. In her previous night's entry, she has confessed to stopping Philip from defying Mrs Finley's god Propriety: 'He spoke with difficulty, trying to be cool and logical so that he might make a better case for Steve; his knuckles white, the veins out purple on his forehead ... I could feel the hot throb of all the years he has curbed and hidden and choked himself – feel it gather, break, the sudden reckless stumble for release – and before it was too late, before he could do what he should have done twelve years ago, I interrupted' (72–3). She is understandably chagrined to find herself as Mrs Finley's fellow worshipper; but she can only vent her frustration on the false fronts which are 'tilted forward, grim, snarling.' And so, after saving her own and, she assumes, her husband's false front, she is at a loss to explain his current drawing: 'in the one last night the town is seen from a distance, a lost little clutter on the long sweep of prairie. High above it dust clouds wheel and wrestle heedlessly.' She cannot, in other words, understand his lofty perspective. Not unless it can be chalked up to passive resignation: 'Here, too, wind is master' (74).

Philip is similarly 'resigned' two months later, just before he is 'supposed' to commit adultery. But in the moment of his apparent confession, she mistakes the real source of his resignation: 'I ran to the bedroom door, flung it open, and showed him the baby. "Your baby!" I cried. "Yours – " and he stopped white a moment, and said in a slow hollow voice, "You were with her then – and she told you – "'' (163). The composure which Mrs Bentley finds so 'heartless' (155) and self-possessed on the night she volunteers to take Judith's baby hardly cracks in his supposed moment of truth. Surely this is all the more surprising for a man who 'still handicaps himself with a guilty feeling that he ought to mean everything he says. He hasn't learned yet to be bland' (4). Or, as his wife says of him elsewhere, '[H]ypocrisy wears hard on a man who at heart really isn't that way' (15). Of course, Philip has already described the importance of illusion in religion and art; in that sense, the illusion he sustains for his wife is one of the most sympathetic guarantees of his art.

The narrator's reproach then yields one of the novel's finer ironies, since she blames her husband for something which is more characteristic of her:

> Guilty himself, is his impulse to find me guilty too? Does the thought that he's been unfaithful rankle? Is he trying to bring us to a level where we must face each other as two of a kind? To do it is he using Paul?
>
> It's hard to believe it of him. It just isn't true of the old Philip, the one I've always known.
>
> It can only mean that the one I've always known hasn't been the real one. I've been a fool like him, just as credulous and blind. I've taken a youth and put him on a pedestal and kept him there. I've taken the extravagances of his boyish dreams and hungers and made a kind of aura of them, through which I've never seen the reality. (135)

Her denial of the old reality only leads to another extremity in which she must impose her image over his. This inability of the narrator to see any face but her own strips the novel of its last vestige of objective realism. But Mrs Bentley's solipsistic reading of the world in terms of her own plot still discloses a larger feature in modernist irony – that spirit 'of scepticism, which questions not only the [artist] figure but indeed the total environment in which modern art is made' (Fletcher 406).

In 'The Sublime and the Beautiful Revisted,' the British novelist Iris Murdoch offers a searching criticism of the modernist view of art as a 'creation of unique self-contained things' (259). Tracing the genealogy of this aesthetics to Kant's theory of the beautiful, she establishes its relation to Kantian ethics in which the autonomy of the will is secured by man's 'ability to impose rational order' (248) upon what would otherwise be the necessity of the sensible world. But the analagous harmony which is struck in aesthetic judgment between the imagination and understanding is no more than an 'analagon of the free rational act,' since reason does not come into play in quite the same way in the making of the art-object (249). Thus beauty, which is the experience of harmony independent of ends, can be like, and yet unlike the moral act which is chosen for its own sake. In such fashion, argues Murdoch, the self-contained work of art becomes the analagon of the self-contained individual. So too in differing ways does Hegel's absolutist 'whole' and Kierkegaard's 'individual' further this idea of self-containment. For Kierkegaard especially, the concept of choice dependent upon intensity of feeling leads to a state where 'the deity and the solitary self between them enclose the whole of reality' (251). More recently in Sartre and other existential moderns, man's freedom of choice and his lonely responsibility disclose 'a terror of anything which encloses the agent or threatens his supremacy as a center of significance.'

Murdoch's analysis does much to explain one strain of modernism – the existential rage for order which leads Sartre to the view that 'a desire for our lives to have the form and clarity of something necessary, and not accidental, is a fundamental urge' ('Sublime' 255). What could be added to her assessment of a 'triumph,' in modern literature, 'of myth as a solipsistic form' (265) is the aestheticism of a Stephen Dedalus. For Joyce anticipates the ethical solipsism of Sartre in Stephen's romantic confusion of beauty and truth by which he seeks to remove the art-object from the world of its maker or audience, making it an autonomous thing whose value consists in its arrest of the mind, dissolvable only by the rhythm of beauty. Here, Dedalus's definition of art as the attempt 'to express, to press out again, from the gross earth or what it brings forth, from sound and shape and colour which are the prison gates of our soul, an image of the beauty we have come to understand' (*Portrait* 206), uncovers the hidden meaning in modernism's quest for the self-sustaining symbol. The artist wants to equate the work of art with his own soul.

Stephen's dramatic response to one such image of beauty charts the course – 'His soul was swooning into some new world ... Glimmering and trembling, trembling and unfolding, a breaking light, an opening flower, it spread in endless succession to itself' (*Portrait* 172). But his carefully reasoned theory of aesthetic stasis reveals a more subtle form of the soul spreading in endless succession to itself, where beauty is reduced to certain relations in the art work 'which satisfy and coincide with the stages themselves of all esthetic apprehension' (209). Thus beauty becomes aesthetic consciousness becomes creative intelligence, which is made even more ominous in Stephen's departure from Ireland 'to forge in the smithy of my soul the uncreated conscience of my race' (253). The artist's self-imposed exile is finally his insistence upon being his own 'country.'

The ironies of Stephen's practice as a poet and a man remark none the less a healthy scepticism in Joyce's own artistic method. Stephen, the poet of aesthetic stasis, rages and lusts while he writes; he fears a malevolent reality behind the 'truth' of substantiation, contradicting his own assertion that 'the true and the beautiful are akin' (*Portrait* 208). Ultimately, the real *claritas* that shines through the conversation of his friend, Cranly, is love and respect for 'the sufferings of women, the weaknesses of their bodies and souls ... Away then: it is time to go. A voice spoke softly to Stephen's lonely heart, bidding him go and telling him that his friendship was coming to an end' (245). This prototype of the modern artist alone and self-contained, creating for the sake of reposeful contemplation 'the purposeless self-contained quasi-object' (Murdoch, 'Sublime' 268), is also the prototype of 'Modernist self-questioning' (Fletcher 407) which points the way back to a world beyond the self.

Joyce's influence in *A Portrait* need inform only indirectly the portrait of the artist in *As For Me and My House*, though Ross has confessed his continuing interest in Joyce and Proust, among others (McMullen 21–2). Even the yoking of the diary with the *Künstlerroman* suggests a likely development from Joyce's *Portrait*, since Stephen himself is left to write a diary in blatant contradiction of his model for impersonality, that fictitious, though obviously Joycean 'old English ballad *Turpin [Stephen] Hero* which begins in the first person and ends in the third person' (215). The sort of diary which Stephen writes even predicts the necessary failure of this type of artist: '*20 March*: Long talk with Cranly on the subject of my revolt. He had his grand manner on. I supple and suave. Attacked me on the score of love for one's mother. Tried to imagine his mother: cannot' (248). It is the diarist herself in *As For Me and My House* who insists that the painter must fail for a similar want of love and lack of imagination. And yet the painter is hardly so solipsistic as she makes him out to be, since 'his' obsession with false fronts that 'stare at each other across the street as into mirrors of themselves, absorbed in their own reflections' (Ross 69) turns out to be her own. She is the one who flees from 'the little town outside [which] was somehow too much like a mirror. Or better, like a whole set of mirrors ... I couldn't escape' (23). The diary, in other words, where she 'keeps' her thoughts is the same self-absorbed and self-absorbing sort of artifice such as Dedalus would have gone on to write.

Mrs Bentley's denial of a world outside herself makes her less a realist than a particular kind of modernist, one whose aestheticism is actually directed *against* the world of her potential audience. Hating her house, her town, and her life, she turns away to her diary and also to her music: 'Tomorrow I must play the piano again, play it and hammer it and charge with it to the town's complete annihilation' (13). It is not that she hates the *idea* of an audience, only that she hates the audience at hand. Her other lost, ideal audience is still contained in memories of Percy Glenn, the world-touring concert pianist, who had answered 'a letter I'd written months before to tell him I was married to a preacher and living in a little prairie town and playing *Hymns with Variations* for the Ladies Aid. He said it seemed a pity, told me how many thousand had heard him play the night before. And I laughed, and worried Philip with amorous attentions in the middle of the afternoon, and didn't trouble to write again' (77). Philip, by contrast, refuses to exalt the artist above his community when he says to his wife, 'You have to put in a word for me – impress them – let them see that your small-town preacher husband has more to him than they can see on the surface – ' (89). It is not that he dislikes the music of Liszt as much as he disapproves of such self-aggrandizing artists.

The diarist, unhappy with the unassuming nature of her 'local' artist, must then find heroism at least in his epic struggle with his subject: 'I'm remembering instead the day he sat bare-headed in the sun up against the problem of putting eternity into his hills' (107). Her vision is in keeping with what William Spanos calls 'the obsessive effort of the modern literary imagination to escape the destructive impact of time and change, of which a disintegrating cosmic order has made it acutely and painfully conscious, by way of achieving the timeless eternity of the esthetic moment or, rather, of "spatial form"' (91). Iris Murdoch also notes how 'Form itself can be a temptation, making the work of art into a small myth which is a self-contained and indeed self-satisfied individual'

('Dryness' 20). Yet Philip is hardly so concerned as his wife with artistic 'immortality' or with what Murdoch calls the 'consolations of form' ('Dryness' 20). His later drawings, for example, include a most earth-bound one of Joe Lawson to which she makes, for once, the appropriate response: 'One of those strong, passionate little things that crop out of him every now and then with such insight and pity that you turn away silent, somehow purged of yourself ... It makes me feel in contrast fussy and contemptible. There comes over me a kind of urge to do something strong and steadfast too' (Ross 139). For a moment, she confirms Philip's cathartic theory of art – that it is meant to take 'a man out of himself' (112). Her feeling of being purged of self, her desire to 'do something strong and steadfast too,' also suggest that the morality of art might not be found in style alone, as Flaubert had first intimated (cited in Becker 94). At least for a moment she can accept the possibility that Philip's subject and audience are united not in himself but in his surroundings. Yet no sooner has she vowed 'that I'll never complain about my clothes and furniture again' than she dreams of renewing his belief 'in himself, in the thousand dollars, in getting away from here' (139). The self-sufficient artist is always better than his subject.

Philip's final two drawings deny, however, that they are 'elegant consolations of their own being' (Fletcher 401), or symbols of the self. The first is a sketch of two horses he has seen frozen to death against a fence: 'The way the poor brutes stand with their hindquarters huddled up and their heads thrust over the wire, the tug and swirl of the blizzard, the fence lost in it, only a post or two away – a good job, if it's good in a picture to make you feel terror and pity and desolation' (153). Not surprisingly, Mrs Bentley translates Philip's tragic vision into something merely personal, and Philip comes along to correct her. He pronounces himself on the side of form and detachment, though he admits that 'You can't be detached about your own work ... You feel it too much' (154). What he has felt in the form of the dead horses is something akin to Kant's theory of the sublime – 'the upsetting glimpse of the boundlessness of nature ... which brings about a sense initially of terror, and when properly understood of exhilaration and spiritual power' (Murdoch, 'Sublime' 268).

The last drawing Mrs Bentley mentions would seem to reinforce this capacity of art to enlarge not the self but the whole relationship between self and world: 'Philip is quiet, finishing a drawing that he's been working on since suppertime. A file of cattle plowing their way across a field piled deep with snow. Off in the distance there's a farmhouse, erect, small, isolated. It's just a pencil sketch in black and white, but you feel the cold and stillness of a winter's dusk. There's that about Philip, his work is bigger than his moods' (157).

Philip, as we discover in his congregation's farewell, has long been the recognized spokesman of that world outside himself. One recalls the narrator's perverse insistence that 'Philip preached well this morning, responding despite himself to the crowded, expectant little schoolhouse … The last hymn was staidly orthodox, but through it there seemed to mount something primitive, something that was less a response to Philip's sermon and scripture reading than to the grim futility of their own lives' (19). The later response of another parishioner is scarcely less ironic:

> It's going to be a chance, she says, for the Lord to show some of the compassion that Philip's forever talking about in his sermons. She has five children. This winter they're going to need shoes and under-wear …
>
> Philip's been changing of late, growing harder, more self-assertive, but today again he winced. He couldn't answer her. He just stood wetting his lips till she saw how it was with him and said, 'You never mind – I'd no right saying such things anyway.' Then she put her hand on his sleeve as if he were a boy in trouble, and without looking up again hurried off to her democrat.   (113)

We see at last that the man's silent forbearance does elicit compassion from some of his accusers. Religion and art can be the same thing after all, though in Philip's case art also opens the way back towards life.

In conclusion, it seems that Ross, like Joyce and other moderns, turns away from 'the analytical interpretation of the natural object,' the province of realism, toward a phenomenological synthesis 'of the naturalism of place with the materials of consciousness' (Lent 65). And yet his ironic handling of point-of-view undercuts one of the greatest dangers in modernist aesthetics – the solipsism of autonomous form – even as his artist-surrogate speaks to the artist's godlike capacity to let other beings exist through him.

7

Looking Homeward in
The Mountain and the Valley

'Oh, it was perfect now. He was creating something out of nothing' (80), David Canaan thinks at one point in *The Mountain and the Valley*. But the artist-as-a-young-actor fails to live up to his godlike power, either in the play or in the book he hopes to write, and the critics have always struggled to explain why.

Claude Bissell, in his 1961 'Introduction' to the New Canadian Library edition, concludes that Buckler's 'portrait of the artist as a young man' (xi) does not proclaim, 'as so many novelists of the century have done, the sacred necessity for rebellion' (xii). And yet Bissell is at a loss to explain the full design of the novel: 'It is the very strength and sureness of Buckler's treatment of the family that makes the last section of the book something of an anticlimax.' In her *Survival*, Margaret Atwood has no such doubt about the integrity of Buckler's design; fictional artists are required to fail in a colony without much taste for art, or in a country without faith in a home-grown culture: 'David has aspirations as a writer, and as his name implies he ought to be both the champion and the incarnation of his culture ... But the champion fails. He is regarded as something of a freak by the members of his family, "different," a little maimed.' The only thing Atwood can't understand is why 'the mountain accords him its vision only at the moment before his death (at the age of thirty, of a mysterious seizure)' (186). A victim of this sort is still the next best thing to winning the lottery in a book subtitled *A Thematic Guide to Canadian Literature*: 'For some reason his author cannot leave him alive with his book even a future possibility, as it is for Stephen Dedalus at the end of Joyce's *Portrait of the Artist as a Young Man*. A great writer, an artist of any kind, is not imaginable in Entremont' (187).

Douglas Barbour notes all the same that 'The Failing Heart' of the young artist is thematically tied to more personal and ethical failures: 'If David is an artist-manqué, it is not because he lacks innate qualities of vision, but because of some moral flaw in his character' (71). And D.J. Dooley glosses the two styles of Joyce's *Portrait* to show how Buckler may even mock the childishness of David's lyrical transports, as well as the 'Joycean epiphany' of the Epilogue. Dooley, however, still locates David's failure in his 'inability to dissociate himself from the standards of the community, to place a high enough value on the written word that he is willing to risk embarrassment for it' (Dooley 682, 680), and so implicitly accepts something like Atwood's 'colonial' (or environmental) explanation for young David's collapse.

In the fullest treatment to date, J.A. Wainwright extends the ironic reading by exploring the 'essentially solipsistic and destructive nature of David's talents' (79), if mostly in terms of his human relationships. But in both instances where David tries to write, only to destroy what he has written, Wainwright gives up his best insight, falling back upon circumstantial explanations of David's behaviour. The first time, 'David's fiction, crafted to breach the silence between him and Chris, is absolutely powerless before the fact of Chris's absence' (81); the second time, the accident of Anna and Toby's return mars his creative isolation, and 'any connection between art and life is immediately cut off' (85–6). In fact, the connection between art and life has been cut off by a critical method which is more content to trace patterns of isolation than to explain the life of such imagery in the novel. What the thematic critic ultimately finds is a community threatened on every side by silence, by isolation, and by death: 'the failure of words ... to breach this silence and prevent or alleviate their entrapment as victims has its matrix in the novel in David's first and ignominious defeat as a potential artist' (Wainwright 73). And so the artist, no matter how 'solipsistic and destructive' his talents, is not nearly as culpable as a world which can't understand his language. Even the family, it seems, makes a victim of the potential artist, at least if 'Buckler's "praise of family" is *always* threatened by his ironic version of life in the valley and of the relationship that exists between the family (community) and the creative individual' (Wainwright 64).

Then again, it could be that no one is to blame in the valley, not if 'David is alone on the stage and the valley inhabitants are isolated from

him as they watch him; this is the basic nature of their relationship'
(Wainwright 73) – though, one might add, it also is the familiar structure of theatrical experience. So who could point a finger at David's
community when 'Buckler's compelling portrait of silence swallowing *all*
words' (82) is so fatalistic? Even Joseph, the best of men, as it turns out,
'could not extricate himself from his fate' (86); so is it any wonder that
'David's fate is certain' (87)? In fact, David's 'struggle to find words
with which to break the silence has been self-deceptive and futile from
the beginning' (89), precisely because words themselves are 'deceptive'
(79), or, to put it more bluntly, because 'the limitations of language'
(76) are too great for any man to overcome. 'In inevitable defeat, the
protagonist who does not become an artist deserves our pity, not an
heroic appellation' (89). Though if defeat were in fact inevitable, would
not the irony of David's fate make him a truly tragic hero?

Lawrence Mathews is not unduly cynical in noting that this whole
process of 'the Ironization of David' ('Hacking' 194) 'says something
either about the quality of the criticism or the quality of the novel itself.'
But Mathews appears to be guilty of reasoning *a priori* that Buckler is a
greater failure as an artist than is David in the book: 'One looks, in vain,
for a thoughtful, comprehensive essay in which a critic demonstrates that
The Mountain and the Valley should, according to reasonably sophisticated aesthetic premises, be considered to possess the qualities that make
it worthy of inclusion in a canon' (191). It rightly seems that the one
premise worth considering for Mathews is the artist's use of language; he
has no doubt that, in Buckler's case, 'the book is *badly written* ' (189).
Did Mathews really mean, then, to say something '*either* about the
quality of the criticism or the quality of the novel,' or, more likely, about
the quality of both? Birds, we know, have to be lined up just so, if there's
only one stone to throw. Thus: 'It is as though, for most Canadian
critics, language scarcely exists' (191). Not that Mathews offers anything more than hearsay evidence of such 'a failure of language' (189) in
The Mountain and the Valley. The satisfactions of the critical *bon mot*
must be sufficient to imply their opposite: 'Somehow a novel gets to be
established as a classic without any "full-scale critical consideration"
having been published. Is there a secret oral tradition?' (188).

The tradition to which the novel belongs – that of the *Künstlerroman*
– is no longer much of a secret, of course. And yet the evidence of
Buckler's style should have been enough to suggest that there really was a

point to 'the manifest overwriting' ('Hacking' 196), since the model for Entremont was obviously not Joyce but Thomas Wolfe – specifically his Altamont in *Look Homeward, Angel* (1929). To be sure, Mathews himself is justifiably hard on critics who pull the 'old "as in Joyce" trick ... If the Joycean *mana* can be transferred to Buckler, then Buckler, too, is beyond criticism' (196). But Mathews also cites, to Buckler's sole disadvantage, a very different critical comparison without bothering to consult his own high standards: 'Buckler's relation to Melville, Faulkner, Wolfe, and Bellow is that of apprentice to master' (189). If Wolfe can be called a master, then Buckler's parody of him in *The Mountain and the Valley* can only be called a masterpiece, worthy of inclusion in any canon, much less one that is constitutionally required (the critic would have us believe) to find a representative from 'Atlantic Canada (best of a poor field)' (Mathews 198). If, on the other hand, Wolfe himself were to be convicted of overwriting, Buckler could only be faulted were he to fail to show the irony of Wolfe's larger aesthetic premises. Here, then, is a probable starting point to search out those 'reasonably sophisticated premises' that are apparently still wanting to prove a book a classic.

'A great writer, an artist of any kind,' it has been affirmed, 'is not imaginable in Entremont.' Then again, a great writer might be more than a little embarrassed to take the Dedalean romantic so seriously. Even a flawed writer such as Thomas Wolfe could have second thoughts about his own imitation of Joyce:

> I believe the character of the hero was the weakest and least convincing one in the whole book, because he had been derived not only from experience but colored a good deal by the romantic aestheticism of the period. He was, in short, the 'artist' ... the wounded sensitive, the extraordinary creature in conflict with his environment, with the Babbitt, the Philistine, the small town, the family. I know that I was not satisfied with this character even at the time: he seemed to me to be uneasy and self-conscious, probably because I was myself uneasy and self-conscious about him. In this sense, therefore, the book followed a familiar pattern – a pattern made familiar by Joyce in *A Portrait of the Artist as a Young Man*, and later in *Ulysses* – a book which at that time strongly influenced my own work. (Braswell 50–1)

Thomas Wolfe died in his thirties, too young to realize his potential greatness as an artist: 'His total work stands, as do so many other monuments of romantic art, as a group of fragments imperfectly bodying forth a seemingly ineffable cosmic vision in terms of the self of the artist' (Holman 23).

Thirty-year-old David Canaan fails to leave behind even fragments of the two stories he writes, though his vision at the end of Buckler's novel certainly moves towards a 'cosmic' vision of the self of the artist: 'They sounded and rushed in his head until it seemed as if he must go out *into* these things. He must *be* a tree and a stone and a shadow and a crystal of snow and a thread of moss and the veining of a leaf. He must be exactly as each of them was, everywhere and in all times; or the guilt, the exquisite parching for the taste of completion, would never be allayed at all' (*Mountain* 292). When Ernest Buckler decided to set his portrait of the artist in a town called Entremont, he might as well have been inviting deliberate comparison with Wolfe's Altamont.

The compositional history of *The Mountain and the Valley* indicates that such an invitation was in fact addressed to Wolfe's editor at Harper's, Edward C. Aswell, who had been left to piece together the manuscripts which were finally published two years after Wolfe's death as *The Web and the Rock* (1939) and *You Can't Go Home Again* (1940). On 10 September 1946, Buckler sent Aswell three stories which, he wrote, were 'connected, my best, and have in them the foetus of a novel' (cited in Young 90). The stories, as Young so ably shows, became the basis of chapters 36 to 38 in the completed novel. Buckler even admits to Aswell that 'the writing' in one – 'Thanks For Listening' – 'is a little over-blown and doesn't quite come off even if the intention is honest' (Young 90). All the same, the story offers a familiar portrait of a roman-tic, self-pitying artist. Here, Buckler implies, is a style with which the editor of Thomas Wolfe will surely be familiar. But Buckler's manuscript was politely rejected, in Aswell's absence, by Elizabeth Lawrence with no more than a few, faint words of encouragement for his planned novel. Evidently the kinship of this novelistic 'foetus' to Wolfe was not yet apparent, not even to quite knowledgeable eyes.

Still, 'the problem of language' (Mathews, 'Hacking' 191) in the novel which Buckler finally completed five years later takes on a much different value when it is compared with *Look Homeward, Angel*. Wolfe's novel has been 'loosely defined as a family chronicle strong in characterization, overcharged with heady poetry' (Walser 48). Claude Bissell says of *The Mountain and the Valley* that 'it is a novel written in praise of the family' (xi) in 'the high metaphysical style – a style of which there have been many examples in American fiction. One thinks of Melville, of Faulkner, of Wolfe, and of Bellow' (x). Though Bissell finally resorts to Dylan Thomas's 'Fern Hill' as 'a fitting epigraph' (xii) to the novel, he glimpses the essential tension in Buckler's style between the dramatic and lyric impulses in fiction.

'When we examine the way Wolfe worked,' writes Richard Kennedy in his seminal essay on genre in Wolfe, 'from the inception of *Look Home-ward, Angel* until the end of his career, we find that he let his mind follow associations from one thought to the next, a method of development that is common to lyric poetry rather than prose narrative' (6). Since lyric pieces tend to be very short, Wolfe had to find for his rambling narratives such devices as 'an autobiographical time scheme to impose control on his material' (Kennedy 8). *Look Homeward, Angel* none the less begins outside of history in a proem which echoes Wordsworth's 'Immortality' Ode. 'If we do not count that as the beginning, but take the opening of chapter one, we still do not begin with a character or an ancestor but with the cosmos and a meditation on the miracle of chance' (Kennedy 8). Throughout the novel there also runs another poetic refrain, '*O lost, and by the wind grieved, ghost, come back again.*' Finally, there are all those prose poems prefacing the more dramatic chapters. For example, chapter 9 of *Look Homeward, Angel* begins in the high, chanting style:

Yes, and in that month when Proserpine comes back, and Ceres' dead heart rekindles, when all the woods are a tender smoky blur, and birds no bigger than a budding leaf dart through the singing trees, and when odorous tar comes spongy in the streets, and boys roll balls of it upon their tongues, and they are lumpy with tops and agated marbles; and there is blasting thunder in the night, and the soaking millionfooted rain, and one looks out at morning on a stormy sky, a broken wrack of cloud; and when the mountain boy brings water to his kinsmen laying fence, and as the wind snakes through the grasses hears far in the valley below the long wail of the whistle, and the faint clangor of a bell; and the blue great cup of the hills seems closer, nearer, for he had heard an inarticulate promise: he has been pierced by Spring, that sharp knife.

And life unscales its rusty weathered pelt, and earth wells out in tender exhaustless strength, and the cup of a man's heart runs over with dateless expectancy, tongueless promise, indefinable desire. Something gathers in the throat, something blinds him in the eyes, and faint and valorous horns sound through the earth.   (78)

All this by way of prologue and lyrical contrast to Eugene's alliance with other boys in 'what they had against the barbarians.' Still, the first, long periodic sentence postpones the social knife, and implies more of a balance in the related syntax of Eugene's life: the social world may be evil but, in the best romantic fashion, nature is still consoling. Even the tedium of repetition in small-town life is clothed in weighty parallelisms. And the emphatic order of the periodic construction ultimately supplies a sense of control, rather than randomness, in the general life of Altamont.

In several chapters of *The Mountain and the Valley* (7, 14, 17, 26), the narrative is also set aside for such lyric flights of voice. As a prologue to David's attempt both to belong to and to lord it over a group of older boys, the narrator offers a lively paean to summer. Beginning 'The summer David was fourteen had every day like August. The sky was so purely blue from morning till night it had a kind of ringing, like the heat-hum of the locusts' (101), the ode moves through several stately paragraphs towards its close:

In the afternoons a steady heat, like Sunday hush, seemed to bring the mountains closer. It gave them dreamy light-greenness. They looked like *pictures* of mountains. The clear blue heat outlined everything with stereoscopic immaculacy. The repleteness in the air, as if the thirst of growing were forever slaked, gave it an almost churchy texture. Even in the stifling backhouse, where a dead fly forever lay imprisoned in an abandoned cobweb, David would feel it. In the stuporous, trancelike afternoons the tools of planting – the spade against the wall or the harrow with the earth of spring caked on its comma-like teeth – lay as if their work would never have to be repeated.

Then in the blue evenings the dew began to make a clamminess in

> the hay while it was still dusk. Scarves of haze blued and exiled the
> mountains. Later, the breath of the whole blue night was bated
> with the pulsating hum of insects.   (102)

Buckler eschews Wolfe's syntax of endless conjunction, and he studiously
refrains from the mythological figure, substituting the concreteness of
'August' for 'Ceres' and the 'hum of insects' for the sound of faery
'horns.' Yet the effect of fullness is the same, issuing from the abstract
diction of 'repleteness' into the homely images of dead flies and harrows
with 'comma-like teeth,' whereas Wolfe moves from the concrete image
(birds, buds, tar, marbles) to the abstract ('dateless expectancy, tongueless promise, indefinable desire'). Buckler's syntax is both more varied,
ranging from simple to complex sentences (including one with a charming compound-appositive clause), and at the same time more detached,
allowing for something approaching aesthetic distance in the midst of so
much sensation ('They looked like *pictures* of mountains'). Though
moving at times in Wolfean rhythms, Buckler's language is less headlong
in its catalogue of boyish sensations, and so is much less given to 'the
fallacy of imitative form' (Mathews 195) than some might think.

Buckler's imagery is also more restrained than Wolfe's, approaching
the precision of an Imagist poet in such sentences as 'Scarves of haze
blued and exiled the mountains.' The 'blue evenings' which are shortly to
become 'the whole blue night' have already been linguistically transformed by 'blue' used as a verb. Moreover, Buckler achieves a greater
unity of effect from the controlling metaphor of sound which is associated with this same blueness. Beginning with a sky 'so purely blue ... it
had a kind of ringing, like the heat-hum of the locusts,' the ode moves
through a more literal 'symphony of heat' where 'the first locust sounded
its brass' to the final 'breath of the whole blue night' which 'was bated
with the pulsating hum of insects.' Wolfe tends, by contrast, to dart from
woods to pavement to thunder in the night, much like his 'birds no
bigger than a budding leaf dart[ing] through the singing trees.' Here, it
would seem, it is Wolfe who is more guilty of the fallacy of imitative
form.

All the same, writes his latest biographer, 'Some of Wolfe's best
effects are, surprisingly enough, on a small scale ... [T]ake his Imagist
portrait of Ben:

My Brother Ben's face, thought Eugene,
Is like a piece of slightly yellow ivory;
His high white head is knotted fiercely
By his old man's scowl;
His mouth is like a knife,
His smile the flicker of light across a blade.'

(Donald xiv)

David Canaan's moment of vision on the mountain leads in corresponding style to a memory of 'the face of my father nights in the kitchen
listening to Anna hear my spellings, hearing a son of his own flesh spell
correctly words he himself didn't even know the meaning of' and to a
Gantian moment of affirmation – 'yes, and my *mother's* face that night'
(*Mountain* 293) – capturing it in a moment of dramatic revelation.
Buckler's novel, in other words, is not limited to the perceptions of the
growing artist any more than is Wolfe's; both are built upon a retrospective sequence of family portraits out of which the mature artist could
discover his likeness and difference.

The more significant family likeness of David Canaan, however, is to
his literary ancestor in Eugene Gant. David 'felt a heightened identity, an
expansive relaxation, in being absolutely alone' (*Mountain* 244). Eugene
looks much the same, once 'The prison walls of self had closed entirely
round him; he was walled completely by the esymplastic power of his
imagination – he had learned by now to project mechanically, before the
world, an acceptable counterfeit of himself which would protect him
from intrusion' (*Look* 167). So, too, 'David's mind deliberately sus-
pended its own nature. It assumed the cast of Steve's. He could synchronize his behaviour with any of theirs now. He could put their thoughts
into words; and hearing them spoken, they'd be as pleased as if they'd
been able to find the words themselves' (*Mountain* 283).

On the other hand, the isolation of the 'Wolfean protagonist' is not as
'entirely subjective and ... entirely solipsistic' as one critic would have it
(Rubin 66), at least not if Wolfe's narrator is to be trusted. Though
Eugene's 'physical loneliness was more complete and more delightful,' he
still 'had a vast tenderness, an affection for the whole marvellous and
unvisited earth, that blinded his eyes. He was closer to a feeling of
brotherhood than he had ever been, and more alone' (*Look* 407). Near
the end of his story, David Canaan likewise 'thought of the people in the

valley. Now they were out of sight, his own face moved kindredly among them. They were pliant in his mind's eye to whatever aspect he cast them in ... He could think of anything now. Everything seemed to be an aspect of something else. There seemed to be a thread of similarity running through the whole world' (*Mountain* 286-7). On the surface, at least, romantic isolation leads for both protagonists to imaginative sympathy.

There is still no denying an accompanying romantic egoism in both characters which outlasts their respective childhoods. The first time David confronts death, he puts the sight of the dead bodies out of mind with a consoling fantasy of his own heroism: 'There were different faces around him. They were lying on the ground and bullets were whining over their heads. And then he got up and ran toward the German trench ... and when the others saw him charging so bravely they all got up and shouted and ran with him. And suddenly, like waking from a muddled dream, he knew exactly what he was going to be. He was going to be the greatest general in the whole world' (*Mountain* 41). Even in conclusion, David still insists ironically that 'When he grew up he'd be the best fiddle player in the whole world'; 'He knew he'd be the most famous mathematician there ever was'; 'and suddenly he knew he'd be the most wonderful dancer that people had ever seen'; 'and he knew he'd be the only man who ever went every single place in the world and did everything in the whole world there was to do' (*Mountain* 290-1). Similarly Eugene, 'With a tender smile of love for his dear self' – if the irony at this point is louder, it is merely temporary – 'saw himself wearing the eagles of a colonel on his gallant young shoulders. He saw himself as Ace Gant, the falcon of the skies, with 63 Huns to his credit by his nineteenth year. He saw himself walking up the Champs-Elysées, with a handsome powdering of gray hair above his temples, a left forearm of the finest cork, and the luscious young widow of a French marshal at his side' (*Look* 445).

It could be said of David, as much as of Eugene, that he 'believed himself thus at the centre of life' (*Look* 160), though a stage-incident common to both novels has a more lasting effect on Buckler's romantic egoist. Eugene is supposed to play Prince Hal in a pageant on the tercentenary of Shakespeare's death, but, because the boy is too big for the costume sent from Philadelphia, he is nearly hooted off the stage: 'Laughter, laughter unleashed and turbulent, laughter that rose flood by flood upon itself, laughter wild, earth-shaking, thunder-cuffing, drowned Dr George B. Rockham and all he had to say. Laughter! Laughter!

Laughter!' (*Look* 312). Still, Eugene is not so deeply scarred by his humiliation as is David who also plays the role of a prince in disguise. As soon as one member of the audience has broken the spell of David's performance with apparent mockery, 'He felt the shame of having spoken the foolish words in this goddam foolish play as he'd felt shame then' (*Mountain* 82). David's artistic isolation, in other words, is more ominous; thus early, Buckler suggests that the fledgling artist will come to reject his art because of the supposed response of his audience.

From smaller elements of style – the medical verb 'encysted' appeals alike to Wolfe (93, 196) and to Buckler (219) – to parallels in character and even incident, we move at last to the largest defining element of structure. Through forty chapters, a growing artist named Eugene Gant seeks redemption from a world in which he feels *'a stranger and alone'* ('Proem'). Then, at the end of his forty 'days' of exile in the wilderness, he has his moment of Mount Pisgah vision (cf. W.O. Gant – *Look* 60) and is called into the promised land of art: the 'vast hills' which earlier appeared to him to be 'like Canaan and rich grapes' (*Look* 383) do stand in conclusion as the summit of his hopes as he 'turns his eyes upon the distant soaring ranges' (522). Through another forty chapters, a very different artist named David Canaan seeks the summit of vision, only to fall dead in the snow. The biblical Moses, after forty years in the wilderness, was granted his moment of vision, too, from the top of Mount Pisgah; but, for his sin, he could not pass over Jordan. Buckler, in other words, seems to have used the same mythology of exile as Wolfe did; but he interpreted it differently. His reduction of Altamont to Entremont suggests that there is something in the very aesthetics of 'Altamont' which necessitates his artist's failure, or at least makes the middle ground of 'Entremont' the surer footing for his own kind of art.

But what could possibly be wrong with Altamont? Already, it was familiar to a generation of readers as the shining peak of the romantic's quest, his symbol in art of the soul's pre-existence and the goal of his return through art: 'Home is Altamont, one's own heart and spirit, wherein lies the potency for artistic creation' (Walser 66). The Altamont artist is veritably Emerson's god in ruins (Wolfe's own phrase is 'a god in exile' – *Look* 426), and he approaches his recovery with an Emersonian self-reliance: 'But in the city of myself, upon the continent of my soul, I shall find the forgotten language, the lost world, a door where I may enter' (*Look* 521). But Wolfe's hero, like a good southerner distinct from merely Transcendental Yankees, is also assisted by family, specifically by his brother's ghost and his father's stone angel: 'The ghost is the source, the brightness, the inspiration of art, and the ghost is ever available to him who is sensitive to its presence' (Walser 67). Finally, what the ghost offers Eugene, beyond the confidence to make his 'own world,' is a vision of 'lost time' (*Look* 519) translated into space: 'And for a moment all the silver space was printed with the thousand forms of himself and Ben … the thousand forms that came, that passed, that wove and shifted in unending change, and that remained unchanging Him' (*Look* 518). This vision of time, like the presence of the angel, is its own proof of the soul's immortality: 'The angel, initially figuring forth the education of the outsetting artist, is ultimately the permanence of art itself' (Walser 67). And so the incipient artist, setting out from a social wasteland which is both the wilderness of Sinai and Bunyan's City of Destruction, 'was like a man who stands upon a hill above the town he has left, yet does not say "The town is near," but turns his eyes upon the distant soaring ranges' (*Look* 522).

Entremont is no accidental come-down from the shining heights of Altamont. To be sure, the 'wounded sensitive' still blames his family and community for making him 'cripple every damn thought' he has (*Mountain* 163). But David also means to wear his scars to his advantage (165). In this, once more, he resembles Eugene who had thanked his family 'for every blow and curse I had from any of you during my childhood,' promising to 'spend the rest of my life getting my heart back, healing and forgetting every scar you put upon me when I was a child,' for 'I shall get me some beauty, I shall get me some order out of this jungle of my life' (*Look* 421–2). Again like Eugene, David turns away from a crass, uncomprehending world to train his eyes 'upon the distant soaring ranges' (*Look* 522), taking his way at the end of his story to an actual mountain top. But from his earliest approach to his final ascent, David's beautiful heights are deadly. Pete Delahunt and Spurge Gorman die the day David's father first leads him toward the top; Joseph himself dies just below the summit, cutting the keel tree; and Anna, in her only peak experience, foresees the death, by drowning, of her husband at sea.

The danger of Altamont does not, however, impress David nearly so much as the grave markers in the valley of certain dead youths: 'He felt almost a jealousy of them. It seemed as if they had done some bright extra thing' (*Mountain* 93). Or hadn't done something, as the case may be, and so not even death could stain their shining promise. In fact, 'They had made the stain brightest of all by their very unconsciousness of having put together the shiveringly matchless words "died" and "young."' So the shivering romantic is hardly affected by Toby's warning that he seeks his inspiration in the wrong place:

> He started to eulogize the mountain, for Toby.
> 'You can see the whole valley up a ways farther,' he said. 'You can't hear a sound, but you can see the whole thing.'
> 'You can't see it as plain as you can when you're in there, can you?' Toby said, with his sudden devastating frankness.   (144)

His faith in himself unshaken, David aspires to the heights till the moment of his death, even coming to a Gantian vision of time frozen into space which offers a hope of his redemption: 'It was as if time were not a movement now, but flat. Like space. Things past or future were not downstream or upstream on a one-way river, but in rooms. They were all on the same level. You could walk from room to room and look at them, without ascent or descent. It was as if the slope of time had levelled off at this moment. It didn't go by while you were reaching out to touch it. It was waiting for you. It waited for you to straighten things out, before it moved on' (287–8).

The proud isolation and exalted individualism of Eugene Gant give way at last in David Canaan to a sense of community and a spirit of forgiveness. Crucially, however, David offers to forgive the members of his community while insisting on his own innocence: 'He felt like the warm crying of acquittal again. Even my mother and my father and all the others who are gone will know somehow, somewhere, that I have given an absolving voice to all the hurts they gave themselves or each other – hurts that were caused only by the misreading of what they couldn't express' (300). So we are not surprised when the priest of eternal imagination dies without absolution himself, slipping as usual into the old romantic egoism, dreaming that his 'book won the prize,' just before he feels 'the beating of his heart' and collapses in the snow. The artist who never cared for the plainness of what you see 'when you're in there' finally has the magic carpet pulled out from under his feet.

The major difference between Altamont and Entremont thus grows out of their differing appropriations of the romantic myth of exile. Wolfe offered a straight imitation of Joyce's 'triumphant' Dedalus (though Joyce seemed to regard him quite as ironically as his Ovidian prototype), while Buckler resorted to the irony of the biblical story of Moses. Wolfe could only see the failure of his character in looking back on the book he had written; Buckler made that failure the subject of his writing.

The inversion of the usual romantic cliché is made clear by Buckler in a letter written to Dudley H. Cloud of Atlantic Monthly Press, the publisher who had just rejected the book: 'It was to be the crowning point of the whole dramatic irony (and, of course, the most overt piece of symbolism in the book), that [David] should finally exhaust himself climbing the mountain, and, beset by the ultimate clamor of impressions created by his physical condition and his whole history of divided sensitivities ... achieve one final transport of self-deception: that he would be the greatest writer in the whole world' (cited in Young 94–5). Young himself is cautious about slipping into the intentional fallacy; but the structure of the novel alone will show how fully David is the dupe of an inflated ego. Ultimately, Buckler's Canadian classic does not follow the familiar pattern of the Anglo-American *Künstlerroman* where the culture proves hostile to art and artist alike; rather, it suggests how a romantic view of art is totally inimical to the Canadian imagination and its sense of community.

The moral and psychological weaknesses in David's character have yet to be understood, however, in terms of his aesthetic weaknesses, in full view of the defining problems of the artist novel: the artist's use of language and his sense of himself in relation to an audience. The story of a romantic artist who dies too young, *The Mountain and the Valley* offers a sensitive critique of Wolfe and of Altamont in particular, and of the larger *Künstlerroman* tradition in general.

The key to the young artist's view of art in *The Mountain and the Valley* is to be found in his view of language: 'All through the year the words of his part in the play kept flushing in and out of David's head like an exalting secret ... The words were something no one else had' (55). Not surprisingly, David plays the part of a prince in disguise; he only stoops to common rags 'to find out what it would be like to play with someone else' (46). The artist-prince begins his career in an a Wildean cult of experience.

Of course, the 'prince' is only a boy in a school play. But already he knows that the words give him 'somewhere outside the moment to go'; he feels pity for the other members of his family 'for being so pitiably, humdrumly, outside it' (56); his words are 'a kind of refuge' to him 'when the moment was bare' (57). In other circumstances, the words are more than a consolation for his deprivation by reality: 'The words gave him a more selfish sort of safety when he was with the ones he *didn't* love' (56). These others 'would seem, beside himself, like people tied' (57). And so the words are deliberately private, since they lift him up above the mob, exalt him to the top of Altamont. Of course, this sort of self-glorification is hard to maintain in public. Little wonder that David won't speak his 'piece' (76) for his mother when she asks, or that the words 'sounded silly to David' when they were overheard by his father in the barn.

Comes the day, all the same, when an artist has to go public or forfeit his pretensions. But in the act of making his words public, David does come to an important realization: 'This was better than the cosiness of doing anything alone. He'd never do anything alone again. He'd take them with him always, in their watching ... There was a bated wonder coming from their faces: to know that this was David, but a David with the shine on him (they'd never suspected!) of understanding and showing them how everything was' (80–1). He doesn't shine for himself, you understand, but for his people. The prince has become the light of the world.

'The Play,' as one critic recognizes, marks a departure from the 'play in the *Portrait* [which] takes on a life of its own ... It is an artistic object which stands apart from normal human concerns; it does not impel Stephen towards a sense of community, but it segregates him ... Similarly at the end of his play David rushes away from everybody, but for a very different reason ... He has found a way to reconcile his own world of make-believe with the common life of others ... No sooner is the way found, however, than it is lost: he oversteps the bounds by kissing Effie' (Dooley 676–7). Yet just before he rewrites the script of the play, David remembers 'the moment in the dream when he climbed to the top of the mountain and looked down' (82). His creative impulse is stirred by a vision of his own transcendence. While his moment at the top is shattered by Jud Spinney, the damage doesn't come exactly from Jud's 'derisive yell: "That's it, Dave. Slap em *to* her!"' (Dooley 677). For Jud doesn't mock; 'He shouted gleefully' (*Mountain* 82), applauding much too well, wanting in on the act. Now even a boy knows that three's a crowd. But where's the advantage of playing king of the hill with the likes of Jud Spinney hard on your heels?

Sharing his 'exalting secret' is obviously a moral problem for young David. But it is also a problem of language as Buckler defines it. For the 'safest sort of exaltation' (65) that David ever knows is the sight one Christmas Eve of the old recluse, Herb Hennessey – *safe*, he thinks, because such isolation could never be his fate; *exaltation*, he knows, because his own position depends upon having such a foil. Even Christmas Eve, with all its trappings of secrecy, is just another mirror of the child's self-absorption. A scant moment before David sees Old Herb, 'The smell of the tree grew suddenly and the memory of the smell of the oranges and the feel of the nuts. In that instant suddenly, ecstatically, burstingly, buoyantly, enclosingly, sharply, safely, stingingly, watchfully, batedly, mountingly, softly, ever so softly, it was Christmas Eve' (65). *Cloyingly*, one is tempted to add to what has to be one of the most overwritten sentences in the language. For one linking verb cannot bear the weight of twelve adverbs, the twelve days of Christmas or no. Not unless the style should happen to be David's.

'The incremental style is particularly appropriate to David's Christmas Eve because it conveys the stretching out of an experience, and the clinging to a sensation, typical of children ... Certainly the hypnotic magic of the lists seems to belong mainly to David, or to the narrator, who is often indistinguishable from David' (Ricou 688). This final, indiscriminate identification aside, David still seems more like the artistic apprentice of Thomas Wolfe who 'told Fitzgerald in a famous letter that he aspired to be ... "a putter-inner" rather than a "taker-outer" ' (Holman 84).

In contrast to David, the narrator of *The Mountain and the Valley* is much more measured when he represents the thoughts of anyone but the child spilling over in his lyrical moods. For example, the day father and son pull a huge rock out of the field, Joseph's 'feelings are not really word-shaped, but they are best conveyed, Buckler makes it obvious, through simple, factual, unelaborate sentences ... The prose is unadorned, and the images are simple' (Dooley 675). In this scene (chapter 24), the point of view alternates between David and his father nine times. Joseph's thoughts are simple and are simply expressed: 'My land fits me loose and easy, like my old clothes' (*Mountain* 157). David's thoughts, though dark, are hardly more complex; only the diction is more abstract: 'When he worked with his father, there was no constraint between them so long as their relationship, whether of harmony or dissonance, was tacit' (158). Joseph's thoughts, concretely expressed, remain perfectly in harmony with his environment. David's thoughts, on the other hand, produce a growing dramatic (and stylistic) dissonance: 'He would grow old here, he thought, like his father. That's what it would be like: the pace of an ox. Lifting their feet with such horrible patience ... He built up the picture and the dismay of himself being old here. It gave him the same self-biting pleasure he'd felt when he let the muddy water stiffen on his face' (158).

While David's narrative perspective occupies 189 of the 290 pages in the novel, there are five chapters in which his point of view is absent. Significantly, one of them is the scene where Anna hears Ellen's story of the sailor she once hid from justice; the story concerns a secret which Ellen shares, not hoards, as David is wont to do. Another (chapter 34) shows Anna giving up her old 'hurting power' (239) once she is 'struck' by Toby's face (240). The thrice-repeated verb emphasizes the new maturity of her response, while David, realizing that 'His brother's face looked struck' (196), never does brings himself to confess his own fault and to make amends with his brother.

As well, there are more than seventy shifts of narrative perspective in the novel to characters other than David, mostly to family members such as Ellen, Martha, Joseph, Chris, and Anna, all of which suggest that the story of the growth of the artist does not belong to him alone. Two such shifts in point of view in chapter 10, the scene of the play, lay bare the essential strategy of Buckler's omniscient narrator. As David listens 'to Anna's opening recitation,' the narrator presents the thoughts of their parents: '(For some reason Martha felt a little catch in her throat when Anna bowed ... And Joseph felt a kind of incredulity that his own Anna had been carrying around all those heavy words, all that time, behind her small soft face).' An ensuing tableau is then presented from David's point of view, before we see it anew through the eyes of an ostracized mother: 'Bess was so startled she almost cried out ... Effie was the loveliest thing anyone had ever seen and she was hers. Even if no one said so to her, they needn't, it was true' (78–9). But then someone does say as much publicly, after all, and Bess's 'defiance wilted. She could scarcely answer for tears: Martha had spoken to her about their two children being beautiful in the same way; she had added a little joke' (79). None of these thoughts is expressed in the 'heavy words' Anna has been asked to speak, but the simple tableau of Faith, Hope, and Love still works its complex magic: people are drawn together in a shared moment of art. Only the boy who thinks he will be 'the greatest actor in the whole world' looks down on his audience, imagining himself as the source of the 'shine ... that went out over everything now. None of all this was consecutive and time-taking like thought. It was glimpsed instantaneously, like the figures of space. And orchestrated in the subliminal key of memory' (81). David, it would seem, is only too happy to exchange his known world for the self-aggrandizing word.

Even Martha, who in fits of jealousy turns most inward and involuted like David, does not corrupt the style of Buckler's prose as much as does her son. In one of several scenes where she withdraws from Joseph because of some imagined slight, her thoughts never really forsake the world, not even in the depths of her own self-absorption: 'She caught her breath and started back to the baskets. But it was faster than movement. Movement couldn't lose or shake the wind of exile. It sprang up from nowhere, and she was helpless, once she had felt it, not to feed it. It was like the blue dusk light of August exiling the mountains; or the cold horizon light of winter exiling the skeletons of the prayer-fingered apple trees; or the retreating October light draining the fields' (128). The alternation of swift, simple declaratives with compound sentences, lead-ing to an extended parallel construction, catches perfectly Martha's flight of thought into endless exile. The earlier poetry of blue light is even repeated in a new and melancholy key; now the woman's mood is naturally keyed, as well, to the coming of winter after the potatoes are in. Only 'the prayer-fingered apple trees' could be considered at all excessive, were it not for Ellen's framing perception of the whole scene: 'She could see him and Martha now. They were on their knees, picking up potatoes in the acre field. Soundless with distance, they looked as if they were praying' (125). While the scene sounds its ironic echo of Millet's romantic painting, *The Angelus*, the image of 'prayer-fingered apple trees' does catch something of the twisted desperation Martha feels, even as it anticipates the later blow of another tree which will 'exile' her from her husband forever.

It would still be hard to deny that the 'delightful collocation of vocables' to which Dooley refers (671) with fitting sarcasm is inappropriate to the thoughts of a thirty-year-old man: 'The afternoon stillness,' though it is said to 'simmer ... soundlessly in the kitchen' (13), is obviously not soundless. And 'The soft flutter of flame in the stove, the heat-tick of the stove itself, and the gentle rocking of the tea kettle,' while representing the synaesthesia experienced by the child, can only be mere sequences of sounds to an adult ear, not significant units of meaning. If the thirty-year-old man is still that much of a child, Buckler dares the reader to see through the irony of his style from his opening page by comparing it with the style of the other chapters.

Likewise, that later example – 'it was Christmas Eve' – helps to show that a child's habit of language still cripples the older David. For the simple declarative clause cannot be the subject which feels ecstatic or bursting or buoyed, much less safe or watchful or enclosed. Rather, every subject refers ultimately to David; the world is entirely enclosed in him, to the point of solipsism. The question is whether his language would ever get beyond this kind of self-reference in its pretence of referring to the world.

'He didn't know why, but the complex magic a letter held for him erased the simple magic of what he'd done with Effie almost utterly' (114). By now, the reader might know why: the thought of a letter, 'with its message to be devoured privately, uncomplicated by the exactions of the writer's face,' carries no hint of possible relationship; the word bears no more than a trace of its absent author, and so is easier to manage. The letter also dignifies him with its secret contents, arriving just in time to repair David's devastating sense of exposure through sexual intimacy. What Effie had given him 'made him feel rich; and it made him feel destitute. There was no room anywhere inside him now where he could keep the things that sprang to life only at his turning of the lock. She too had a key' (110). The self is like a safety-deposit box where great varieties of psychic wealth are stored. And when Effie finds the key, only a new and private set of words will serve as a refuge. Except that Toby Richmond's letter 'baffled him. He could find almost no message in it – where then did he get the feeling that this was some kind of turning point in his life?' (115). The turning point is not just Toby's attraction to Anna, his twin and his narcissistic double; the boy from Halifax represents an actual incursion of the outside world into David's solipsistic fantasy.

The challenge that Toby presents to the young artist is summed up in his single objection that 'You can't see it as plain as you can when you're in there, can you?' But the problem is not confined to the question of objective realism; what is at stake through the whole scene of Toby's first visit is the issue of subjective authority. David wants, on Toby's arrival, to retain 'all control of the greeting' (134). He even resents the camaraderie of Toby and Anna who have come to the farm together: 'He had the sense of the one who is never there, who is told only. He felt the inhibition you feel when someone whose laughter has always been conspiratorial with you alone, tells you of laughing with another' (135). Anna comes home with her own story, with Toby. But that story doesn't refer to David. He might even have to listen to someone else doing the telling. Definitely not exalting. Now we know why it is better to give than to receive.

The question of authorial control has plagued David since the beginning of his career in 'The Play.' Back then, 'You planned how it would be with someone, seeing ahead how their part must go as certainly as your own. Then when the time came, they started off with an altogether different speech or mood, and your part became useless and wooden' (45). But now, as he plays Lothario before a group of uninitiated boys, he cannot afford to let Effie have any more will of her own: 'He crept up behind her. He felt that funny guilt and power you feel, watching someone for whom you have a plan' (107). His plan is not merely to use Effie in a sexual sense; he uses her to make himself the star of his own script. His 'art' imposes on life, forces other people to play the roles he assigns to them, makes their lives imitate his art, even as his language imposes on experience, forces it to reflect his own 'superior' consciousness.

It is Toby's indifference to one such performance that makes David painfully aware of his lack of control in these real-life dramas: 'And in that moment David knew he could never outdistance Toby in anything he thought Toby would envy, however he might be willing to betray himself trying. Toby would always remain ahead, by not having to make the effort at all' (146). Worse, Effie's death from pneumonia makes him face the consequences of his 'aesthetic' method: 'It taught him that secrecy about anything (even a hateful thing like this) made it a possession of curious inviolability, and tempted him to collect more' (152). Secrecy of this sort is hardly exalting either. But with his usual perversity, David embraces a secret to make himself inviolable. He intends, it would seem at first, to punish himself: 'He had a savage urge to do it with Bess, in this very room. To stoke his frustration (as always) with bitter and bitterer self-destruction' (151). And yet, paradoxically, he also wears his albatross to make sure he won't be destroyed.

David martyrs himself to Effie's memory for much of the rest of the novel. He has to; in a very real sense, she steals the show. But martyrdom is also his new 'exalting secret,' his means of controlling others by having them take the blame. When, in 'The Rock,' he provokes his father to strike him, 'the fascinating whisper told him not to move ... to let the blow dry on his face like the muddy water. It was more grindingly sweet than anything he'd ever known. He didn't move. Oh, he'd never wipe *that* blow off his face ... They made out they thought he was so smart. Then they called him a goddam snot. Oh, he'd never wipe that off either ...' (165). Much more subtle after Effie's death, the controlling 'artist' now grants his characters the illusion of free will. But they still serve to identify him as the hero; the artist who is too precious for this world martyrs himself on nothing more than the stake of a finer sensibility.

His secret struggle for control helps to explain David's abrupt refusal of the one chance he has of escaping his restrictive environment, of going out into a world which speaks his language. Riding in a car with strangers who offer to take him to Halifax, he thinks, 'They were *communicating* with him. They were all talking together as if they were all alike. He talked to them their way. There was nothing angular about their speech. They laughed as if they *decided* how much anything should amuse them' (169). Though he will not admit it, his immediate decision to return home is prompted by a sudden threat of equalization; he will perforce give up his social advantage in the city. Earlier, before he had pronounced the shibboleth which admits him to their company, his resentment of their self-possession was transparent: 'These were the people the town people tried to imitate. They had that immunity from surprise the town people could never quite catch. That automatic ease. These were city people' (167). Even when he wiped off his muddy feet getting into their car, 'He thought: I am wiping off my feet. I left mud all over Mother's stairs. She had just scrubbed them. He almost hated these people' (168). As he watched the woman 'commenting casually to the man beside her and then selecting, as if the landscape were on a tray, something else to look at. He saw the fraying of his father's sweater at the cuffs' (168), and he felt pity for more than his father; for his lot is hard who forsakes a small pond for the ocean. He also 'thought of having used words like "shall" against his father, who had none of his own to match them or to defend himself with' (170). And so he 'sacrifices' himself out of loyalty to his own people. So he says, at least, having tracked mud across his mother's floor and then blamed city people for it. Of course, he is incredibly well-versed in methods of establishing his control by blaming others. So the martyr who wearily turns back is hardly at a disadvantage: 'He watched them out of sight. He looked toward home. He felt as if he were in a no man's land' (170). A moment of self-pity is all he needs to re-establish his customary authority.

On both occasions in the novel when David actually sets pen to paper, he is trapped by the logic of this secret drama. If he writes, his hidden means of control is exposed; if he plays out his role as the martyr, the story cannot be written. 'The Scar' nicely figures his whole predicament:

> He wrote quickly, 'Roger was angry with his brother.' He hesitated. When he did, a listening seemed to spring up in everything around. It stiffened him. But he forced himself to go on. 'He didn't want to climb the ladder, but something made him. His brother's face looked ...' He thought: sad? ... sober? ... hurt? ... *struck*. Yes, sure. 'His brother's face looked struck.'
>
> He couldn't go any farther. The cleansing cathartic of the first accurate line (*there* was the thing itself, outside him, on the page) made him close his eyes. He felt as if he were going to cry.   (196)

Why did 'Roger' climb the ladder? The 'first accurate line' David has written is actually a confession. He knows he is not the one who has been hurt the most; he wanted to fall to hurt his brother.

The pattern of punishing himself to punish others is the real stigmata of 'The Scar.' If David is angry at hearing Chris say, 'Dave don't like to see anything killed,' his fury swells at 'Their exposing a whim of his he'd thought secret [which] left him as shameful for the whim's transparency as for the whim itself' (189). He knows that Chris has tried 'to save even a joke going against him. It was one of those times when Chris came out with that odd perceptiveness you'd never suspected in him. You wondered suddenly how much he understood about everything else' (191–2). But to be understood is the last thing David wants. Tearing his hand on a nail, he wills his blood to be on their heads: 'the throb of his ignored hand seemed to synchronize his anger in a steady track. The calm, biting, beautiful part of it began' (190).

The real beauty of David's part is that no one can figure him out. Chris may be sensitive to David's pride, knowing his tendency to ' "git dizzy when you climb." ... But Chris didn't open his mouth. It was that assaulting perceptiveness again' (192). All the others, however, 'denied him the danger. They assumed so unconcernedly (because it was no one close to them) that he would *not* fall – and coming back, not having fallen, where was the achievement in walking fifteen feet or so of beam?' The real achievement lies twenty feet straight down. That should make his brother's face look 'struck.'

Yet in his 'first accurate line,' David realizes he must tell the truth to be a writer. For once, he actually lets someone else be the hero (or the victim) of his story. Then what perverse impulse could make him black out the truth he has just confessed, 'obliterating even the loops of the letters' (199)? Rachel Gorman at the door is perverse enough, blaming Chris for knocking up her daughter. For the truth has not yet become public knowledge: 'And if the scribbler were in sight, she'd be sure to pick it up. She'd open it to that very page. She'd never come into the house that she hadn't brought up something that someone wanted to keep hidden' (196). But the fear of public confession is nothing compared to the fear of exposing a deeper identity. For Rachel is just the kind of martyr who can make a man despise himself: 'No, dear,' Rachel heaps her coals of fire in her son-in-law's ear, if not on his head. 'I got lots a clothes to last me out, fer all I go. I won't be here *too* many more years' (205). David has to blot out the words to avoid a fatal identification with this kind of martyr. How far is he expected to go, anyway, once he starts telling the truth?

The only other story David writes is a contrary attempt to identify himself with Toby. As much as he pretends to live for his dead comrade, 'Tony,' he is at least aware that his narrator 'was ... sick; he'd never been *any*where, but he had to make them believe it was his face in all the pictures, so he could have the war over with. He couldn't have it over with, like the others who'd been there and returned got it over with, unless they believed he knew how every bit of it was' (260). The narrator still believes that he puts his face on 'Tony's' picture for the sake of his friend, 'that somehow I'd save his part of the pain and the laughing in the world for him always, fiercely somewhere, where it could never be lost' (263). But there is a deep ambiguity in his sense of accomplishment: 'And in a minute like that when it's clear how another can have *for* you the things you might have had for yourself, the meaning of everything else is clear too.' The meaning that is suddenly clear to the reader is that 'Tony' is the 'sick' narrator's only means of getting the things he might have had for himself. He lives vicariously through 'Tony,' far more than the fallen comrade lives through him. What is worse, the original of 'Tony' isn't even dead. David himself might be guilty of wishful thinking, were it not for his careful pattern of dramatic irony. But he cannot trust that narrative pattern when Toby stumbles on the newly completed manuscript. Faced with the question of whether he is writing his 'will' in more than just the sense of 'testament,' David has to burn the story. After all, he wouldn't want anyone to get the idea that *he* was sick.

'Thanks For Listening' brings to a crux the governing problem of the novel. Does the artist exist to speak for his community? Or does the community serve to gratify the heroic fantasy of the artist? At the end of *A Portrait*, a romantic aesthete such as Stephen Dedalus could believe that he goes away from Ireland to 'forge in the smithy of my soul the uncreated conscience of my race' (Joyce 253). And even Eugene Gant goes away hoping to find 'the forgotten language' (*Look* 521) which could awaken the slumbering human spirit. At the top of his mountain, David Canaan also looks back on a time when 'he had composed a petition from all the men in the village, asking the government for a daily mail. When he read it back to them they heard the voice of their own reason speaking exactly in his' (*Mountain* 298). But the 'legislator' who is acknowledged by others in writing his petition seems to have had other intentions all along in fashioning his art. For the sudden intrusion of Toby and Anna into the final act of 'Tony's' story makes him feel an 'instant denuding when he saw them. The mirror of his consciousness was stripped of everything but the reflection of his own face: pale, tentative, and struck with the long burning scar' (263). The artist who can see only his own face in the mirror is more than physically disfigured; he is the moral cannibal of a community for which he still pretends to speak.

On his final ascent of the mountain, David is pursued for good reason by a horde of voices that 'began to swarm. They asked, and then listened, to be heard exactly. He had felt this insistence of theirs before, but never as now. Never so bold and relentless, giving him no quarter whatever' (291). Toby's remembered face offers an especially sharp rebuke: '[W]hy was the challenge just to listen to it exactly, so much sharper than the old challenge to make his own like it?' (294). The irony of David's title, 'Thanks For Listening,' now recoils on him with a vengeance. Since he has never listened in all his urgent concern to make himself heard, he must finally hear the world's story or lose his own voice: 'As he thought of telling these things exactly, all the voices came close about him. They weren't swarming now. He went out into them until there was no inside left. He saw at last how you could *become* the thing you told' (298). But even this is a 'final transport of self-deception' (Young 95), for the pattern of dramatic irony in David's story – 'this wouldn't come out till the end' (*Mountain* 260) – turns out to be Buckler's own. Just as David had said of his character's motive that 'It wouldn't be credible, but he was ... sick' (160), so too Buckler says of him, 'He didn't consider *how* he would find it.... Nor how long it might take. (If you took a hundred years, then – though neither this thought was explicit nor reason's denial of it, for the swelling moment to transcend – he would live a hundred years.) He knew only that he would do it ... It would make him the greatest writer in the whole world' (299).

Defenders of the Romantic faith are wont to see a gulf between art and life that mirrors the old Platonic chasm between the ideal and the real. One way or another, the romantic artist is always obliged to bring the world of essences down into a world of clay: 'Like Plato, Wolfe wants to get at the essence of things. But unlike Plato, he does not want to transcend sense or escape time. He wants instead to root his essences in the loam of sense impressions, like a tree that can ascend toward heaven only because it is firmly planted in the earth' (Gurko 134–5). Buckler's character, on the other hand, seems to remain more of a dualist: 'David is caught in Keats' dilemma. The vision and art, like the Grecian Urn, offer beauty and permanence in an ideal world of "slow Time," an image peculiarly appropriate to Buckler's novel. But there is something inhuman about their "Cold Pastoral." David finds the emotions of art appealing because of their eternity, but they have nothing of the warmth found in his family. He is thus torn between the promise of the eternal in art and the passionate involvement which he craves in life' (MacDonald 208). Yet if David fails to 'achieve the union of art and life,' it can hardly be because he 'is not strong enough to bear the spiritual isolation of the artist' (MacDonald 208); for David is one of the most isolated characters in modern fiction, most wilfully so. On the road to the top of the mountain, he thinks: 'Now he was absolutely alone. He said, "It's perfect here." Involuntarily. Aloud' (*Mountain* 286). If the 'Pastoral' is cold, it is because the egoist himself lacks warmth.

Another sort of artist in the novel refutes this idea that art emotions, being permanent, must be cold as stone. The day David begins his quest for 'Altamont,' his grandmother is left to console Anna with a story: 'Ellen thought for a minute. She looked as if a frightening idea had come to her. One of those secret things you are suddenly tempted to tell no one else but a child' (32). The telling of her secret does not exalt Ellen, since she refuses to cast herself as the heroine hiding the refugee from authority. Most of her concern is still for the young sailor who, in stealing a beautiful peacock feather to show his mates, has had to flee an unjust punishment: ' "His flesh was strong enough," she said, "but young flesh is soft. They would have split it" ' (34). In a sense, she identifies his youth with her own: 'Someday my youth would be gone. I wouldn't even notice when. So I hid him. I only meant to hide him for one night' (33). But she is not only saving her own youth by protecting him; she is also defending an aesthetic impulse to share what is beautiful, whatever the risk. Though we catch her, like David, looking in the mirror, the face she sees is a 'face that's lonesome for just you' (34). What Anna receives from her grandmother's story is a legacy not of narcissism but of love. And Anna grows up to live this shared, though secret, story: 'Grammie ... I think I'll marry a sailor' (35).

Finally, the image of the sailor helps to resolve the question of artistic identity in the novel – whether the artist gives a voice to others or uses other people only as masks for himself. The night David tries to run away from home, Ellen sees in him the likeness of her long-lost sailor. She gives David a locket bearing a portrait of her secret love, apparently authorizing his quest for beauty. David 'knew where he'd seen a face like that. He was looking at it right there in the mirror' (172). Anna, on the other hand, understands her grandmother's legacy of love: ' "It looks like Toby," was all she said' (180). But to the romantic egoist, there can only be the one old story: the whole world exists simply to wear his face.

Ellen, who is the only person left on the farm at the end of the novel, hooks a rug whose round pattern is nothing like the deadly circle of

David's 'Prologue' and 'Epilogue.' For her rug-making has long involved a sharing of her memories: 'Anna chose the rags as she began to hook – so nearly the ones Ellen would have chosen herself that almost none had to be rejected. She told Anna some little thing about the garment from which each rag had come' (52). But David seems oblivious to Ellen's story-telling, even though her poor 'scraps' of clothing in the 'Prologue' might redefine the course of his 'career.' Her memories, slighted and ignored by the young artist, still offer aesthetic alternatives in a chapter (33) otherwise given over to the 'awful challenge' of his art to 'name' a thing exactly, 'as if it had been put there for him, and him alone, to see exactly and to record. As if in having neglected to perceive *every*thing exactly he had been guilty of making the object, as well as himself, incomplete' (233). For Ellen's own art, faced on every hand with absence, is founded all the same on a tacit metaphysics of presence: 'More than ever, lately, her hooking had become a kind of visiting. Memory could bring back the image of the others, but not the tune of them. These pieces of cloth which had lain sometime against their flesh could bring them right into the room' (224).

Fittingly, then, it is the rug-maker who, by recalling the story of each rag she uses, binds the generations of the family and the community together. Ultimately, it is she who sits at the centre of the novel, a scrap of whiteness at the centre of her own rug, an 'absolute white, made of all the other colours but of no colour itself at all' (300). Surviving in story, in the middle of her community, Ellen embodies Entremont. But the body of the young romantic is buried in its 'Cold Pastoral' of snow, is finally erased by the transcendental blank of Altamont.

8

Imagism and Spatial Form in
The Road Past Altamont

In her autobiography, *Enchantment and Sorrow* (*La Détresse et l'enchantement*, 1984), Gabrielle Roy paints a familiar portrait of the artist fleeing the nets of family and a narrow provincial capital to seek the boundless realm of art. The scene on the platform of the old Canadian Pacific station in Winnipeg recalls Stephen Dedalus at the end of Joyce's *Portrait* and, more particularly, Eugene Gant at the beginning of Wolfe's *Of Time and the River*, waiting to catch the train that will carry him off to destiny. But what makes Roy's scene unique is the apparition of some faces in the crowd who have gathered to see her off:

> Then, at the end of the platform, there appeared a little crowd from the past, dressed in black. There were my forebears, the Landrys and the Roys too, the Connecticut expatriates, their ancestors who'd been deported from Acadia, their descendants repatriated to St-Jacques-l'Achigan, my St-Alphonse-de-Rodriguez relatives and those at Beaumont, even my Savonarola grandfather whom I had time to recognize beside Marcelline, his eyes dark and smouldering as in his photograph ... the terrible exodus my mother had introduced me to one day ...
>
> Can I deny finding in my heart that perhaps I'd always wanted to break the chain, escape from my poor dispossessed people? ... Perhaps it was the bitter taste of desertion that made me cry.   (193)

The author's confession predicts the shape of her career. The dead will not gladly suffer her exile into art. They are the unforgotten conscience of her race, imploring her to forge a link across the generations, to give them a voice with which to speak. Naturally she would like to forget the bitter taste of her desertion, rationalizing it as an obligation 'first to save myself. If you drown, what use are you to anyone else? Then time to return and save the others' (193). But what she will learn is that she cannot possess herself without first returning in art to those whom she has helped to dispossess. At the outset of this belated modernist quest, the artist carries lost time away with her, even though she hopes to lose it at once on her way to the future.

Christine, the aspiring writer of *Street of Riches* (*Rue Deschambault*, 1957), is literally pulled between the poles of past and future by parents who hold opposing views of life. On the one hand, her mother shirks her wifely duties in 'The Gadabouts' to run off with Christine to the childhood home of the father in Quebec. On her return, Eveline vindicates herself in a triumphant proclamation to her husband: 'Without the past, what are we, Edouard? ... Severed plants, half alive! ... That is what I've come to understand! ... Those Quebec houses, low-lying, with their narrow windows near the ground and their tall, pointed roofs perhaps do not let in as much daylight as ours in Manitoba, but they preserve better the warmth of memories ... Perhaps ... the generations of the dead still breathe around the living in that ancient land of Quebec' (*Street* 71). In 'The Well of Dunrea,' on the other hand, Christine recognizes in her father, a Colonization officer of the Dominion government, the same attitude he admires in his Ruthenian immigrants: 'Certainly the past counted for something in their lives – a past deeply wretched – but it was in the future, a wonderful and well-founded future, that the Little Ruthenians above all had faith when they came to Canada. And that was the sort of settler Papa liked: people facing forward, and not everlastingly whining over what they had had to leave behind' (*Street* 73). These paired stories sketch a binary opposition in *Street of Riches* – between facing forward or forever looking backward – which is only resolved in later work.

At the end of that beautifully melancholy novel, *The Road Past Altamont* (*La Route d'Altamont*, 1966), Christine appears to have sided with her father in settling on the future, despite the objections of her mother: 'In the first place, if you want to write, you don't need to rush to the ends of the earth to do it ... A writer really needs nothing but a quiet room, some paper, and himself ...' (*Road* 136–7). But past and future no longer seem to make up the same binary opposition, at least not in the mind of Christine's mother:

> 'Haven't you understood yet that parents truly live over again in their children?'
> 'I thought you chiefly relived the lives of your own parents.'
> 'I relive their lives and I also live over again with you.'
> 'That must be exhausting! You can't have much time to be yourself.'
> At any rate, it's perhaps the most illuminated part of one's life, situated between those who came before us and those who follow after us, right in the middle ...'   (*Road* 135)

While the younger Christine feels 'some sort of irksome interference with the personality and individual freedom' (130) in this idea, the retrospective narrator finds a new answer to one of her earliest questions: 'When one is very old ... does one have to die?' (76). For the road to the future stretches away inevitably towards death; yet the dead remain alive among those who are situated 'right in the middle.' Somehow the once excluded middle of the present negates the usual opposition of past and future.

In literary terms, too, *The Road Past Altamont* might resolve another opposition in aesthetic ways of recovering 'lost time.' For it does not seek to recover the merely personal time of the Proustian self; more like Wolfe's *Of Time and the River*, it chronicles the quest for the lost time of the generations. And yet Altamont, an actual hamlet in Manitoba, symbolizes more for Roy than Wolfe's ideal permanence of art. It is a road, a progression, a process, as well as a destination. This very tension between a linear view of time and some timeless realm where 'the dead still breathe around the living' has formal, as well as thematic, implications for the narrative which make it utterly different from the infamous formlessness of Wolfe's vision.

Of course, *Altamont* is not a unified novel in the traditional sense, but a linked story-sequence. Each of the four stories represents a dramatic moment in time which has the emotional impact of an epiphany. And the epiphany, in every instance, is compressed into an image. In 'The Old Man and the Child,' Christine gains the confidence to ask about death from an image of the eternal lake given her by old Monsieur St-Hilaire:

'The end or the beginning? Such questions you ask! The end or the beginning. And if they are fundamentally the same ...'

He was also looking into the distance as he spoke, and now repeated, 'If they are the same ... Perhaps everything finally forms a great circle, the end and the beginning coming together.' (68)

But in 'The Move,' Christine's 'nostalgic longing for the lost years' (95) is actually betrayed by her mother's use of a spatial image, and Christine accuses her most bitterly: 'Oh why have you said a hundred times that from the seat of the covered wagon on the prairie in the old days the world seemed renewed, different, and so beautiful?' (106). And so her mother's insistence, in the title story, that the past catches up with us in ways which are not so different or beautiful is all the more threatening: ' "Later," said Maman, "with the first disillusionments of life, I began to detect in myself a few small signs of the personality of my mother. But I didn't want to resemble her, admirable as she was, poor old thing, and I fought against it. Only with middle age did I catch up with her, or she caught up with me – how can you explain this strange encounter outside time?" ' (129).

The temporal problem Maman tries to articulate is not so different from the formal problem of Roy as a novelist: how are the disconnected and even contradictory moments of the individual stories to be reconciled in a structure which is not as concerned with causality and sequence as it is with 'this strange encounter outside time'? In other words, how can the straight line of temporal narration be drawn out into the circle of 'eternity'? At first glance, Roy's strategy for solving this formal problem doesn't look so very different from the familiar forms of male modernism, though the metaphors used by Christine's mother increasingly suggest the bearing of another person inside oneself in a maternal act of spiritual gestation.

In earlier attempts to make use of the image in short fiction, as, for example, in Sherwood Anderson's story of the growing artist in *Winesburg, Ohio* or in Hemingway's *In Our Time*, the idea of timelessness had hardly figured in the usual pattern of the *Bildungsroman*. Only in Hemingway's 'The Snows of Kilimanjaro,' which forms a brief *Künstlerroman*, does imagism offer anything quite so ambitious as the 'fusion' of time and timelessness. For Harry, the dying artist, is haunted by images of all the things he has saved to write – mostly a series of moments united by loss and death. Having sold his talent, he mentally tallies up the record of other people's 'lost time' with a painful awareness that his old refusal of suffering makes it impossible for him to redeem either it or them. And yet this very *agon* of memory helps to redeem him, at least, since at the end, 'all he could see, as wide as all the world, great, high, and unbelievably white in the sun, was the square top of Kilimanjaro. And then he knew that there was where he was going' (27). The epigraph to the story has already led us, in four sentences of prose poetry, part way up Kilimanjaro, preparing us to answer the sort of question which naturalism could never ask: '*Kilimanjaro is a snow covered mountain 19,710 feet high, and is said to be the highest mountain in Africa. Its western summit is called by the Masai "Ngàje Ngài," the House of God. Close to the western summit there is the dried and frozen carcass of a leopard. No one has explained what the leopard was seeking at that altitude*' (Hemingway 3). The artist, purged by the pain he has tried to avoid all his life, climbs higher than the leopard to the very 'House of God.'

Nicholas Joost notes, however, that 'Such a method constricted unbearably the range of poetic expression' (37) in Hemingway's longer fiction. For the novel, like the long poem, was built out of a temporal sequence and so resisted the simultaneous perception required by spatial figures. Pound, one recalls, had almost arrested the development of any linguistic sequence in poetry by making the sculptured instant into the raison d'être of the poem. 'An "Image,"' he wrote, 'is that which presents an intellectual and emotional complex in an instant of time.' But 'How was more than one image to be included in a poem? ... Or was the poem itself one vast image, whose individual components were to be apprehended as a unity? But then it would be necessary to undermine the inherent consecutiveness of language, frustrating the reader's normal expectation of a sequence and forcing him to perceive the elements of the poem juxtaposed in space rather than unrolling in time' (Frank 227).

To a certain extent, time continues to be 'unrolled' in *The Road Past Altamont*. Roy holds to many of the narrative conventions of naturalism which make each story a self-contained sequence of setting, character, and plot. The stories also succeed one another in chronological order, offering portraits of the young artist at six, eight, eleven, and twenty-some years of age. Still, the moment of epiphany in each story has the sculptural quality of a frozen instant. The imagist novel, it seems, is more easily built out of the linked story form and its series of lyric instants. For each of these instants, as in Pound's doctrine of the Image, manages to present 'an intellectual and emotional complex in an instant of time.' More than once, in fact, Christine sees time turned into space, flattened into geometric shapes. And yet to her the image is never an intellectual abstraction; rather, it is so breathtakingly felt that, as in the case of M. St-Hilaire's circle, it fuses intellect and emotion into a timeless instant of sculptured stasis. In the very 'vibrations of the light on the water' (67), the reader actually glimpses eternity for a moment on Lake Winnipeg.

One recalls Pound's larger attempt at fusion in the doctrine of the Image: 'In a poem of this sort one is trying to record the precise instant when a thing outward and objective transforms itself – or darts into a thing inward and subjective' (*Gaudier-Brzeska* 89). Pound's formulation is an early version of phenomenology, of what can be defined as the removal of 'the subject-object division that constitutes all perception' (Iser, *Reader* 293), or of what another reader-response theorist has described as the sense of being 'occupied' by an alien consciousness: 'The work lives its own life within me; in a certain sense, it thinks itself, and it even gives itself a meaning within me' (Poulet 355). Phenomenology, in other words, tends to universalize the (typically) gender-based experience of being inhabited by another (whether a child or a lover). Roy's method, which is at once mentally phenomenological and physically feminine, is to emphasize the profound interpenetration of the object with the subject: 'I saw then – or believed I saw – an immense sheet of tender blue, deep, glossy, and, it seemed to me, liquid. My soul stretched wide to receive it' (58–9). Christine's mistaking the sky for the lake only prepares her for the moment when the 'thing outward and objective' is transformed into 'a thing inward and subjective,' when an 'unknown joy held me in a state of intense astonishment. I learned later on, of course, that this is the very essence of joy, this astonished delight, this sense of a revelation at once so simple, so natural, and yet so great that one doesn't quite know what to say of it, except, "Ah, so this is it" ' (64–5).

Pound himself had searched for words to describe what the sight of several beautiful faces in a station of the Metro had meant to him, though 'I could not find any words that seemed to me worthy, or as lovely as that sudden emotion' (*Gaudier-Brzeska* 86).[1] Only in the tre-

---

1 Evidence of such a 'feminine' sensibility in the younger Ezra's work is not atypical – not when one considers, for example, 'The River-Merchant's Wife: A Letter,' that deeply moving free translation of a poem by the eighth-century Chinese poet, Li Po.

mendous compression of the image could he finally record the precise instant of subjective-objective alchemy. 'So this tiny poem, drawing on Gauguin and on Japan, on ghosts and on Persephone, on the Underworld and on the Underground, the Metro of Mallarmé's capital and a phrase that names a station far more than it need ever specify' (Kenner, *Pound Era* 185), expands the sudden, finite emotion toward infinity.

Christine's sense of revelation leaves her likewise speechless in the moment, though the narrator later finds a way to show her private emotion set against something eternal: 'Alone now on this long beach before immensity, we slept shoulder to shoulder' (83). Because the 'precise instant' of transformation in *The Road Past Altamont* is almost always a figure of time turned into space, the novel offers a particularly self-conscious example of what Joseph Frank, in a seminal essay, called 'Spatial Form in Modern Literature.'

The defining formal feature of modernist art is its requirement that it be apprehended 'spatially, in a moment of time, rather than as a sequence ... But since language proceeds in time, it is impossible to approach this simultaneity of perception except by breaking up temporal sequence' (Frank 225, 231). Pound and Eliot had both contributed to this method of spatial juxtaposition which demanded 'a complete reorientation in the reader's attitude to language. Since the primary reference of any word-group is to something inside the poem itself, language in modern poetry is really reflexive' (Frank 229). Joyce likewise forced the reader 'to read *Ulysses* in exactly the same manner as he reads modern poetry – continually fitting fragments together and keeping allusions in mind until, by reflexive reference, he can link them to their complements' (Frank 234).

Perhaps the most subtle form of this method of juxtaposition is to be found in *À la recherche du temps perdu*, where, 'Obsessed with the ineluctability of time, Proust was suddenly visited by certain quasi-mystical experiences – described in detail in the last volume of his work, "Le temps retrouvé" – which, by providing him with a spiritual technique for transcending time, enabled him to escape time's domination' (Frank 235). The narrator's intuition of 'a reality "real without being of the present moment, ideal but not abstract"' leads him 'to dedicate the remainder of his life to recreating these experiences in a work of art' (236). But 'the novel the narrator decides to write has just been finished by the reader; and its form is controlled by the method that the narrator has outlined in its concluding pages ... Instead of being submerged in the stream of time – which, for Proust, would be the equivalent of presenting a character progressively, in a continuous line of development – the reader is confronted with the various snapshots of the characters "motionless in a moment of vision," taken at different stages in their lives; and the reader, in juxtaposing these images, experiences the effects of the passage of time exactly as the narrator has done' (Frank 239).

In a similar fashion, little Christine at the end of 'My Almighty Grandmother' begins 'to understand vaguely a little about life and all the successive beings it makes of us as we increase in age' (*Road* 30). The grandmother, whose powers of creation once made her seem greater than 'God the Father' (16), has been paralysed and is helpless to move anything but her eyes. The juxtaposition of such contrary faces is too much for the child to assimilate; for some time, she clings to her 'idea of the substitution of persons' (24). Only when the mute appeal in the old woman's eyes grows unbearable does Christine cast about for something with which to comfort her. A phrase of her mother's suddenly makes her think 'of a poor old oak, isolated from the others, alone on a little hill ... Then an odd picture came to me. I seemed to see, lower down, some young trees, which were perhaps born of the old tree on the hillside but, still decked in all their leaves, sang in the valley. It was this image, I believe, that gave me a most brilliant idea. I ran down to the living room to fetch the photograph album' (28–9).

Quite literally, the family album presents to the child a spatial arrangement which demands more and greater understanding of its juxtapositions: 'And so it came about that, as I turned the pages, I found her there herself, still young, seated beside her husband, among her children, some of them standing behind her, the younger ones on the grass at her feet. This old photograph fascinated me so much that I forgot everything else' (29–30).

Christine has come face to face once more with her grandmother, the 'Creator,' though this youthful face was formerly hidden from her. On every side she has already recognized people who, 'as the expression goes, descended from Mémère' (29). She has even tried to catalogue them all, feeling that 'the more names I had to offer Mémère ... the more enclosed she would feel.' And yet the sight of Mémère as a young mother stops her short, bringing the story to a close. The snapshots have made her feel the full impact of time; they prove to her that no one is eternal or is even one person. But the retrospective narrator now puts the passage of time into a new perspective, using the later confession of Maman that 'Only with middle age did I catch up with her' (129) to explain why her mother looked 'so pleased with me. I was only playing, as she herself had taught me to do, as Mémère also had played with me one day ... as we all play perhaps, throughout our lives, at trying to catch up with one another' (30). The sculptured instant, the narrator suddenly assures us, must still be open to time's flow. But she is not the only one who will have to catch up with it.

The reader of these four juxtaposed stories is then put in quite the same position as the narrator. For the face of M. St-Hilaire in 'The Old Man and the Child' bears little resemblance to the grandmother 'lying in her coffin, her face hard as rock, surrounded by people who prayed in voices whose accent tore my heart' (37). Neither is the time-haunted child much like the little girl who had catalogued the descendants to make an old woman feel enclosed; all her former assurances are lost: 'How could I make him understand about the weight of grief that had come to me, now that the brilliant color of things was extinguished, at seeing them look so dull and as if forsaken? And above all at having come so close finally to understanding the truth about old age and what it leads to?' (75). The stasis of the photograph in an album full of stories may serve to collect and preserve the changing faces of each character; but the image of just one rock-hard face proves that stasis is also deadly. So the prospect of catching up with that face must inevitably seem dreadful.

Now even the old man, who has given Christine a glimpse of eternity, will not let her rest in abstract consolations. When she asks, 'Why ... did we not all reach the same age at the same time' (78), he insists on the need for plenitude in a whole variety of ages, even though this same variety guarantees the separation of death. Refusing to exempt her from the grief of time, he none the less offers her another way of 'catching up with one another' through time. For his stories of the many countries to which he has travelled inspire in her a desire for imitation:

'Someday I'll go and see what Bruges is like.'
'Oh you will like it very much,' the old man promised. 'And when you're there, will you think for a moment that it was I who sent you to see Bruges?' (79)

In effect, he says, *This do in remembrance of me*. And so he would seem to institute a sacramental means of overcoming time.

And yet his story of the most enchanting country of all, the country of love, eliminates any transcendent model from the usual *imitatio Christi*:

> As if it too were a country to be explored, he told me that everything shone with a special light there, that even ordinary humble things were illuminated by this light. Because, a single human being having been given to us, it was as if henceforth we possessed the earth.
>
> It seemed to me that he was speaking of the two of us. But no, he said, this was an entirely different sort of thing. For the country of love was the most vast and profound there was, leading us from one point to another so far away from it that we could no longer even remember the point of departure. (80–1)

His own love seeks no possession for himself; he simply offers the child this other country to possess at some future date for herself. Anyway, they both know that in this instant he has found his lost childhood in her: 'He too was much too happy to speak. But his eyes were no longer watching the great open stretch of water spread out in the distance. They were watching me instead, as if I were the huge lake we had come to see' (61). He 'imitates' her, in other words, as much as she will ever imitate his journeys to distant lands. And so his stories are not truly sacramental but patrimonial: he bequeaths to her his experience of love when it will no longer be his own to possess. And so the old man, who has come full circle to catch up with a child, starts her off along the circle by which she will 'catch up' to him.

The terrible disillusionment which Christine experiences in 'The Move' demonstrates none the less that such quests might be abstractions after all. Driven wild by her mother's romance of westward migration, she is now frantic to enter that long-lost childhood herself: 'That night the intensity of my desire wakened me from sleep. I imagined myself in my mother's place, a child lying, as she had described it, on the floor of the wagon, watching the prairie stars – the most luminous stars in either hemisphere, it is said – as they journeyed over her head' (95). But her ride on M. Pichette's horse-drawn cart becomes a parody of the old man's bequest to her: 'We, with our cumbrous and reflective gait, passed like a slow, majestic film. I am the past, I am times gone by, I said to myself with fervor' (97). Perhaps her failure comes from her will to repeat the past, instead of rediscovering, as Proust had done, the lost time through *la mémoire involontaire*. But Roy, it seems, is also suggesting something else about the false consolation of spatial form: 'Once more we were in sad little streets, without trees, so much like the one from which we had taken the Smiths that it seemed to me we had made all this journey for nothing and were going to end up finally at the same shack from which I had hoped to remove them' (103). In this ironic inversion of M. Saint-Hilaire's 'the end and the beginning coming together' (68), Christine discovers 'a life of which I knew nothing, terribly gray and, it seemed to me, without exit' (99). What she learns, in fact, is that there is no exit from time for anyone; history cannot be transcended. But how, then, is she to interpret the whole idea of 'catching up with one another'?

The 'lost hills' of family history in 'The Road Past Altamont' renew her problem of interpretation in a way that finally leads to resolution. She wonders, did Maman 'believe she had been carried back to the land of her childhood, returned to her starting point with her whole long life to be lived over again? Or did it seem to her that the landscape was mocking at her desires, offering her only an illusion?' (117). Only when she sees her mother stand on one of the hills beside a small tree can she begin to explore her fallacy of excluded middles: for her mother revives the image of the grandmother as that ancient tree upon a hillside. Back then, Christine had felt 'such an unutterable confusion about ages, about childhood and old age' when she heard her 'mother, old as she seemed to me at that time, speaking with this child's word to someone who could no longer eat or drink alone' (27). But now she has to face the possibility that what one 'lives over again' is really someone else's life instead of one's own.

The retrospective narrator, of course, can already report the discovery that the young woman has still to make for herself: 'And why is it that a human being knows no greater happiness in old age than to find in himself once more the face he wore as a child? Wouldn't this be rather an infinitely cruel thing? Whence comes the happiness of such an encounter? Perhaps, full of pity for the vanished youthful soul, the aged soul calls to it tenderly across the years, like an echo. "See," it says, "I can still feel what you felt ... love what you loved ..." And the echo undoubtedly answers something ... but what? I knew nothing of this dialogue at that time' (119). Till now, the only dialogue between youth and age has taken place, as in 'The Old Man and the Child,' between two people. But the greater need of dialogue appears, to the aging narrator, to develop among the changing faces of the self. And yet nothing in her experience prepares her for Maman's assertion that the greatest dialogue of all takes place with the *other* person whom one becomes.

In the dramatic time of the narrative, Christine is not at all ready to accept 'the idea of "My Mother/Myself"' (Hesse 51), for it brings with it the terrible threat of determinism. Even as she argues with her mother about 'living over again' the lives of parents and children, her jibe shows most clearly where she stands: 'You can't have much time to be yourself' (135). This is the crux; she wants to be only herself. She also wants her mother to remain who she is, which, of course, means wanting to keep the past as it was. But even the story which her mother used to tell is becoming

> a sort of canvas on which she had worked all her life as one works at a tapestry, tying threads and commenting upon events like fate, so that the story varied, enlarged, and became more complex as the narrator gained age and perspective ...
>
> Sometimes we interrupted her.
>
> 'But that detail didn't appear in your first versions. That detail is new,' we said with a hint of resentment perhaps, so anxious were we, I imagine, that the past at least should remain immutable. For if it too began to change ...
>
> 'But it changes precisely as we ourselves change,' said Maman.
>
> (123)

History, it seems, is not so much what happened as what is remembered. The past, in other words, cannot die so long as its only being is among the living. But then, as the present changes, the past must also change with it. So, rather than adopting Proust's method of juxtaposing 'various snapshots of the "characters motionless in a moment of vision," taken at different stages in their lives' (Frank 239), Roy creates a method of juxtaposing differing versions of the past as characters come to see it at different stages of their lives. Maman retells the story of the journey west not from her former viewpoint of the child, but from the point of view of her own reluctant mother; and Christine now tells the story of leaving her mother behind from the vantage point of the one who stayed, as well as the one who left.

Here, at the very end of the modernist period, that most familiar icon of male art – the 'well wrought urn,' a form itself forever unchanging, forever consoling – is supplanted by the ancient (and mythologically feminine) 'loom of time.' Or, to change the figure, the romantic's 'Grecian Urn' gives way to a medieval tapestry where the frozen moment is always open to a continuous line of development, and where the 'arrested' figures succeed one another throughout time. But, since the tapestry preserves the notion of time as artifice, as distinct from natural process, it would be reductive to say that, in *The Road Past Altamont*, 'Essentially time is conceived as a cycle, so that the future contains the past while the past anticipates the future' (Hesse 43).

To argue that time is in some sense artificial is not to say that art, for Roy, is superior to nature, or even that it is antithetical. For what Christine has to learn is how nature itself can be joined to human acts of perception and creation. Once again, Maman poses some hard questions for the romantic individualist:

'And now can you honestly say that I don't bear an astonishing resemblance to that picture we have of Grandmother when she was just my present age?'

I gave her a troubled look and could not help admitting that there was something in what she said.

'In your face perhaps, but not in your character.'

'In my character too, believe me. Besides, I'm no longer angry about it, since, having become her, I understand her. Ah, that is certainly one of life's most surprising experiences. We give birth in turn to the one who gave us birth when finally, sooner or later, we draw her into our self. From then on she lives in us just as truly as we lived in her before we came into the world. It's extremely singular. Every day now as I live my own life it's as if I were giving her a voice with which to speak.' (129)

Christine might have seen that Maman's story of the journey west is still, in a sense, being told by the dead woman who made it. For 'Maman appeared to be listening to someone invisible, a soul that had vanished perhaps but had not yet stopped trying to make itself heard' (125). The dead do not exist in some timeless eternity but only within a living heir. And so the story becomes an act of parturition as well as an act of fabrication.

In that case, the ultimate spatial form for time in Roy is necessarily feminine: it is quite literally 'the womb of time.' For the living bear past generations in themselves even as they bear the seeds of the future. They live forwards and backwards, as Maman says, in 'those who came before us and those who follow after us' (135). That is why time is neither cyclical nor lineal but both: the round womb of time gives birth again to linear development.

As a lineal descendant, Christine still has to learn what it means to repeat her mother's and her grandmother's lives. For, even as Mémère was deserted by most of her family, Maman herself is left in exile when Christine goes away to Europe. Now Maman accuses Christine of making the same, historic mistake:

> 'Do you mean to wear me down as we all combined in the old days to wear down my poor mother?'
> 'You're beginning to be like her, as a matter of fact,' I said unkindly, to which her only reply was a wounded look.   (137)

But then Maman has to confess that she was once guilty of what her daughter now says to her:

> So a hundred times a day I said to Maman, 'Rest. Haven't you done enough? It's time for you to rest.'
> And, as if I had insulted her, she would … say, 'You know, I spoke that way to my own mother when she seemed to me to be growing old. "When are you ever going to give up and rest?" I used to say to her, and only now can I see how provoking it must have been.'   (115)

Perhaps Christine is guilty of a greater desertion, however, than the one Mémère had suffered. For Maman is left with no one to mother her, as she had once mothered her own parent. Christine virtually glosses over her mother's death in conclusion, since it is almost too painful to be borne in her absence:

> My mother failed very quickly. No doubt she died of illness, but, as so many people do fundamentally, of grief too, a little.
>
> Her capricious and youthful spirit went to a region where there are undoubtedly no more difficult crossroads and no more starting points. Or perhaps there are still roads there but they all go past Altamont.   (146)

And yet this consolation may not be as easy as it seems. For the whole novel has been the story of Maman's place 'right in the middle,' between the generations, living over again the lives of her own mother and daughter. So too, Christine, who seems to have had no children, gives birth to her dead mother, gives her a voice in her novel with which to speak. In that sense, the novel itself is at once mother and child to all these generations of loving women.

Now the portrait of the artist as a medium between the generations puts the reader in an analogous position as the medium between succeeding stories. Joseph Frank's conclusion about Proust contains new possibilities: 'The reader, in other words, is substituted for the narrator, and is placed by the author throughout the book in the same position as the narrator occupies before his own experience at the reception of the Princesse de Guermantes' (Frank 239).

To such a lucid anticipation of reader-response theory in the work of Georges Poulet and Wolfgang Iser, we might add T.S. Eliot's observation in 'Tradition and the Individual Talent' that 'the historical sense involves a perception, not only of the pastness of the past, but of its presence' (Eliot 49). This male, modernist idea of the past as an active force in the present is close enough to Poulet's sense, in the 'Phenomenology of Reading,' of an extra-individual identity at work in the reading experience: 'Reading, then, is the act in which the subjective principle which I call *I*, is modified in such a way that I no longer have the right, strictly speaking, to consider it as my *I*. I am on loan to another, and this other thinks, feels, suffers, and acts within me' (Poulet 354). Poulet's sense, however, of being possessed is finally too submissive; it is quite as passive as Eliot's suggestion that quotation is the essence of the poet's individuality, since we might 'find that not only the best, but the most individual parts of his work may be those in which the dead poets, his ancestors, assert their immortality most vigorously' (48).

While Christine discovers in the writing of *The Road Past Altamont* that her dead mother does assert her immortality most vigorously, such 'immortality' does not depend on the daughter's passive bearing of it; it is also a labour of love, in a way that Christine's uncle cannot understand. In one sense, this act of recreating one's legacy is also central to Eliot, as well as to the other great moderns: 'Now cut off from the past, disinherited from it, the poet can choose to accept the imperative and responsibility "to make it new" or else remain without any authentic sense of past or present culture at all' (Con Davis 13). And yet for Roy the *I* which is 'on loan' to another *I* is not reducible to a 'shred of platinum' which permits 'an escape from personality' (Eliot 58); rather, the *I* for Roy is more like an historical descendant who finds her identity as the self and heir and parent together. Neither a self-made man nor simply the heir of all the ages, the artist has to become her own mother before she can be truly herself.

The reader who is 'occupied,' in Poulet's sense, by the thoughts of the author is left very much in Christine's position of allowing another voice to speak through her. But since 'in reading, the reader becomes the subject that does the thinking' (Iser, *Reader* 292), it is clear that the reader does not fully surrender her personality any more than the narrator does. Instead, the reader may discover in the linked-story form of the novel just what it means to 'give birth in turn to the one who gave us birth when finally, sooner or later, we draw her into our self' (129). Here, Roy's metaphor for imaginative conception and reproduction finally shows the limits of the reader-response idea that 'such acts of conception are possible and successful to the degree that they lead to something being formulated in us ... The production of the meaning of literary texts ... does not merely entail the discovery of the unformulated, which can then be taken over by the active imagination of the reader; it also entails the possibility that we may formulate ourselves and so discover what had previously seemed to elude our consciousness' (Iser, *Reader* 294). For the emphasis on the maternal body in *The Road Past Altamont* suggests that it is not only the self, but also some *other*, who is formulated in the act of reading. And so 'the dialectical structure of reading' (Iser 294) has to be understood in terms which are also relational, and can make room for other kinds of union – of the subject with the object, of the past with the present, and, strangest of all, of the living with the dead. So it may well be that the 'most illuminated part of one's life,' for the reader as for Christine's Maman, is to be 'situated between those who came before us and those who follow after us, right in the middle' (135).

The reader, then, by finally juxtaposing all the disconnected and contradictory moments of the novel, learns how to square the circle, or how to play, as the narrator was 'playing, as she herself had taught me to do, as Mémère also had played with me one day ... as we all play perhaps, throughout our lives, at trying to catch up with one another' (30). Thus the linear and temporal act of reading becomes as well the spatial act of juxtaposition, becomes our last, best way of 'catching up' with that *other* whom we are destined to become.

Part Three

SNAPSHOTS OF
THE PARODIST

9

Beyond Photography:
Parody as Metafiction in the
Novels of Alice Munro

At the end of Alice Munro's *Lives of Girls and Women*, Del Jordan outlines the 'black fable' (206) she had once hoped to write about the people in her town: 'I knew from my reading that in the families of judges, as of great landowners, degeneracy and madness were things to be counted on' (203). And so 'I did not pay much attention to the real Sherriffs, once I had transformed them for fictional purposes' (206). Because this term 'real' is narratively hedged, however, by a distinction as old as Plato, Del's definition of what is 'true' might better help to explain her artistic failure: 'All pictures. The reasons for things happening I seemed vaguely to know, but could not explain; I expected all that would come clear later. The main thing was that it seemed true to me, not real but true, as if I had discovered, not made up, such people and such a story, as if that town was lying close behind the one I walked through every day' (206). As Lorraine York observes, this comment 'has caused some difficulty for critics who see only one level of reality in Munro's creative act.' It seems to have caused some difficulty for York herself who concludes that 'The "real" is, in Del's terms, becoming "true"' (23). For the mature narrator has discovered that what she thought was 'true' was in fact a wilful subversion of the 'real.' As she is forced to admit, 'It is a shock, when you have dealt so cunningly, powerfully, with reality, to come back and find it still there' (*Lives* 209).

What is 'real' in the novel Del eventually writes – presumably the *Bildungsroman* we have been reading – might well depend on the problem of photographic truth raised by Munro's 'Epilogue: The Photographer.' If 'the photographs reveal what is present – whether in the past or in the future – or what is potentially true' (York 38), then the camera becomes an analogue of Plato's cave, letting in the truth of an ideal world. But if the camera should prove to be an analogue of the imagination, then the 'truth' of what is seen is more doubtful, because poets, as Plato would remind us, tell lies.

In fictional 'fact,' the images registered by Del's photographer turn out to be neither ideal nor natural; they can only be described as subjective perceptions or fictionally constructed notions of truth, conforming to the negative intention of Del's 'black fable': 'The pictures he took turned out to be unusual, even frightening. People saw that in his pictures they had aged twenty or thirty years. Middle-aged people saw in their own features the terrible, growing, inescapable likeness of their dead parents; young fresh girls and men showed what gaunt or dulled or stupid faces they would have when they were fifty. Brides looked pregnant, children adenoidal. So he was not a popular photographer' (*Lives* 205). The retrospective narrator has to confess that her imagination was not then disciplined by the *real*, was in fact ignoring what was *there*: 'For this novel I had changed Jubilee, too, or picked out some features of it and ignored others.' And so her cameraman sees only what she wants him to see: 'It became an older, darker, more decaying town, full of unpainted board fences covered with tattered posters advertising circuses, fall fairs, elections that had long since come and gone.' In the language of her technology, she has refused to make a positive print out of the negative image.

Of course, the fictional photographer does not survive a meeting with the 'real' Bobby Sherriff, certainly not with Bobby speaking so sanely about diet as the cause of his mental breakdown: 'Damage had been done; Caroline and the other Halloways and their town had lost authority; I had lost faith' (208). But the question of what is real is not decided simply by reference to appearance or to the surface world of 'objects.' If the maturing writer now finds that only '*Real life*' (201) in all its marvelous complexity can supply her with her truth, 'real life' is still to be found only *inside* Plato's cave, not in the transcendent light of the sun outside it: 'People's lives, in Jubilee as elsewhere, were dull, simple, amazing and unfathomable – deep caves paved with kitchen linoleum' (210). The 'truth' of reality, in other words, is necessarily located inwardly in subjective perception. So if Del is to find what is 'radiant [and] everlasting' (210) in human life, she must seek it in a vision of immanence, not of transcendence. For there is no world *above* this one;

'everyday existence reveals nothing beyond itself but is simply marvellous in itself' (Hoy 108). Philosophers, it turns out, can lie just as eloquently as poets.

The problem of the poetic lie is not done away with, however, by banning Plato from the republic of Jubilee. While the camera of 'black fable' may fail to register what is 'really' there, so may a poet with notoriously better intentions. Del quotes a sentimental line from Tennyson to express the duplicity (L. *duplex*) of more than her feelings for Garnet French: 'I said it with absolute sincerity, absolute irony. *He cometh not, she said*. From "Mariana," one of the silliest poems I had ever read. It made my tears flow harder' (200). It is not just that the conventions of sensibility are as threadbare as the gothic conventions. Art emotions necessarily turn paradoxical, like Del's own grief, the moment they are objectified or made the object of consciousness. Art thus distorts life by locating itself outside its source, by doubling the subject as an object.

Paradox, of course, can be too easily thematized in Munro's work, even by a critic who chooses 'to concentrate on the photograph as a partaker in a system of signification which is, like all other such systems, necessarily rooted in culture' (York 12–13). For if Del develops a kind of '[p]hotographic vision' which 'is, by definition, all-inclusive' (30), then the definition itself becomes a self-fulfulling prophecy: 'The inevitable result of this all-inclusive, photographic vision is paradox. The world becomes at once ugly and beautiful, familiar and strange, innocent and threatening. Indeed, Susan Sontag's *On Photography* is couched in terms of paradox: the photograph brings us closer to objective reality and distances us from it; the photograph is both realistic, she argues, and surrealistic' (York 32).

'The Language of Paradox,' of course, is the title of the introductory chapter to Cleanth Brooks's *The Well Wrought Urn*. York herself barely swerves from this method of New Criticism in finding a series of themes and images in recurrent patterns of opposition throughout Munro's work: ' "Epilogue: The Photographer" in *Lives of Girls and Women* is Munro's most systematic and sustained attempt to describe the paradoxes of surfaces and depths, and of the familiar and the grotesque, using the metaphor of photography' (York 38); 'Munro's acute consciousness of human transience is closely connected with yet another paradox in her art – the paradox of control and helplessness, fixity and flux' (44); 'The photograph is the meeting place not only of power and helplessness, the familiar and the grotesque, but of motion and stillness as well' (45). By such means, the formal paradoxes of photography are actually transformed into the content of Munro's work.

The dual status of the photographic image – as a representation *and* a transformation of the world – may in fact invite this sort of critical method which seeks to reconcile the binary oppositions of photography. York's allusion to Susan Sontag, however, misses other critical possibilities: 'Surrealism lies at the heart of the photographic enterprise: in the very creation of a duplicate world, of a reality in the second degree, narrower but more dramatic than the one perceived by natural vision' (Sontag, *Photography* 52). It seems that Del's photographer does make this sort of 'surrealistic' attempt to create a duplicate world; his 'unnatural' vision is an extension of Baudelaire's 'voyeuristic stroller,' of whom the modern 'photographer is an armed version' (Sontag 55). This contemporary '*flâneur* is not attracted to the city's official realities but to its dark seamy corners, its neglected populations – an unofficial reality behind the façade of bourgeois life that the photographer "apprehends," as a detective apprehends a criminal' (Sontag 55–6).

The fictional 'Photographer' is not alone in *Lives of Girls and Women* in displaying a surrealist sensibility; from the time she was a girl, Del would catch glimpses of 'unofficial reality' from some of her 'real-life' neighbours. As early as the first story, 'The Flats Road,' she had apprehended another world 'lying alongside our world ... like a troubling distorted reflection, the same but never at all the same' (22). This world – identified at first with Uncle Benny – is a place where 'people could go down in quicksand, be vanquished by ghosts or terrible ordinary cities; ... defeats were met with crazy satisfaction. It was his triumph, that he couldn't know about, to make us see.' What Uncle Benny makes Del see from the outset is really another way of seeing, one which questions the sufficiency of ordinary views of reality.

This 'duplicate world' created by photographers and other kinds of 'surrealists' is hardly a reaffirmation of Platonic ontology, celebrating the 'truth' of a transcendent world. As Sontag says, 'The powers of photography have in effect de-Platonized our understanding of reality, making it less and less plausible to reflect upon our experience according to the distinction between images and things, between copies and originals' (*Photography* 179). In effect, photography has become a language, like any other, whose signifiers and signifieds contain by definition only themselves, not reality: 'To possess the world in the form of images is, precisely, to reexperience the unreality and remoteness of the real' (*Photography* 164).

The real problem presented by photography is likely to be epistemological in nature, since the knowledge it offers is based on a culturally determined code. This epistemological problem comes into exceptionally sharp focus in Sontag's comparison of Chinese and Western views of the medium:

> While for us photography is intimately connected with discontinuous ways of seeing (the point is precisely to see the whole by means of a part – an arresting detail, a striking way of cropping), in China it is connected only with continuity. Not only are there proper subjects for the camera, those which are positive, inspirational (exemplary activities, smiling people, bright weather), and orderly, but there are proper ways of photographing, which derive from notions about the moral order of space that preclude the very idea of photographic seeing. Thus Antonioni was reproached for photographing things that were old, or old-fashioned – 'he sought out and took dilapidated walls and blackboard newspapers discarded long ago' ... – and for showing undecorous moments.
>
> (Sontag, *Photography* 169–70)

This perceptual difference is more than an ideological conflict between idealism and realism (or what the Chinese might see as the nihilism of 'black fable'); it is at root an epistemological difference between 'continuous' and 'discontinuous' ways of seeing. 'The Chinese resist the photographic dismemberment of reality. Close-ups are not used' (*Photography* 172); 'Our society proposes a spectrum of discontinuous choices and perceptions. Theirs is constructed around a single, ideal observer; and photographs contribute their bit to the Great Monologue' (173).

Del's 'photographic' language, like Uncle Benny's, resists the conventional idea of a monolithic world; reality in the language of each is multiple and discontinuous. But if the visions of both 'surrealists' displace what is *real* by an inverted world, the tone of their shared language is very different. Uncle Benny passively seeks an explanation for his failure in a world where 'luck and wickedness were gigantic and unpredictable,' where his only choice is to meet his defeat with 'crazy satisfaction.' Del, on the other hand, is open to the criticism made by the Chinese of Antonioni: 'He racked his brain to get such close-ups in an attempt to distort the people's image and uglify their spiritual outlook' (Sontag, *Photography* 171). Del openly admits to such an intent to ridicule: 'Once as we walked over the trestle a car full of people from our class at school passed underneath, hooting at us, and I did have a vision, as if from outside, of how strange this was – Jerry contemplating and welcoming a future that would annihilate Jubilee and life in it, and I myself planning secretly to turn it into black fable and tie it up in my novel, and the town, the people who really were the town, just hooting car horns – to mock anybody walking, not riding, on a Sunday afternoon – and never knowing what danger they were in from us' (*Lives* 206).

And so Del's 'photographic' doubling is not quite the same, after all, as Uncle Benny's, since he surrenders to his vision of a duplicate world. In view of his male version of gothic fantasy, Coral Ann Howells asks whether there is in Del's vision 'anything about the content or the form of fantasizing which is distinctively female' (78). Choosing content as the more likely difference, she decides that 'The power of fantasy to create alternative worlds whose design conforms more closely to desire is keenly scrutinized in the central female fantasy of falling in love' (80): 'Both Del and Rose grow up with dual visions of themselves as exiles or spies in their hometowns, resisting the social and gender constraints imposed on them and needing to invent more glorious possibilities than their ordinary lives seem to promise. It is only through fantasy that they can recreate the world and themselves' (79). Both characters do seem to conform to a 'typical' pattern of submission, followed by resistance, to fantasy; yet this pattern of 'distrust of fantasy' is never claimed as a distinctively female form. Howells says only that Del 'rejects her gothic novel about Jubilee as an "unreliable structure" which cannot accommodate the multiple resistance of contingent reality' (Howells 86–87).

Of course, Del's refusal of the old ideology of 'transformation through sex' (Howells 84) does lead to other ideological refusals – some of them distinctively literary. For the 'unreliable structure' of the gothic novel proves quite un-gothic, anyway, in Del's projected use of it. Her prior quotation of Tennyson's poem 'with absolute sincerity, absolute irony,' already suggests that she is tempted more by parody than by any purely gothic sentiment. And since she can no longer speak the words of the poem with only their manifest intent, she will use henceforth what Linda Hutcheon calls 'double-voiced parodic forms' (*A Theory* 4). For Del's continuing 'desire' is to escape more than the body's authority; she wants to be free of the authority of social convention and morality. As the allusion to 'Mariana' suggests, her future method will be to parody both the conventions of paradox and of gothic melodrama. The story, in other words, will exploit a more ironic form of doubleness.

The surreal kind of 'doubling' which we see in 'The Flats Road' and 'The Photographer' is meant for now only to free her from the tyranny of expectation, whether this should come from the fantastic expectations of Uncle Benny or from the forced marriages of friends such as Naomi. By parodying the conventions of life in Jubilee, Del plans to destroy (at least for herself) its whole conformist mentality. And yet the danger, as she sees in yoking her project to Jerry's interest in nuclear physics, is that parody may also lead to annihilation of one form or another. For, like 'The Photographer' she invents, her duplications threaten to destroy her originals in life: the mocker discovers that she might be turning into the real gothic monster.

There is already something inherently dubious, anyway, in the nature of photographic 'doubling' which makes it morally doubtful as well. For the photograph is 'co-substantial' (Sontag, *Photography* 155) with the subject – an actual emanation of its light rays – though still quite different from it. In this respect, photography has an innate capacity for parody, since 'the textual doubling of parody (unlike pastiche, allusion, quotation, and so on) functions to mark difference' (Hutcheon 53). Thus, because its 'co-substantiality' involves the 'real' subject, Del's 'photographic' parody necessarily assaults the freedom (and reality) of others at the very moment it establishes her independence from their world.

Del's most 'gothic' subject, Bobby Sherriff, exposes the ethical limitations of such a method when she goes to his house looking for 'some secret to madness, some *gift* about it, something I didn't know' (210). Unintentionally (and most kindly), he also parodies the novel she is planning, since his prosaic discussion of the chemicals in white flour and his poverty in college destroys all her gothic expectations about insanity. Still, he does not leave her without a sign, or a 'gift' as she puts it, of something extra in his experience beyond what the (camera) eye can see, as 'he did the only special thing he ever did for me. With those things in his hands, he rose on his toes like a dancer, like a plump ballerina. This action, accompanied by his delicate smile, appeared to be a joke not shared with me so much as displayed for me, and it seemed also to have a concise meaning, a stylized meaning – to be a letter, or a whole word, in an alphabet I did not know' (*Lives* 211). By playing out a role she seems to expect, though in a language she cannot spell – and here Del's Ur-novel foreshadows Rose's predicament in 'Spelling' – Bobby Sherriff subjects her plot to the ' "double-voiced" word' of parody (Hutcheon, *A Theory* 72). With one 'surreal' gesture, he invalidates the gothic story of *The Photographer*.

Del's abandonment of her novel signals her final reconciliation to reality, heightened and 'radiant' as it appears to her. Still, her discovery of the 'real' Bobby Sherriff does not mean that her way of seeing has suddenly become continuous or monolithic. Rather, it is as if Bobby's 'madness' offers yet another world than the one Uncle Benny has discovered within or alongside this one. Thus her heightened 'realism' turns out to be 'surrealism' of a brighter kind than, for example, in *Les Fleurs du Mal*, because she still sees a duplicate world contained within the familiar, surface one of everyday reality, a world which is both more dramatic and more radiant than the one seen by natural vision: 'I would try to make lists. A list of all the stores and businesses ... a list of family names, names on the tombstones ... And no list could hold what I wanted, for what I wanted was every last thing, every layer of speech and thought, stroke of light on bark or walls, every smell, pothole, pain, crack, delusion, held still and held together – radiant, everlasting' (210).

Readers who expect more 'heightened realism' in *Who Do You Think You Are?* tend to regard it, rather as George Woodcock does, as 'a much less convincing book ... in both emotional and aesthetic terms' ('Plots' 248). Woodcock makes the 'hard objectivity' of the novel 'with its relentless social documentation of low life' a result of the shift in narrative point of view to the third person: 'In *Lives of Girls and Women* the sense of familiar authenticity was sustained by the fact that the aspirant writer as central character was assumed to be both participant and observer.' Now the supposed absence of the retrospective artist-observer takes all depth out of the realism, leaving only a dreary version of the former *Bildungsroman*: 'In this respect Alice Munro has remained fundamentally unchanged, applying the same realist techniques with the same impeccable skill and merely varying the human situations. Her potentialities have always been major; her achievements have never quite matched them because she has never mastered those transformations of form with which major writers handle the great climactic shifts of life' (Woodcock, 'Plots' 249–50).

Rose, however, will insist on 'discontinuous ways of seeing' in a manner which, recalling young Del's surrealist version of photography, must signal a major transformation of form in Munro's art. At the end of 'Privilege,' Rose even wonders whether her photographic memories of childhood have any accuracy at all: 'When Rose thought of West Hanratty during the war years, and during the years before, the two times were so separate it was as if an entirely different lighting had been used, or as if it was all on film and the film had been printed in a different way, so that on the one hand things looked clean-edged and decent and limited and ordinary, and on the other, dark, grainy, jumbled, and disturbing' (*Who* 38). Though Rose clings to her faith that the break is really in history, not in her imagination, her photographic metaphor reveals the same habit of textual doubling by which Del meant to break with her past. Rose's dual ways of seeing, like the ones which Del renounces, prove to be discontinuous with each other as well as in themselves, a series of images on film.

Rose has another connection with photographic ways of seeing at the end of 'Simon's Luck'; she plays the part of a 'pseudo-mother' (175) in a TV drama. Significantly, she depends on narrative continuities to assume that 'People watching trusted that they would be protected from predictable disasters, also from those shifts of emphasis that throw the story line open to question, the disarrangements which demand new judgments and solutions, and throw the windows open on inappropriate unforgettable scenery' (177). But in the middle of filming, she discovers that the lover she thought had deserted her was really dying of pancreatic cancer. And so 'Simon's dying struck Rose as that kind of disarrangement' (177). The interplay between life and film reinforces, though it also qualifies, her earlier discontinuous way of looking at things.

No doubt this same 'technique of "disarrangement" ' helps the reader to 'perceive that the aesthetic pattern is possibly, and often probably, "false," in the sense that it does not provide an adequate rendering of the full truth of that experience' (Mathews, 'Disarrangement' 184–85). Yet it is not as fair to say that the disruptive epilogue to each story will not 'allow us to devise a new, definitive pattern which yields the story's "real meaning." Instead, the presence of the information raises questions about the validity of any pattern we might find in the story' (185). For Simon's death shows Rose as wanting to blame fate or events, more than herself, for her crippling lack of self-knowledge: 'It was preposterous, it was unfair, that such a chunk of information should have been left out, and that Rose even at this late date could have thought herself the only person who could seriously lack power' (*Who* 177). The final relative clause may be the first indication in the novel that Rose is on the verge of finding out the 'real meaning,' not the perpetual undecidability, of her story.

If Rose is becoming aware of ironic disarrangements in her view of things, she is still slow to recognize how much she actively distorts experience through the narrative lens of story-telling. She appears, on a dramatic level, to be a narrator very much like Del in 'The Photographer,' and for much the same reason: 'The change in Rose, once she left the scene, crossed the bridge, changed herself into chronicler, was remarkable' (41); 'This is the sort of story Rose brought home' (42); 'Here is the sort of story Flo told Rose' (43); 'When Rose told people these things, in later years, they had considerable effect. She had to swear they were true, she was not exaggerating. And they were true, but the effect was off-balance. Her schooling seemed deplorable' (28); 'Rose knew a lot of people who wished they had been born poor, and hadn't been. So she would queen it over them, offering various scandals and bits of squalor from her childhood' (24). The narrative sequence suggests that Rose continues to chronicle such clichéd schoolyard horrors because she would like to transform herself through the telling. Once upon a time, on the dramatic level, she was humiliated by Cora, the scornful schoolyard queen, who rejected her offered tribute. But on the narrative level, 'happily ever after,' she survives Cora who has become 'swarthy, hairy, swaggering, fat' (37). Rose is not even 'much bothered by this loss, this transformation,' since narrative allows her to take Cora's place. Out of her discontent with reality, she recreates herself as the new queen of a 'surrealist' fiction.

'In the past, a discontent with reality expressed itself as a longing for *another* world. In modern society, a discontent with reality expresses itself forcefully and most hauntingly by the longing to reproduce *this* one. As if only by looking at reality in the form of an object – through the fix of the photograph – is it really real, that is, surreal' (Sontag,

Photography 80). In *Lives of Girls and Women*, Del had already given more than a hint of such motives in her longing to reproduce this world. Oppressed by an uncle's dogmatic 'notions of time and history' (25), she had kept his manuscript hidden 'inside a large flat copy of *Wuthering Heights* ' (52), that epitome of gothic, even surreal, longing for another world. Yet her later abandonment of her uncle's local history, 'so heavy and dull and useless' (52), was not as final as Del had assumed: 'Voracious and misguided as Uncle Craig out at Jenkin's [sic] Bend, writing his history, I would want to write things down' (210). Her final making of lists becomes a need to reproduce *this* world without conforming to her uncle's mere 'hope of accuracy.' For what she seeks is not a mimesis of this world but its transfiguration, a 'fix' which is real on her terms, that is to say, surreal.

Refusing to conform to other people's notions of reality, Rose likewise rejects inherited conventions of story-telling: 'She knew that those little dark or painted shacks were supposed to be comical – always were, in country humor – but she saw them instead as scenes of marvelous shame and outrage' (*Who* 24). Discontented with the 'real' world, she struggles to reproduce it – with a vengeance. Her strategy is not so much to deflect reality through laughter, but to display the unofficial reality of horror behind a conventional façade of amusement. This act of negative transfiguration thus gives her power – makes her 'queen' – over those who submit to more polite ways of seeing.

The strategy Rose takes up is precisely the one young Del had found so appealing in 'The Photographer.' At base, it is a habit of mockery intended to displace 'reality,' not a habit of comedy meant to produce a reconciliation with it. If Rose is somewhat slower than Del to reconcile herself to reality, she would appear none the less to come to the same conclusion. Only now, the refusal of parody is begun by someone else; it is the reluctance of a former schoolmate, Ralph Gillespie, to imitate Milton Homer that precipitates her own rejection of mockery: 'But when Rose remembered this unsatisfactory conversation she seemed to recall a wave of kindness, of sympathy and forgiveness, though certainly no words of that kind had been spoken. That peculiar shame which she carried around with her seemed to have been eased. The thing she was ashamed of, in acting, was that she might have been paying attention to the wrong things, reporting antics, when there was always something further, a tone, a depth, a light, that she couldn't get and wouldn't get'

(209). Rose, who wants as much as Del to mock her town out of existence, still has to learn how to give up 'black fable.'

The radical change of form in *Who Do You Think You Are?* is not apparent to readers like Woodcock because it looks so much like a recycling of the old themes and 'realist techniques' of *Lives of Girls and Women*. And yet the timing of Rose's refusal constitutes the whole of the difference between the two novels. Though both women decide in the last chapter of their respective stories to give up mockery, Del does so before she tells her story, Rose only after her story has been written. And so *Who Do You Think You Are?* becomes the 'black fable' that Del decided not to write, the voyeuristic side of the surrealist vision which presents a far more dissociated way of seeing than anything in *Lives*.

The subject of *Who Do You Think You Are?* now has less to do with the *Bildungsroman* than with the sort of parody which was left unwritten in *Lives of Girls and Women* – parody both as a social strategy and as a literary device. Rose is in fact a highly self-conscious parodist, one who claims only to be imitating 'Ralph Gillespie *doing* Milton Homer' (195). The parodist clearly understands the function of her art, observing how the idiot's 'contribution to any parade was wholly negative; designed, if Milton Homer could have designed anything, just to make the parade look foolish' (196). In social terms, Milton Homer's function is more satiric than parodic; it is an imitation which comments on life, not on other art. And so his satire, directed against the high and mighty of the world, unwittingly undercuts the pretensions of his own aristocratic family: 'In short, he had made himself so comical a sight that the petition which nobody really wanted could be treated as a comedy, too, and the power of the Milton sisters, the flax-mill Methodists, could be seen as a leftover dribble....."That was the end of them thinking they could run things," Flo said' (202).

Flo's terms are only a little more salty than those of the Russian formalist who says that parody 'introduces the permanent corrective of laughter, of a critique on the one-sided seriousness of the lofty direct word' (Bakhtin 55). For the idiot unwittingly helps to break the spell of his aunts' biblical language, thus making his function truly parodic: 'language is transformed from the absolute dogma it had been within the narrow framework of a sealed-off and impermeable monoglossia' (Bakhtin 61). Milton's need to imitate is an 'authorized transgression of norms,' a folk remnant of the medieval carnival which 'Bakhtin describes

... as actually being "consecrated by tradition," both social and ecclesiastical' (Hutcheon, *A Theory* 74). He thus appears in the novel as that most Bakhtinian of figures, the 'comic double' (Bakhtin 58) who is the antidote to high, mythic seriousness, a revolutionary agent in the process of change. But Milton Homer, so little conscious of what he does, is also more clown than artist, a figure satisfying the formalist's concept of function rather than the pragmatist's idea of 'encoded intent' (Hutcheon, *A Theory* 23). Ralph Gillespie, on the other hand, is the truly self-conscious artist who, if he commits an 'authorized transgression,' also introduces a genuine aesthetic distance into his campaign to make the town look foolish. For he pretends that he is only mocking the village idiot, all the while using him to disgrace the old authorities. In that sense, Ralph, like Bakhtin's impersonal novelist, is 'a third party in a quarrel between two people (although he might be a biased third party)' (Bakhtin 314).

So, too, Rose's imitation of Ralph offers a more artistic form of this 'folkloric disgracing and ridiculing of the old – old authority, old truth, the old word' (Bakhtin 82). Her parody of a parody even creates the necessary aesthetic distance to allow her to pretend to the virtues of realism; evidently her performance supplies the single occasion when her brother 'could put up with Rose's theatrics[–]when they were about Hanratty' (*Who* 195). Realism thus becomes a self-saving mask for Rose, since it keeps the true design of her fiction at one or two removes from herself.

Finally, it is this distance which is so unsettling to a critic like Woodcock, since *Who Do You Think You Are?* parodies both the matter and manner of *Lives of Girls and Women*. Rose's narrative method is hardly meant to create the empathy of Del's method of telling; instead, her stories have the effect of Del's imagined photographs, or even those of one of Munro's favorite photographers, Diane Arbus, whose 'work shows people who are pathetic, pitiable, as well as repulsive, but ... does not arouse any compassionate feelings' (Sontag, *Photography* 33). Until, of course, Rose finds an unexpected sympathy in the reformed parodist who shows her how to give up parody.

Because Ralph Gillespie is not introduced before this last, title story, his chapter takes on something of the function of an epilogue to the whole novel. All the briefer epilogues offering their retrospect on the action of each story are now replaced by a flashback, not the usual flashforward, which helps to explain Rose's use of parody throughout her life story. The reader who has failed to see story-telling itself as the subject of the novel has, like Rose, evidently 'been paying attention to the wrong things' (209). For the ' "vital" link between art and life' is 'reforged on a new level – on that of the imaginative process (of storytelling), instead of on that of the product (the story told)' (Hutcheon, *Narcissistic* xvii, 3). Now the retrospective observer shows up in the very structure of her stories, inviting us to see, long before the participant does, not only how the story line is open to question, but how story itself (such as in Rose's self-protective fiction of Simon's absence) can become a telling defence against self-knowledge. Parody thus works, on both a dramatic level and a covert narrative level, 'to prevent the reader's identification with any character and to force a new, more active, thinking relationship upon him' (Hutcheon, *Narcissistic* 49). In that sense, *Who Do You Think You Are?* becomes a metafiction which is 'not about "reality," but about the imaginative processes of coming to grips with it in formal aesthetic terms' (Hutcheon, *Narcissistic* 45).

Flo's mimicry presents in little the multiple uses of parody in Munro's later novel: 'Among the people she listened to were Mrs. Lawyer Davies, Mrs. Anglican Rector Henley-Smith, and Mrs. Horse-Doctor McKay. She came home and imitated them at supper: their high-flown remarks, their flibberty voices. Monsters, she made them seem; of foolishness, and showiness, and self-approbation' (10–11). In social terms, Flo's imitations belittle the high and mighty, bringing complacent authorities down to her level. But naming these women ever more exactly for the occupations of their husbands is also a linguistic feat: 'mimicry rips the word away from its object, disunifies the two, shows that a given straightforward generic word – epic or tragic – is one-sided, bounded, incapable of exhausting the subject' (Bakhtin 55). The question of genre is all the more relevant because Flo rips self-styled 'heroic' characters away from heroic language, making them over into that 'black fable' which doubles back on (or doubles over) their more pretentious story. In literary terms, Flo thus anticipates the surrealist voyeur who apprehends an unofficial reality behind the façade of bourgeois life.

Flo's plots bear out this duplicative purpose of her mimicry as well as of her language: 'Becky's old father was a different kind of butcher from her brother according to Flo. A bad-tempered Englishman ... A skinflint, a family tyrant. After Becky had polio he wouldn't let her go back to school. She was seldom seen outside the house, never outside the yard. He didn't want people gloating. That was what Becky said, at the trial' (7). Still, the matter-of-fact appeal to public history comes as a bit of a shock after Flo has invoked so many conventions of melodrama. The black fable shrugs off, as it were, its status as fiction, asking to be taken for real. Yet even Rose knows better than to confuse the two: 'Present time and past, the shady melodramatic past of Flo's stories, were quite separate, at least for Rose. Present people could not be fitted into the past' (8). Except that Rose herself still seems willing to reduce 'times past,' if not her present, to 'the shady melodramatic past of Flo's stories.'

'Royal Beatings' shows, in fact, how much Rose has acquired from Flo in the art of parody: 'The word Royal lolled on Flo's tongue, took on trappings. Rose had a need to picture things, to pursue absurdities ... she pondered: how is a beating royal? ... In real life they didn't approach such dignity' (1). Rose's mimicry, much like her master's, 'rips the word away from its object, disunifies the two'; Flo is caught looking every bit as pretentious as Mrs Horse-Doctor McKay. Rose, of course, would tend to regard this as the victim's right when she has endured such a beating as Flo stage-manages. And yet Flo, who does so much to humiliate others, has ironically complained that Rose ' "humiliates me." ... There it is, the explanation. "She humiliates me," she repeats with satisfaction. "She has no respect" ' (15–16). Flo is hardly mistaken; but as Rose looks back on this painful moment of her childhood, she can only see herself as an innocent martyr. Her stepmother, on the other hand, turns into a monster of cruelty and self-approbation.

Flo, however, has hardly been standing by in the dramatic moment of the story, letting Rose use her own tricks of parody against her: 'Flo goes beyond her ordinary scorn and self-possession and becomes amazingly theatrical herself, saying it was for Rose that she sacrificed her life' (13). The daughter's response to the mother's sacrifice suddenly exposes what 'the household struggle' is really about: who has the superior claim to martyrdom. 'I never asked you to do anything,' Rose says smugly. 'I wished you never had. I would have been a lot better off' (14). The moral debt of the orphan might be figuratively erased if only she can prove herself the true martyr, the stepmother the false one.

Flo's theatricality is a fairly easy target of parody, but Rose's position is as soon compromised by her own 'theatrical unconcern' (13). And the father, forced to play the villain, likewise helps to expose the theatrical conventions of the scene: 'He is like a bad actor, who turns a part grotesque. As if he must savor and insist on just what is shameful and terrible about this. That is not to say he is pretending, that he is acting, and does not mean it. He is acting, and he means it' (16). The duplicity of these various roles is nicely anticipated by Del's quotation in *Lives* of sentimental verse 'with absolute sincerity, with absolute irony.' For Rose's little drama is just as sincerely felt, and every bit as ironic. Since she doesn't even see her villain acting out of his own volition, but out of aesthetic conventions proper to the women's staging of the scene, the family drama becomes a virtual parody of itself.

'Parody, according to the formalist theoreticians, is the result of a conflict between realistic motivation and an aesthetic motivation which has become weak and has been made obvious' (Hutcheon, *Narcissistic* 24). In that sense, even the part Rose plays, the part of a victim, is pure aesthetic convention, and so it can only be offered as parody: 'The very last-ditch willing sound of humiliation and defeat it is, for it seems Rose must play her part in this with the same grossness, the same exaggeration, that her father displays, playing his' (17). Real motives cannot be admitted or Rose will forfeit her role as the martyr; so she is left at the mercy of weakened aesthetic conventions. Now even she can't believe in the situation she has created; but with the strap stinging her flesh, she can't possibly disbelieve either. She can only play 'his victim with a self-indulgence that arouses, and maybe hopes to arouse, his final, sickened contempt.' Through the excess of her own humiliation, she cannot help but humiliate. And so her parody of martyrdom belittles as much as Flo's mimicry ever did.

Forgive them for they know not what they do. The true martyr forgives the trespass in the moment it is committed. But 'Rose is hanging on to advantage as long as she can,' refusing the blandishments of peace because then 'all advantage will be lost' (19): 'She floats in her pure superior state as if kindly drugged' (18). Clearly the apprentice teller of black fables knows how to elevate herself by discrediting everyone around her. But what Rose seems to have forgotten from Flo's stories of shame and outrage is that 'Becky herself, town oddity and public pet, harmless and malicious, could never match the butcher's prisoner, the cripple daughter, a white streak at the window: mute, beaten, impregnated. As with the house, only a formal connection could be made' (8).

The artifice of formal connections in the novel is finally underscored at the end of 'Royal Beatings' by the apparent absence of formal connection. Hat Nettleton, the fabled horsewhipper who drove Becky's father to his death, turns up rather belatedly on a morning radio show to evade the 'truth' of his own history. Not surprisingly, the conventions of the interview encourage him to remember only buggy races and a rather vulgar rural idyll having nothing in common with Flo's 'black fable.' So Rose is left to muse with savage irony: 'Oldest resident. Oldest horsewhipper. Living link with our past' (22). Still she fails to see that this 'discontinuous way of seeing' undercuts her own story of being a poor, abused child. She is hardly a more valid link herself with the past than is Hat Nettleton; for her own version of history is just as self-saving, just as much a defence against real self-knowledge.

From the outset, the narrator signals that Rose is not ready for the 'real meaning' of her story. Not yet, at least; not before she learns from Ralph Gillespie to renounce her scorn for people like Hat Nettleton who so blatantly deceive themselves: 'It was Flo who would enjoy hearing. She thought of her saying *Imagine!* in a way that meant she was having her worst suspicions gorgeously confirmed' (22–3). Only Flo has slipped into one of her own black fables, 'sitting in a corner of her crib, looking crafty and disagreeable, not answering anybody, though she occasionally showed her feelings by biting a nurse' (23). The humiliations of age are hardly qualification enough, in Rose's belittling habit of mind, for martyrdom. But then Flo is not the only one who has a habit of biting her nurse.

Much of Rose's story is structured by this same habit of denial which turns into a virtual refusal of identity. What Rose most wants to deny, of course, is Flo and her dogmatic story of the world. For instance, that insane little cautionary tale about 'White Slavers' in 'White Swans': 'Flo had mentioned people who were not ministers, dressed up as if they were. Not real ministers dressed as if they were not. Or, stranger still, men who were not real ministers pretending to be real but dressed as if they were not' (65). The problem is not merely that evil is more bewildering than Flo's hackneyed intuition of it. The indeterminate identity of the lecher also allows for something in Rose's imaginative response to him akin to deconstructive freeplay – that 'joyous affirmation of the freeplay of the world and without truth, without origin, offered to an active interpretation' which, in Derrida's terms, 'surrenders itself to *genetic* indetermination, to the *seminal* adventure of the trace' (264). More literally even than in Derrida's reading, indeterminacy offers to the active interpretation of a young girl wanting to be free of her stepmother and all her old wive's tales a fictive world without origin and without truth. Yet, much to Rose's chagrin, Flo's story comes 'true': the fabled undertaker who sings, '*Her brow is like the snowdrift/Her throat is like the swan*' (58), shows up in the guise of a minister 'saying *snows*, a poetic-sounding word' (60), and talking of swans. Rose must try to take credit for this situation – make it her own fiction – if she is to avoid believing anything Flo has told her: 'Her imagination seemed to have created this reality, a reality she was not prepared for at all' (62). But if this is so, her 'shameful smells; humiliation' (63) are bizarre proof that 'truth' has not receded as she hoped, and that she can only sabotage herself by refusing to heed Flo's warnings. Unless, of course, her consent might still turn the whole shameful business into parody.

By making herself 'Victim and accomplice' (64) both, Rose manages to reify her usual ideology even as she mocks Flo's naïveté. For, should the minister prove to be Flo's imagined 'White Slaver,' Rose's escape would subvert the usual conclusion to the story; on the other hand, a truly reverend minister would be in quite as much danger from Lolita as she from him. Stranger still, by making the minister a paragon of her own scorn, Rose could actually flout the conventions of decency and indecency alike: 'But he remained on call, so to speak, for years and years, ready to slip into place at a critical moment, without even any regard, later on, for husband or lovers. What recommended him? She could never understand it. His simplicity, his arrogance, his perversely appealing lack of handsomeness, even of ordinary grown-up masculinity?' (65). Probably it is the minister's contempt which puts him beyond good and evil, which serves to make her superior, too, to hobgoblin little minds. Though 'the little bag with ten dollars ... rubbing its reminder against her skin' is there to insist on her close call: 'She couldn't stop getting Flo's messages, even with that' (65).

Ultimately, Rose can only resort to indeterminacy to escape, after the fact, the threat of what *might* have happened. She now affirms another version of 'the freeplay of the world and without truth, without origin' through Flo's story of a friend named Mavis who once assumed the name Florence Farmer, 'To give everybody the idea she was really the other one, Frances Farmer,' the movie star. But, this time, she need not even worry about 'the tension of freeplay with presence' (Derrida 263), since, like a good parodist, 'Florence' has altered her model just enough to let the viewer take the blame for the mistaken identity. Rose admires such daring, in other words, because the origin of 'Florence's' name, like the origin of Derrida's sign, 'is "always already" absent' (Fischer 34), and so she would not be responsible for any consequences. It is a technique which Rose has learned long ago from Ralph Gillespie, this 'magical, releasing way' (204) of transforming herself by self-consciously doubling someone else. This, after all, was what she always wanted, 'to manage a transformation like that. To dare it; to get away with it, to enter on preposterous adventures in your own, but newly named, skin' (66).

Rose's ability to make meaning undecidable – or to find a contemporary means of self-invention – is still the source of one of her most desperate self-deceptions in 'The Beggar Maid.' Here, the plot concerns Rose's decision to marry Patrick Blatchford, a man whose 'chivalric notions, which he pretended to mock' (76), help to throw a romantic haze over both her poverty and his own social condescension. For Patrick only pretends to be a parodist undercutting old authorities; secretly, he dreams of Rose taking the part of the Beggar Maid, 'meek and voluptuous,' in the painting by Burne-Jones, while he plays King Cophetua, 'sharp and swarthy ... even in his trance of passion' (79). The image, of course, is false to both of them, creating impossible expectations for their marriage. Rose has no illusion that, wanting to worship her, he really believes in her superiority. To the contrary: 'You despise me. You despise my family and my background and you think you are doing me a *great favor* – ' (94). But then we have seen her play the victim before – to Flo. In fact, Rose despises Patrick *and* she wants to be worshipped. Her secret desire to substitute *The White Goddess* (80) for the painting of *The Beggar Maid* shows, in its very reliance on aesthetic conventions, how both partners can only pretend, at this point, to love. Yet Rose's motives prove ultimately to be further than Patrick's from 'real' love, unless narcissism counts, as metafiction does, as a self-reflexive form of the 'real thing.'

Years later, Rose will ask 'friends and lovers and party acquaintances whom she might never see again' (96–7) to choose among several possible motives for her marriage in spite of her better knowledge: she herself will reduce these motives to 'pity or greed or cowardice or vanity' (98). Of the four, she confesses, 'it was really vanity, it was vanity pure and simple, to resurrect him, to bring him back his happiness. To see if she could do that. She could not resist such a test of power' (97). And yet 'What she never said to anybody, never confided, was that she sometimes thought it had not been pity or greed or cowardice or vanity but something quite different, like a vision of happiness. In view of everything else she had told she could hardly tell that' (98).

Rose's tactic of discrediting others is finally turned against herself; she makes herself look worse in public than she really is. But her private vision approaches the reformed Del Jordan's heightened view of reality: 'Then it was as if they were in different though identical-seeming skins, as if there existed a radiantly kind and innocent Rose and Patrick, hardly ever visible, in the shadow of their usual selves' (98). What she wants to believe is that she alone is martyred to a vision of love which other people, including Patrick, cannot share.

In the dramatic moment, however, her immediate motive had been rather different: 'She was so moved, made so gentle and wistful, by the sight of him, that she wanted to give him something, some surprising bounty, she wished to undo his unhappiness. Then she had a compelling picture of herself. She was running softly into Patrick's carrel, she was throwing her arms around him from behind, she was giving everything back to him. Would he take it from her, would he still want it? ... This was a violent temptation for her; it was barely resistable [sic]. She had an impulse to hurl herself. Whether it was off a cliff or into a warm bed of welcoming grass and flowers, she really could not tell' (96). The emphasis, in both versions, falls on a variant of the word *irresistible*; but what she can't resist is a 'compelling picture of herself.' Narcissism is really the only emotion she seems to feel. How, then, has she still managed to deceive herself in the narrative moment?

The narrative disruption of the epilogue shows how actual motives have been masked by a continuing strategy of narrative undecidability (though Rose decides in the moment that Patrick's motives are at fault). Some nine years after her divorce (and eighteen years after her engagement), she has had a chance to repeat the experience: 'She knew that was how she had seen him; she knows it, because it happened again ... And she had the same feeling that this was a person she was bound to, that by a certain magical, yet possible trick, they could find and trust each other, and that to begin this all that she had to do was go up and touch him on the shoulder, surprise him with his happiness' (98). Patrick, of course, is not as eager to repeat the experience; the 'face' he makes at her, 'a timed explosion of disgust and loathing' (99), bears no resemblance to his former, radical innocence. Many more people than he, however, long 'to sabotage themselves' (99); she knows this from her experience as an interviewer. 'But she was not really able to understand how she could be an enemy. How could anybody hate Rose so much, at the very moment when she was ready to come forward with her good will, her smiling confession of exhaustion, her air of diffident faith in civilized overtures? Oh, Patrick could. Patrick could' (99). It seems that the only radical innocence she can allow is her own. But even this latest portrait of the martyr offers a new and 'compelling picture of herself' by which she merely tries to soothe her wounded vanity.

The narrator's strategy of making meaning undecidable turns out to be little more than the character's last-ditch attempt to avoid self-knowledge. And so narrative disarrangement comes to offer far more than 'its continual commentary on its own tentativeness' (Mathews, 'Disarrangement' 192), since it is Rose's self-saving tentativeness which is finally discredited. The usual intentions of the realist narrator are none the less transcended by Rose's decision to take her hearers into her confidence, since she demonstrates how their understanding of life can only be fictive. Munro's implied invitation to the reader to share in the necessary fabrication of meaning suggests her growing preference for a more contemporary, more self-conscious style of narration: 'What has *always* been a truism of fiction, though rarely made conscious, is brought to the fore in modern texts: the making of fictive worlds and the constructive, creative functioning of language itself are now self-consciously shared by author and reader. The latter is no longer asked merely to recognize that fictional objects are "like life"; he is asked to participate in the creation of worlds and of meaning, through language' (Hutcheon, *Narcissistic* 30). The object of such narrative self-consciousness, however, is not freedom from meaning, much less from self-knowledge. As fiction begins 'to internalize or constitute a self-criticism of its own form' (Hutcheon, *A Theory* 72), it forces a latent self-consciousness on the teller. Rose's narrative 'narcissism' begins to deconstruct the whole ideology of her martyrdom; the 'martyr' wants to escape self-knowledge by her very profession of it.

Rose is even able to resume this martyred role before she is quite done blaming herself: 'She could not resist such a test of power. She explained then that she had paid for it ... She hopes she did not tell people (but thinks she did) that she used to beat her head against the bedpost, that she smashed a gravy boat through a dining-room window ... Sometimes she flew at him; sometimes he beat her' (97). Here, too, what she leaves out of the public story – 'What she never said to anybody' – shows how, in her heart of hearts, she is really justified, an innocent believer in happiness, while Patrick is the one convicted of rejecting love. The frame of what is *told* about her thus turns into an ironic double of what she *tells*, creating 'discourse *within* and *about* discourse' (Hutcheon, *A Theory* 72). Munro's parody of Rose's act of narration therefore invites us to decode a story which is far more self-questioning than the one in which Rose 'confesses' a truth she doesn't even believe.

At the end of 'Mischief,' Rose finds herself in almost the same dramatic situation, though now there is no one whom she can 'take' into her narrative 'confidence.' And so her reasons for taking a lover can have no public elaboration outside of what she recalls about her disgrace; this time she has to face the fact that it was 'vanity pure and simple': 'On the bus going home Rose looked down her dress at the sweat blooming between her breasts and could have fainted at the splendor of herself' (115). Unfortunately, for the sake of her dawning self-knowledge, she is betrayed by Clifford who says, 'It's only mischief' (124). Humiliated more than she is devastated, she manages to humiliate Patrick in his turn by pretending to have consummated the affair. Her 'mashed pride' (132) casts desperately about for some covering to her wounded vanity: 'She would rather not think of any of this. She prefers to see through metal window-frames of dripping cedars and salmonberry bushes and the proliferating mortal greenery of the rain forest some small views of lost daily life. Anna's yellow slicker. The smoke from Jocelyn's foul fire' (133). But this belated return to the narrative strategies of realism is transparent, even to her, as an evasion. For how can she possibly imagine herself as the *femme fatale* when the adultery took place, *literally*, under the wife's nose? Her yearning to flout the conventions of married love has only led her into unintentional self-parody.

The usual ironic epilogue puts the story of 'Rose's immaturity, ambivalence and shilly-shallying' into quite a new perspective this time, rebutting the criticism that the story has only a 'single axis' which makes it 'too static' (Martin 114). For Rose, who has had a habit since childhood of 'play[ing] a superior, an onlooker's part' (*Who* 41) – much like Wilde's spectator aesthete, Lord Henry Wotton, in *Dorian Gray* – is literally supplanted by Jocelyn who 'seemed to hover above them making comforting noises of assent' (134). Now the dilettante is no longer shielded 'from the sordid perils of actual existence' (*Intentions* 174), as Wilde would have it. Rather, Rose is well aware 'that they had made a fool of her, cheated her, shown her a glaring lack' (135), first of all because she is hardly a dispenser of happiness any more, dizzy with her own power, but needy and vulnerable; secondly, because she is known in more than the carnal sense, has in fact been stripped of her usual advantages of disguise and deceit. Though she tries to make herself the victim again, and accuses them both more bitterly than she had Flo, she can no longer even pretend to virtue. For the wife has the better claim to be a martyr. And so she must hate Jocelyn for exposing her self-deception, not to mention her real lack of power.

It is only Simon's death which makes Rose see at last that she is not 'the only person who could seriously lack power' (177). Yet Flo's earlier stories might have prepared her, if only she had known, for the sort of disorder which is a harbinger of death: 'Flo used to say she could tell when some woman was going off the track' (178). But Flo's own terrible decline and derangement merely revive Rose's cherished fantasy: 'She pictured herself going to Hanratty and looking after Flo, living with her, taking care of her for as long as was necessary ... She wasn't so far gone as to imagine Flo fitting comfortably into this picture, settling down to a life of gratitude. But the crankier Flo got, the milder and more patient Rose would become, and who, then, could accuse her of egotism and frivolity? The vision did not survive the first two days of being home' (184–5). The old story of who is going to be the better martyr has become totally irrelevant; the role can have little meaning once Flo's condition puts it out of reach. Now only a new sort of story can appease Rose's terror of disorder, since a senile inmate of the County Home whom she finds spelling every word she hears not only shows 'some woman ... going off the track' (178) but also finding another way through the maze: 'It seemed she had only the thinnest thread to follow, meandering through that emptiness or confusion that nobody on this side can do more than guess at. But she didn't lose it, she followed it through to the end' (187).

To this point, Rose herself has always seized upon the failures of language to determine meaning, as in the example of 'the War (called, in Rose's earliest childhood, not the First, but the Last, War)' (3). Her father's incomprehensible words had likewise revealed people as being mastered by language, or language even speaking with purposes of its own, beyond the speaker's intent:

> 'Macaroni, pepperoni, Botticelli, beans – '
> What could that mean? Rose used to repeat such things herself. She could never ask him. The person who spoke these words and the person who spoke to her as her father were not the same, though they seemed to occupy the same space.   (4)

But the sceptic who has been made profoundly aware of 'the gulf' (190) that lies between herself and her past is forced to reconsider the source of this gap between words and things. For what she discovers in the old woman 'waiting, in the middle of her sightless eventless day, till up from somewhere popped another word' (187–8), is that language also bears whatever powers of communication (or community) we are willing to assign it: 'Rose wondered what the words were like, when she held them in her mind. Did they carry their usual meaning, or any meaning at all? Were they like words in dreams or in the minds of young children, each one marvelous and distinct and alive as a new animal? This one limp and clear, like a jellyfish, that one hard and mean and secretive, like a horned snail. They could be austere and comical as top hats, or smooth and lively and flattering as ribbons. A parade of private visitors, not over yet' (187–8). The rhetorical shift from interrogation to assertion suggests that words, for Rose at least, have begun to close the gulf, since the gap lies in the user's intent – in what she wants to believe (or disbelieve).

Even Rose is now surprised by a latent connnection which she herself will make. After the 'obscene or despairing' words which come to her mind,

> without prompting came another.
> 'Forest. F-O-R-E-S-T.'
> 'Celebrate,' said Rose suddenly.
> 'C-E-L-E-B-R-A-T-E.'   (187)

Sensing for once that life makes victims of us all, Rose is finally chastened by the old woman's lack of self-pity, by a total absence of 'egotism and frivolity.' And suddenly she knows that life, even life reduced to its lowest common denominator, is still shared, is still worth celebrating.

The transfiguration of Rose's whole way of seeing is now signalled in a subsequent dream about Flo, 'radiant, satisfied' in 'a throne-like chair, spelling out words in a clear authoritative voice ... and looking pleased with herself, for showing powers she had kept secret till now' (188). People, it seems, do have some power over language, not just the other way around. But it would also seem that Flo's lingering power is ultimately vested in the language of Rose's consent to it. While this is hardly Del Jordan's old vision of things 'held still and held together – radiant, everlasting,' Rose's darker truth of human decay spells out what is 'real' without divorcing it from the 'true.' The author of 'black fables' discovers mystery and magic in the very 'obscenity' to which we are reduced by life.

Finally, Rose accepts the body of the (parodic, step-) mother she has rejected all her life. By donning Flo's motley wig, she assumes her likeness to Flo instead of her superior difference: 'Rose stuck it on her own head, to continue the comedy, and Flo laughed so that she rocked back and forth in her crib' (191–2). In this willingness to laugh at herself, and to rejoice in the face of her mortality, Rose could be the daughter of Hagar Shipley in Margaret Laurence's *The Stone Angel*. Her final acceptance of the mother even comes about in her playing of a role to comfort the dying woman. For Flo, who has begun to wander in a past where Rose's father is still alive, now frets about the

> 'gallstones they took out of me[.] Fifteen! One as big as a pullet's egg. I got them somewhere. I'm going to take them home.' She pulled at the sheets, searching. 'They were in a bottle.'
> 'I've got them already,' said Rose. 'I took them home.'
> 'Did you? Did you show your father?'
> 'Yes.'
> 'Oh, well, that's where they are then,' said Flo, and she lay down and closed her eyes. (192)

Once she rediscovers the mother's 'body' as her own, Rose, like Laurence's 'stone angel,' finds her ultimate truth in a lie.

Only when she learns to stop 'reporting antics' (209), does Rose find another purpose in story beyond parody. The 'wave of kindness, of sympathy and forgiveness' that she feels from Ralph Gillespie leads her past her scorn and mockery of others to see story-telling as a window, if not a bridge, to other lives: 'What could she say about herself and Ralph Gillespie, except that she felt his life, close, closer than the lives of men she'd loved, one slot over from her own?' (210). On the narrative level, Rose has finally become the story-teller who, looking back on all her previous tellings, acknowledges the truth of her own duplicity, the self-concealment of her parodic doublings. But on the dramatic level, the teller, even while allowing for the fact of human sympathy, affirms a reality which can only, ever, be *other* and so, in that sense, be ungraspable.

'Her imagination,' Rose had once insisted, 'seemed to have created this reality, a reality she was not prepared for at all' (62). The ultimate success of *Who Do You Think You Are?* is that it manages to uncover the process by which 'reality' is necessarily imagined. By means of this largely interrogative method, Munro parodies the comfortable narrative strategies and judgments of *Lives of Girls and Women* without denying the ultimate mystery of existence. Because its answers are harder won, the metafictional questions asked by *Who Do You Think You Are?* linger in the mind long after the 'radiance' of *Lives* is but a fading glow.

10

'Roll Me Over':
Parodic Repetition and Freedom
in *Badlands*

History is a more complicated muse in Robert Kroetsch's *Badlands* than many readers want to believe. The usual critical commonplace about the novel is that, by throwing away some old field notes, 'Anna frees herself from the dead past, reverses her father's will, turns the Badlands upside down and reaches the source' (Grace 31), or that she is finally 'free from the past that has held her prisoner' (Davidson 136). Yet Kroetsch, responding obliquely to his critics in an essay on the Canadian novel of the 1970s, suggests that the past remains to be confronted: 'Our genealogies are the narratives of a discontent with a history that lied to us, violated us, erased us even. We wish to locate our dislocation, and to do so we must confront the impossible sum of our traditions. Like the Spanish-American writers from whom we presently learn so much, we recognize that we can be freed into our own lives only by terrible and repeated acts of perception' ('Nationalism' vi).

At the end of her story, Anna Dawe writes, '*We sang together, that awful song about rolling over in the clover, because that was the only song we both remembered and could sing long enough to see us through. We walked out of there hand in hand, arm in arm, holding each other. We walked all the way out. And we did not once look back, not once, ever*' (270). 'This,' writes Robert Lecker, 'is the most ironic statement in the book, and also its greatest lie – one that should alert us to the beginning of a grand inversion process. For no sooner has Anna announced that "*we did not once look back*" than she proceeds to tell us the story that brings her to the point at which she tells us she did not look back' (*Robert Kroetsch* 81). 'Parody,' as Kroetsch says in another context, 'becomes a way into ending' ('Nationalism' x) – though not, he would add, without 'terrible and repeated acts of perception.'

Roll me over in the clover and do it again.

The 'awful song' does not even free the virgin from her inhibition, much less from her father's ghost. Dramatically speaking, it is mere whistling in the dark, 'long enough to see us through'; in that sense, her journey west has not enabled her either to reach her dead father or to free herself from his will. But in terms of the story Anna is about to tell, the 'song' announces her intent, at least, to transgress his words by rolling them over and embedding them in her narrative. Her second, literary journey is an attempt to free herself through parody.

What Lecker sees as 'the beginning of a grand inversion process' does not, however, go nearly far enough in defining the nature and function of parody in the novel. While '[i]ronic inversion is a characteristic of all parody' as Linda Hutcheon defines it (*A Theory* 6), its chief characteristic is the 'historical awareness' (4) that it entails. Parody does not so much reject the past as transform it; it offers 'a workable and effective stance toward the past in its paradoxical strategy of repetition as a source of freedom' (Hutcheon 10).

The nature of parody, in Lecker's view, is characterized solely by rejection: Dawe refuses 'to be storied' (88), and so his field notes reject 'the female claim in time that comes to be synonymous with storytelling' (79). 'Anna's account of the Dawe expedition becomes a sustained parody of the quest motif, and a sustained mocking of the figure who believes that she can find her form by giving form …To grant Anna her freedom we must argue that, like Dawe, she rejects the written word from the start, that she is not searching for a cathartic retelling of her father's story, but for a nontelling, for a form of narrative that defies conventional narrative expectations' (Lecker 84, 94). If the function of parody is limited to negation, however, then the only possible new telling is antistory, 'the death of narrative Dawe so ardently pursues' (93).

If Dawe's silence could free him to live in antistory, we would understand 'why none of the male characters in *Badlands* ever speaks except through Anna's imagining, why what Dawe "writes" is "undecipherable," and why we learn, ironically, that Dawe had discovered "the end of words" right from the start' (Lecker 80). But Dawe's silence is, in fact, his suicide. In 1962, at the age of eighty-one, he takes his daughter's canoe out on the lake, though '*I couldn't swim a stroke ... Still can't*' (*Badlands* 233). '*And we found the canoe all right,*' Anna notes sardoni- cally, '*at least we didn't lose eighty dollars worth of canoe. But we never found the body*' (269). The man who kept daily field notes for the last forty-six years of his life has obviously not come to 'the end of words right from the start'; his belated rejection of words is really a refusal to live. So to name Dawe as the hero of parody is really to identify the genre as a mode of textual suicide.

For another theorist, parody originates in the 'primordial struggle between tribes, cultures and languages' which first gave rise to 'the novelistic word' (Bakhtin 50). Alongside the more 'straightforward Greek genres' such as epic and lyric 'there flourished parodic and traves- tying forms that kept alive the memory of the ancient linguistic struggle' (Bakhtin 67). Mockery, even for the Russian formalist, is none the less a single element in the function of parody; its larger use is 'dialogic.' The language of parody, like the language of the novel, becomes 'a dialogue between points of view, each with its own concrete language that cannot be translated into the other' (76). But the 'quarrel' in parody is formal as well as linguistic; parody creates a dialogue between historical texts and forms as much as between persons and languages.

The language of *Badlands* is clearly that of a dialogue; Anna Dawe serves as a first-person chorus on the third-person narrative of her father's expedition. From the outset she presents herself as a different, more literary, kind of archaeologist from her father, working in a field com- posed of his old field notes: '*I don't know that I ever received a letter from my absent father. He sent us instead, left us, deposited for me to find, his field notes*' (2). Later, she elaborates more fully both her corre- spondence to and difference from her father: '*Surely, yes, I worked at the waiting; as he had worked at his starting out. I studied the documents*' (138). And so her role as reader – as the decoder of these old field notes – requires her to enter his 'field':

> But somewhere in the course of that first journey that was his own –
> somewhere, somehow, he shook himself free of any need to share
> even his sufferings with another human being. His field notes, after
> that summer, were less and less concerned with his crew, his
> dangers, his days of futile prospecting, his moments of discovery,

his weariness, his ambitions, his frustrations. They became scientific
descriptions of the size and location of bones, of the composition of
the matrix, of the methods of extraction and preservation ...

And I had to visit those badlands where his success began.
Because, there, in that beautiful and nightmare season – he ceased to
dare to love. (139)

Anna enters her father's 'field' in still another literal sense – as a note-
taker – as she implies one time when she forgets to make the necessary
note: '*And if the stories I heard fifty-six years later in Drumheller were*
true, then the two women were sisters, and the blonde was not really
named America – nor for that matter was she blonde – and the dark-
haired woman in green had a name I didn't bother to write down and so
lost from memory' (76). But because the commentator is sceptical of the
'narrative tricks' of her father's field notes, she remains cautious about
the narrative impulse: '*And I assumed the occasion would demand of her*
a formal telling, would sponsor the curious little narrative tricks of a
male adventure' (27). And yet her own attempt '*to mediate the story*' (3)
must implicate her in her father's methods; the archaeologist has left her
nothing but fragments which she must piece together. And so she lets him
speak for both of them when he says to Sinnott, the photographer,
'There is nothing that does not leave its effect. We study the accumulated
remains' (118).

Anna Dawe's study of her father's literary 'remains' is unusually conscious, all the same, of the mechanics and process of their production:
'He broke off the enlarging sentence, surprised at his own unscientific
noting of the world. He scratched, righteously, pompously, in his
cramped hand on the next line' (11); 'And he wrote quickly, staving off
the words that swarmed into his mind, *He is safe and sound*; and he
shoved the pencil and field book into his pockets' (37); 'Dawe, pretending he was busy, pretending he wasn't afraid: *The hole is empty. Redun-*
dant. Be careful of the sun. Redundant. A hunchback will, easily, if
exerting himself beyond the natural, suffer from anoxia. He looked at
what he had written. He felt safer. *Redundant*, he dared to add' (142).
Anna's obsession with her father's act of writing thus implies a virtual
mirroring of her own narrative processes, confessed more fully, if still
obliquely, when Dawe can no longer write *in* the field: 'Sullen, then,
sullen, in the last clinging gesture, absurdly, he unreeled to his mind's eye

the field notes he had faked for the world from Web's reluctantly postulated observations: *Sixteen pairs of ventral ribs*. He clung to that, trying to imagine the neat bones arranged neatly' (196). In a sense, all of Anna's story is made up of such field notes she has 'faked for the world,' since she has not been as close to the 'source' as even her father had been in the weeks he was laid up with a cast on his leg.

Anna's need to mirror her father's process of writing is further elaborated, at one point, as her desire to *become* the product: 'And then, holding the field book on his knee like a baby, a child, he recognized, understood, admitted that this, finally, might be his way of communicating with his unborn descendants' (34). And yet she cannot hide the anger which accompanies this false consolation: 'He was jealous rather of a found armful of bones of *Ornithomimus*, fragments of turtle shells, the teeth of Upper Cretaceous fish: and he wrote, in a fit of love and jealousy that should have been a poet's, scrawled in a quiet prose that hardly contained his only enduring passion, his furious need to dispossess and recover' (58). Her 'quiet prose' has finally exposed her own 'furious need' to dispossess the self-possessed hero, as well as to recover an absent father.

The linguistic dialogue of Anna's narrative thus threatens at times to slip formally into monologue. For, as much as she tries to let the men have their say, several stylistic signatures are carried over from her announced monologues to the men's purported story; her personal voice begins to impose upon the 'impersonal' narration. Anxious in the first-person to distinguish herself from her father's mistress, Anna Yellowbird, she refers to her as 'that Anna' (2, 25, etc.); but Anna Yellowbird appears as well in the third-person story as 'that Anna' (230, 248, etc.) Likewise, Anna Dawe's private grammatical fondness for the 'yes' appositive shows up in the telling of the male story: '*Yes, he was not born with his famous limp*' (210, and cf. 259, 269), she says in her own voice, though not before the third-person narrator comments on 'young Tune who had learned to worship – yes, that was hardly too strong a word – Tune worshipping the old master' (171, and cf. 183, 192). There is more than a little irony, then, when she breaks off the story of the men to comment on it: '*Total and absurd male that he was, he assumed, like a male author, an omniscience that was not ever his*' (76). No matter how much she gives herself up to the men's language, she is guilty of projection; she assumes an omniscience that is not hers in her very attempt to reproduce the conventions of male narrative for them. If *Badlands* does not turn into Anna's quarrel with herself, that is only because she quotes so extensively from 'actual' documents; her father's words speak for themselves, even when they are taken out of context. The field notes thus work to prevent monologue, always forcing her back into real dialogue with her own family history.

At the same time, Anna's story suggests that she is not just her father's daughter, but also the daughter of Sinclair Ross's Mrs Bentley. This larger dialogue between texts helps to govern the reader's expectations about inner dialogic form in *Badlands*, though Anna herself has not read a word of *As For Me and My House*. A minor parallel of names ('Dawson's store' in Ross) first points to the larger parallel between 'fathers' who lose their adoptive sons in the two novels (Kroetsch 108–9, Ross 115–16). The boys, Steve and Tune, are both characterized by their love of music, though the nickname of the second signals a parodic function: his piano-playing in a whore-house becomes the inversion of young Steve's fascination with the piano-playing of the minister's wife (Ross 47, 69). By such means, we are advised how to read the parallel narrative situations in each book, since both male protagonists, who are seemingly silent and evasive, have managed to exclude a wife and a daughter, respectively, from their affections. Thus each woman writes to possess a reluctant male, though Anna Dawe is at once more open, and more openly mocking, about the 'virtues' of such a hopeless desire.

The exegetical strategy of both narrators also happens to depend on an enigmatic document – whether a wordless painting or a hoard of '*cryptic field notes*' (259) – which must be deciphered or expanded to solve the problem of relationship. Here, however, begins a double process of inversion: in *Badlands*, the male takes over authorship of the daily field note from the diarist in *As For Me and My House*; and the field note as historical document undercuts the future-oriented plot of the diary, itself a scheme for second-guessing the future. For the field notes left to Anna Dawe are mediate, not immediate in time, leaving the peruser historically marooned, '*born one generation too late*,' like old Dawe himself on the trail of '*those first great collectors of dinosaur bones*,' equally determined '*not to be deterred by a mere error in chronology*' (138). Mrs Bentley, in other words, has the living man on whom she tries to project her will into the future, while Anna has only the legacy of his written words.

The differing functions of form in the two novels should not obscure an essential likeness in the two narrators. Anna Dawe, as we have already seen, wants to make her father's writing over in her own image: 'And then, holding the field book on his knee like a baby, a child, he recognized, understood, admitted that this, finally, might be his way of communicating with his unborn descendants' (34). Her hope, however, is immediately denied in one simple sentence by which her father evades her: '*I despise words*, he wrote: he stared at the sentence, enjoying it. Writing it down had freed him, in some way he did not fully comprehend' (34). So, too, Mrs Bentley wants to make her evasive husband and his pencil drawings over in her own image as an *artiste manquée*, although other narrative witnesses see strength in his 'fatalism' instead of defeat (see above 133–4). Even the prospect of the 'fossil remains of the prehistoric lizards' (Ross 100) in these same badlands makes Mrs Bentley despair, perverting her husband's 'strength and fatalism' into her own view of 'futility' (Ross 102–3). Anna Dawe's similar desperation comes from her sense that she is left in the ambiguous position of the paleontologist himself, reconstructing fragments of narrative even as he had tried to put together 'the skeleton that was not the beast, not even the bones of the sought beast but the chemical replacement of what had been the bones' (56). On this level, parody convicts Anna of Mrs Bentley's folly of trying to replace her husband's view of life with her own.

William Dawe's final silence forces his daughter all the same to reconsider his 'text' and to 'confront the impossible sum' of her 'tradition.' His death, in other words, enforces a likeness she wants to reject, that hidden kinship which makes her whole legacy impossible. For on the day he died, Anna, who was vexed at being found drunk, '*dwelt on the occasion of Tune's death. Perhaps because my father reprimanded me and I wanted, in turn, to reprimand him. Or because, when I started to cry, he would not say one word, give me one glance, that confessed he was sorry*' (233–4). After the fact, she does understand '*why he looked so* bad,' why she '*should have guessed [why] he was lying*' about what '*[b]roke his heart*' (234). For the death of Dawe's surrogate son is still as real and as hurtful as it was on that day forty-six years ago. No matter how long he tries, his responsibility for Tune's death cannot be evaded. Anna only means to wring a confession from him, not knowing that he would rather die than confess. But what if he is forcing her to bear a like responsibility in driving him to his death? Could his suicide be a means of shifting the blame? The field notes refuse to say. In the circumstance, how could she help but mock such a deadly legacy?

Quotation is her only remaining tool, not just to mock, but to extort a confession from the grave. Dawe writes: '*A cave is a pocket of night, cooling and dark, saved from the day. But a cave smells* – He could not write it. Of death' (149). She can thus fill in the blanks with her own view of things, make herself superior to his fear. And so she adds with a vengeance, 'A cave smelled, as he had not expected, of a denned coyote, a wintering snake. Of death.' Death, after all, is the medium in which the paleontologist has to work. His inability to face it makes his whole livelihood more than a little suspect. The outlook which Anna imposes upon her father turns out to be, like Lecker's critical view, a strategic series of deferral, resistance to closure, evasion, silence, antistory, and even parody itself, all designed to escape the taint of generation and the anxiety of influence. Anna's only redeeming grace in such a bald manipulation of her father's words is that she shows promise of the courage she will need to face up to her part in his death.

The postmodern critic would still promote an escape from mortality by having Anna share her father's preference for parody, for rejection of 'the written word' (!) in exchange for 'the tall-tale tradition' (Lecker 94): 'The writer who becomes the oral poet is freed from the conundrum: everything is possible when spoken by one whose aim is to embellish, backtrack, invite interjection, refuse closure' (Lecker 95). This ingenious notion of orality as freedom from death is oddly contradicted by the notion of silence as freedom. But then Anna, who is neither silent nor oral, is not particularly flattering to men who hold escapist notions: '*As if we didn't know all the answers long before they asked their absurd questions ... They have their open spaces, and translate them into a fabled hunting. We have only time to survive in, time, without either lies or mystery or suspense; we live and then die in time*' (27).

Anna, given to the temporal sequence of narrative, *writes*; nothing could be more obvious. But the very idea of writing is associated with permanence. For the text survives the moment of writing and reading; Dawe's notes continue to speak though he is dead. Anna's own chapter titles might even be a sign of her 'desire for permanence and closure' since she has borrowed the technique from Sinnott, the photographer, who offers a way 'to frame experience ... In fact, the structure of her story can be seen as a set of frames enclosing the scenes she wants to preserve' (Lecker 89). And yet photographs, as Susan Sontag suggests, can only 'give mock forms of possession: of the past, the present, even the future' (167).

Sinnott's claim that he alone captures the vanishing moment is mocked at once by Dawe who says, 'You make the world stand still ... I try to make it live again' (128). Yet Sinnott also ridicules Dawe's notion of restoring the past: 'Then let me save you from your inevitable failure ... Tell me where you might possibly be reached and I'll send you the consolation of my masterpiece: The Charlatan Being Himself.' Sinnott's 'Travelling Emporium' is the work of one who well understands how 'Cameras miniaturize experience, transform history into spectacle' (Sontag, *Photography* 109–10). Though he cheerfully confesses himself to be a charlatan too, he continues his assault on the world, *taking* its picture and substituting it for the reality. He seems to know that 'the force of photographic images comes from their being material realities in their own right, richly informative deposits left in the wake of whatever emitted them, potent means for turning the tables on reality – for turning *it* into a shadow' (Sontag 180). And so he presumes, through a collection of images, to capture time itself.

The writer inevitably takes a different attitude to time from the photographer. As Kroetsch remarks in critical commentary on Michael Ondaatje's *Coming Through Slaughter*, the photograph of Buddy Bolden and his band is only a 'static arrangement,' enclosed in 'a grave-like frame ... Here is the "real thing," anticipating, refusing, creating, destroying the fiction that is to come. Photo: arrest. Killing. Going' (*Treachery* 112). Photography and realism, for Kroetsch, both end in fixity, in death; language, as he notes in quoting Foucault, at least breaks the silence, ' "erects itself vertically against death" ' (*Treachery* 109).

Still, there is another temporal problem with the image, as opposed to language, which Susan Sontag defines: 'Photography implies that we know about the world if we accept it as the camera records it. But this is the opposite of understanding, which starts from *not* accepting the world as it looks ... In contrast to the amorous relation, which is based on how something looks, understanding is based on how it functions. And functioning takes place in time, and must be explained in time. Only that which narrates can make us understand' (Sontag, *Photography* 23). While Lorraine York identifies Sontag's position with the 'bullying word' of modernist poetics, York herself mistakes the nature of this freedom allowed by a poststructuralist semiotics of photography: 'the viewer,' she says, 'is not forced to understand [through words], but free to create for himself or herself a variety of readings of the visual image' (York 17). And yet the viewer does not create 'a variety of readings' through still more visual images; the writers she mentions all use words – by definition. So, too, Anna Dawe's decision to 'mediate the story' defines her need to explain her father in time, through the temporal medium of words set in succession, rather than to accept his image in space.

There seems to be only one way for Kroetsch in which the photographer's art can be a surrogate of the writer's – in the text which accompanies the image. Anna and the photographer both make witty use of titles; as it turns out, they even have one in common. Sinnott, composing a portrait, 'announced his title: "Chinese Cook and Cookstove on Open Deck" ' (125); Anna's fourth chapter is shortened simply to 'Chinese Cook on Open Deck' (12). It is their common tone, however, which points to a shared practice of parody; through Sinnott, Anna can explore new ways of 'framing' the 'hero' as villain, of ripping the heroic 'word away from its object, disunif[ying] the two' (Bakhtin 55).

'Pilot Looking for Trouble' (125), Sinnott offers his ironic tribute to Web, the irrepressible clown. 'Vanishing Man Makes First Appearance' (111), Anna declares with equal irony of the photographer in chapter 22. 'Leader Awaiting His Calling' (126), Sinnott scoffs at Dawe, while Anna scoffs at her father too in a subsequent chapter title, 'Looking for Fossils' (142). Now Dawe, who is hunting bones, turns into one of his own fossils as Anna tries to flesh out something he wrote 'on page 39, Book A, of his field notes for 1916, then tore off the bottom half of the page' (143). Of his picture of a vulture in flight, Sinnott likewise remarks sardonically, 'Waiting Bird'; 'Flatboat and Waiting Birds' (235), Anna deliberately insinuates her father's guilt into a 'still' of Tune's unmarked grave. Though Sinnott's titles are not likely to be recorded in Dawe's field notes, Anna's comic invention becomes a playful twist on her father's claim to Sinnott that 'You make the world stand still ... I try to make it live again' (128). 'See the Monsters Returning to Life' (246), Anna and the photographer finally mock with the same voice.

Anna has reason, none the less, to fear the 'Monster' returning to life: for her initial desire to follow in her father's footsteps seems to have been incestuous. Writing about the stone house where the men once spoke to a woman who was hostage to her husband's jealousy, she finally admits on the narrative level what had to be repressed before she came west: '*I was like that woman. Except that my fortress, my prison, was on the shore of Georgian Bay, and ships not flatboats came by in the night ... And when the stranger came to my shore, he, my father, was that stranger. There are no truths, only correspondences*' (45). But on first approaching that stone house, she had lacked the ironic distance she needed to control a sudden flood of memories. She said simply, ' "*I was frightened. But I touched his back. And he kissed my breasts –* " ... *And I had to ask her then. I was pulling up my panties, straightening my white skirt, when I saw against the glare – the sun shines in hell too – a deserted stone house ... "What was he – like?" I asked her*' (262–3). In the dramatic moment, she is still eager to collapse her difference from the old Indian woman into virtual identity with her father's lover. And so this first repetition of her past is not at all parodic; it has the character of a repetition compulsion.

The second journey does not even begin until Anna Yellowbird wilfully misunderstands her. Then, she '*had saved me; in that instant had brought me back, turned me around, somehow.*' After '*a lifetime of wondering*' (263), the daughter is freed from a love which is narcissistic and self-reflexive. Anna Yellowbird makes her '*ready for real laughter*' (264), inverts the whole direction of the quest, leads her away from sterile repetition of her father's voyage down the Red Deer River to a quest for '*the high source of the river.*'

Anna Yellowbird stands at the beginning of Anna Dawe's journey into narrative as a version of the muse of parody. Flinging the photographs '*up at the bear's balls*' (269), she mocks the potency and authority of the threatening male. '*And then I could do it too. I opened my purse, took out the field book I had carried like a curse for ten years ... And I took that last field book with the last pompous sentence he ever wrote, the only poem he ever wrote, a love poem, to me, his only daughter, and I threw it into the lake where it too might drown*' (269–70). Inspired at this point by rejection of his love, Anna Dawe none the less throws away just the one field book – the same one that contains the threat of incest as well as that last pompous sentence. What she rejects, finally, is Dawe's evasive form of closure: '*He had written on the last page of his last field book*: I have come to the end of words'(269). It is both an indication that her accusation about Tune's death has left him with nothing to say, and an ultimate sign that she writes to force his hand, to make him say more than he has been willing to reveal. Evidently she has a whole car trunk full of boxes of field notes remaining to rework as she will; but to prevent the *monster* from returning to life, she has first to profane a number of self-absorbing memories.

Roll me over, lay me down, and do it again.

After Anna Yellowbird goes home, Anna Dawe stays on '*in the mountains, where I can look to the east, and downward, to where it is all behind me*' (264). The critical difference in this second repetition of her father's journey is finally apparent in her assured first sentence: '*I am Anna Dawe*' (2). Once, she had felt named out of existence by her father's own insistence on repeating the past: '*Just as my name was determined in that season eleven years before I was born, so were my character, my fate*' (138). Now she defines her difference from 'that Anna' in order to escape being a mere extension of the couple's 'fossil' love life.

All the same, a genuine repetition compulsion is not so easily left behind. Fairly late in the novel, Anna Dawe indulges in unmaidenly thoughts of her father's entry into 'that Anna's' body, 'her quick hand taking him to the secret gate; then her mouth opening into a soft smile as she eased him into her cunthair' (195). Narrative itself supplies a new temptation to close the distance, to put herself in the 'mother's' place. Nor is the narrative temptation done away with by an earlier acknowledgment of Anna Yellowbird's priority in time: '*Any relations of mine, mother?*' (262). Still, her confession of kinship does help, as much as her giddy laughter, to establish her unique identity. The name 'Anna Dawe' offers repetition with a critical difference; she is neither one person (Yellowbird) nor the other (Dawe), though she is somehow both. But in the moment of her writing, she has to keep her distance from both of them.

Web helps as much as Sinnott to keep the threat of her father at bay: '*Web was the man I imagined most often. He was the one person whom my father could never destroy*' (4). Web, in fact, is her father's antithesis: '*His indifference was his secret weapon. For my father, years later, could fly into a rage, remembering Web's indifference about the past they were seeking together*' (162). It is no accident that her first chapter is entitled '*Web's First Discovery*' (5). For Web is both her alter ego and her ally in her fight with her father. Web, as young Tune recognizes, is a genuine artist, albeit 'a natural-born bullshit artist' (137). So, as much as possible, Anna tries to mimic him, becomes the bullshit artist herself.

Web is almost as narcissistic and egomaniacal in his own way as old Dawe. The difference is that he expects no one to take him seriously: 'I suppose you think I'm bullshitting?' (136) he says, before Tune confirms him in his art. What Anna admires in the teller of tall tales is his way of recreating himself out of disaster. For Web, the buffoon, the joker, the accident on its way to happen, is a self-made man. Having burned down the shack his father lived in (and maybe the old man with it), he heads down the road into a world no less hostile to his will. And yet he goes on *'dreaming grandly, boast[ing] his trivial failure into magnificent success'* (94).

The tall-tale artist's ability is more than a talent to compensate for his failures. Caught with his pants down by some vindictive gentlemen, he clothes himself in the most outrageous story. Ay, there's the rub, for no matter how hard he tries to turn his liabilities into assets, the shoe polish won't go away: ' "Don't plan to get clean. Stove blacking makes your prick grow. Ever look at a stovepipe?" Web talking himself out of his anger, or his fear, beginning to laugh ... "Sheee-*yit*" ' (93). The real triumph of his laughter is his mockery of himself.

More than just talk, Web's tall tales are also a cheerful profanation of Dawe's ambition. His noise becomes an 'antic reproof' (Thomas, *Kroetsch* 90) to Dawe's silence. Even though his prowess with words confesses his impotence against reality, or though his tall tales mock probability, imply their impossibility, he happily degrades the myth of the hero by celebrating another sort of victory. For he confesses at every turn his true vulnerability, no matter how self-aggrandizing he seems. He even laughs in the face of his own mortality, whereas Dawe must try to shake *'himself free of any need to share even his sufferings with another human being'* (139), still seeking 'the lost bones ... [to] immortaliz[e] the mortal man' (36).

The victory of Web's attitude becomes a model for Anna to recreate herself against a fate supposedly determined for her by her father. Dawe is not likely to write down the details of Web's 'bullshit,' either, feeling little but antipathy for one who so loudly proclaims his failings. Rather, he seems to have commented on Web's capacity for self-invention; reading his notes, Anna discovers a personal way to elaborate. Through Web, she creates space for her own story, even though '*women are not supposed to have stories. We are supposed to sit at home, Penelopes to their wars and their sex. As my mother did. As I was doing*' (3). Dawe, the 'hero' who '*removed himself from time*' (139), is thus cheerfully contradicted by Web whose lyrical transport inside a tornado mocks the whole notion of transcendence. Web's travesty of hierogamy, the sacred marriage, becomes a comic acceptance of profane mortality. His laughing 'indifference' is what gives his scepticism power; for Web is as likely to get Dawe's goat as he is to get the girl.

As much as Anna shares this instinct to get her father's goat, her ultimate difference from Web is summed up at the outset of her story: ' "*There is no such thing as a past*," Web, his father forgotten, said to mine. *There is nothing else, Web. That you should misunderstand is unfortunate; on that one issue, on that issue only, my father perceived correctly. And he went out and looked for that past*' (4). So does Anna. Her obsession with that past is finally what distinguishes her mode of parody from Web's sort of travesty. For Web, as for the ferryman he meets, 'Dead is dead' (54). But the words of a dead man manage to live on in Anna's quotations, no matter how ironic and mistrustful she may be of the documents themselves, 'the field notes he had faked for the world' (196). Anna's quarrel with her old man, in other words, is not meant entirely to cancel her likeness to him.

In fact, Anna begins to see a symbiotic relationship between her own act of writing and that of her father. For example, there is this central explanation at the centre of her book: '*But I was left always with the mystery of his own first season ... And I had to visit those badlands where his success began. Because, there, in that beautiful and nightmare season – he ceased to dare to love*' (139). Now her very next words in the opening to chapter 26 are 'Dawe writing.' Even as she writes, her father appears to write again in her words. But Anna, who has not ceased to love, also runs the risk of wanting to incorporate him into her text, just as she had wanted before to take him into her body. Symbiosis only threatens endless repetition of the past.

That Anna understands her dilemma is clear from a mirror image she uses to imagine her father writing: 'The burdened boat, Dawe motionless and writing in its centre, seemed to move of its own: it floated square and lifeless on its own image while the three figures half immersed in the water themselves both fled the image and dragged it along behind them'

(240). Dawe's field notes, as Peter Thomas says, are 'consistently Narcissistic, an attempt to provide an historical record of devotion to scientific aims which is really Dawe's "heroic" self-projection' ('Silence' 34). But the image of the writer floating on his own image bears out the observation in another way. Though Anna may feel condemned, as a daughter, to drag her father's image along into the future, she is tempted as a writer to float 'square and lifeless' on her own image, to make her father the endless replication of herself. The assertion of difference in parody is one thing; an acceptance, through repetition, of likeness is quite another. So how are the two to be reconciled?

A healthy convergence of Dawe's story with his daughter's begins in chapter 42, appropriately entitled 'Daweosaurus': 'Anna heard the blast. It sounded to her like thunder, out of a cloudless sky' (215). There is even some ambiguity about which Anna does the hearing, let alone an ambiguity about what is heard. The blast, of course, is the one that kills Tune: Anna 'knew that her confrontation with the dead, the moment for which she had travelled so far, waited so long, was at last arrived' (215). But Anna Yellowbird, who has followed her shaman all this way, does not discover her dead husband; it is Anna Dawe, travelling back into the past through narrative, who confronts her own dead – both the surrogate brother and the father she has driven to suicide by '*dwell[ing] on the occasion of Tune's death*' (233).

So well along in her record of independence, Anna has suddenly to face the possibility that she's misread her father all this time. His field notes offer unexpected and painful new possibilities of meaning. Earlier, she had said she '*left home, determined to set straight the record*' (45); but in the record itself she finds new evidence '*that confessed he was sorry*' (234), evidence that she refused to see because of her own guilty sorrow. '*Crushed. He must have been. Beyond.* Dawe not finding a sentence, a word, that consoled him into the community of his attendant slaves: *Will notify the proper. Hire and send in.* The sentences breaking in the middle of creation. The pencil freezing in his shovel-stiffened hand. *Dead. And buried. I found one finger. I think. I. Kicked the dirt. Over –* ' (239).

The broken syntax shows better than anything else the broken spirit of the man, his numb incomprehension, his total inability to think his way through to a conclusion. His only virtue is that he can find no consolation. But the broken words also open up new possibilities of meaning. 'I think I found one finger.' 'I think of little else.' 'I think and think.' 'I.'

The intolerable sense of self, utterly disconnected from everything and everyone. 'Kicked the dirt.' Who kicked? No subject. Hard to know whom to blame. *I. Kicked the dirt*. Nearly a confession here of who did bring down that hill of clay on the poor boy's head. Who grieved. 'Bit the dust, kicked the bucket.' 'Over.' It's hard to be more final than that.

Yet 'Never,' Dawe responds in his daughter's narrative to his own hand-written intuition that it's over. Anna, after all, needs some word to go on to account for his lifelong silence. Not to mention the turning away, his ‚continuing pursuit of ambition. Still, his own last written word is hardly one of rejection: '*It was an unfortunate accident*. Dawe crossing out the word, *unfortunate*. Starting again: *No doubt the boy was. Careless. Didn't follow*' (241). No doubt the boy *was*, had been. But who, then, was careless? The ruptured predicate divides the boy from blame. It didn't follow. The boy didn't follow – orders? Or the boy's fate didn't, shouldn't, follow from a moment of carelessness (yet whose?)? The record refuses to choose among alternatives. All are true. And even a likely impulse to justify himself is arrested by feelings Dawe can't control: 'He, Dawe, smashing the period down onto the page as if he would pierce it, penetrate, nail the book to the box' (241). That helpless anger, neither justifying nor consoling. Though protesting his sorrow all the same. The past is evidently still alive and open to change. Only the reader has to be open to her own grief, to get rid of her anger and guilt.

The beauty of Anna's story is that she can finally incorporate her father's confession into a double peace-making with the dead (Dawe with Tune, she with her father). The confessional structure of the book is made more pointed, paradoxically, by Anna Yellowbird's preventing her halting confession of incest, thus forestalling even more regret. For Anna Dawe is forgiven before she asks, is turned around, 'saved,' freed to make her own journey into forgiveness. Finally, she learns to be as tactful as 'that Anna' in absolving her father before he asks. And so the third act of the journey inverts the second one of mocking and of blame. It is in this sense that parody as a 'paradoxical strategy of repetition' becomes for Anna 'a source of freedom' (Hutcheon, *A Theory* 10).

Finally, in Anna Yellowbird's naive wonder at the magic of a photograph, we see the true duplicity of Anna Dawe's art:

Anna staring at the picture of a boy, a comb and a piece of paper pressed to his mouth. She turned the photo over and looked at the blank side, then looked again at the young face framed in its mop of curly hair, the two almost pudgy hands. She straightened her drying red dress over her hips. She took the picture to Sinnott; Sinnott busily moving his camera.

'But he's dead,' Anna said.

'I assumed as much,' Sinnott said. From under the cloth.

'You can bring him back – '

Sinnott moving out from under the focussing cloth, straightening. 'It's only a picture – ' Sinnott, then, seeing her luminous eyes, the unfeigned praise of his magic, the simplest hope recovered –

(250)

Although 'A photograph is both a pseudo-presence and a token of absence' (Sontag, *Photography* 16), the grief of the photograph is that it cannot make present what is absent. Yet absence, the blank side of the photograph, happens to be just half the truth; the other side holds a 'chemical replacement' which is the perfect analogue of the dinosaur hunter's bone.

In reconstructing the 'beast' from the 'bones,' Anna Dawe takes up the work of her father; she goes beyond the 'duplicate world' of the photograph, which almost brings Tune to life again, to a rewriting of her father's text which allows him to speak in the silent spaces between his own words. The younger, unsophisticated Anna Yellowbird holds to the photograph as way of restoring 'the most primitive relationship – the partial identity of image and object' (Sontag, *Photography* 158). For 'Our irrepressible feeling that the photographic process is something magical has a genuine basis. No one takes an easel painting to be in any sense co-substantial with its subject; it only represents or refers. But a photograph is not only like its subject, a homage to the subject. It is part of, an extension of that subject; and a potent means of acquiring it, of gaining control over it' (Sontag 155). And yet the older Anna Yellowbird who throws her photographs away does not really reject the past, only her feeling that she should be able to control it. What Anna Dawe learns from that gesture is that she must also surrender control of her father's field notes, or better yet, open them up to the voice which speaks otherwise than she thought in that deconstructed, broken language.

Much earlier in her story, the writer had been anguished by the absence of truth, by the very inability of narrative to re-present its subject: '*Action and voice: how strange they should have so little connection. Or is there any at all, any familiar knock at the closed door, between the occurrence and the most exact telling? ... There are no truths, only correspondences*' (45). Her passing statement could still serve as a provisional definition of parody. Yet our experience of the gap between the event and later tellings of it helps to define the space in which the past is transformed by 'terrible and repeated acts of perception' ('Nationalism' vi). What the narrator finally learns is that her written 'correspondence' with her father's story *is* her subject. In the act of telling itself, she creates an unexpected empathy with her father writing which helps to proclaim her own identity, and even, perhaps, to bridge the great divide of death.

11

The Aesthete's Reply:
'A Prose Kinema' in
Famous Last Words

Mauberley's Windsors belong squarely in the William Hickey
school of historiography: beings brought to life by a thousand
flashbulbs.

> Boyd Tonkin, 'Hitler's Understudy'

The 'age demanded' chiefly a mould in plaster,
Made with no loss of time,
A prose kinema, not, not assuredly, alabaster
Or the 'sculpture' of rhyme.

> Ezra Pound, *Selected Poems*

To an age who had already written his obituary, Pound addressed *Hugh
Selwyn Mauberley (Life and Contacts)* (1920) as a parody of what 'The
Age Demanded' (*Poems* 184). Mauberley, the self-confessed 'hedonist'
(*Poems* 186), became an ironic spokesman for his age, writing off 'E.P.'
in the 'Ode Pour l'Election De Son Sepulchre' as being 'out of key with
his time' (*Poems* 173). ('The worst muddle they make,' Pound would
finally say of his readers, 'is in failing to see that Mauberley buries E.P.
in the first poem; gets rid of all his troublesome energies' – cited in
Brooker 188.) In consequence, *Hugh Selwyn Mauberley* is Pound's own
reply to the age, one of his truly 'great self-justifying poems' (Kenner,
Poetry 164).

In *Famous Last Words*, Timothy Findley's Mauberley is the one who is
accused, in 'A PORTRAIT' by the leftist critic Julia Franklin, of being 'OUT
OF KEY WITH HIS TIME' (*Words* 128). The bulk of the novel is Mauberley's reply to her charge that 'his departure from the literary scene is no

loss to culture. His works, all along, were paste' (129). His final work, etched in plaster and 'made with no loss of time' on the walls of a grand hotel in the Austrian Tyrol, appears to fictional readers within the novel to be either (and only) apologia or genuine confession. One of these readers, Captain Freyberg, vehemently denies that Mauberley's story can be anything more than 'an apology' (54), while his subaltern, Lieutenant Quinn, is initially convinced that 'after years of silence ... Mauberley was a writer at the last' (58), most of all because he tried to '*Tell* the truth. About himself. Including the mistakes he made' (154). Self-knowledge thus becomes an explicit test of heroism in the novel, just as it was in Pound's poem where the 'modes of self-knowledge' are so complex that, at 'its deepest levels the poem is still virtually unread' (Kenner, *Poetry* 169). The major difference, however, between the novel and the poem is that Pound is the one who comes to know himself through his character's failure, while in the novel it is Mauberley who is thought to have found himself through his summing up. Apparently, the aesthete's confession in *Famous Last Words* is meant to reverse that 'complete divorce between Pound and Mauberley' (Espey 16) which takes place in the sequence of poems by letting Mauberley get free of Pound in the novel.

There are other ironic reversals in Findley's portrait of the artist which recommend the novel as a parody of a parody. For example, Pound's Mauberley is a miniaturist who has but one 'fundamental passion':

> This urge to convey the relation
> Of eyelid and cheek-bone
> By verbal manifestations;
>
> To present the series
> Of curious heads in medallion –
>
> (Poems 183)

'*Medallion*,' the finale to Pound's suite of poems, even 'presents Mauberley's values in Mauberley's voice' (Witemeyer 163). But 'this sample Medallion in its very scrupulousness exemplifies his sterility. His imagination falls back upon precedents; his visual particularity comes out of an art-gallery and his Venus Anadyomene out of a book' (Kenner, *Poetry* 181). The art of Findley's Mauberley, by contrast, depends almost exclusively on first-hand experience. He not only moves freely among the central personages of his age, but is drawn to teeming humanity as the source of his art: 'Shanghai drew me like a motherlode of dreams and I thought I had found the ultimate source, the wellspring of every fiction known to man. It was there in that massive, visible throng that I found my *Crowd Invisible*, and thus my first success' (*Words* 67).

Similarly, where Pound's Mauberley reduces life to the exquisite sterility of a medallion, Findley's Mauberley magnifies it to mythic proportions, as when he describes his royal couple arriving in Dubrovnik as 'icons walking on the earth – choosing the people of Dubrovnik to bask in. This was the new mythology, I thought. Homer might have written it' (63). The part he chooses for himself in the scene is likewise drawn from heroic lore – 'Cadmus ... the guardian of myth and literature' (62). Apparently he maintains this mythic role to the end of his famous last words, reassured by a belief out of folklore 'that Cadmus was the Phoenix, or a sort of lizard-Lazarus, rising from the flames of some forgotten human rebellion; an assurance that, in spite of fire, the word would be preserved' (62). Cadmus-Mauberley, the heroic bard of the novel, thus seems to have superseded Pound's aesthete type, Pisanello-Mauberley, since the former is evidently not 'lacking the skill/To forge Achaia' (*Poems* 182).

Wallis Simpson, one of the 'icons' of Cadmus-Mauberley's new mythology, still helps to identify the heroic bard with the hedonist in a manner perhaps not fully intended by Findley. Pound's aesthete, one recalls, was inclined to 'the strait head/Of Messalina' (*Poems* 182) for his 'series/Of curious heads in medallion.' The empress Messalina, wife to Claudius, happened to be one of the most dissolute women in Roman history. Not that Pound's miniaturist was likely to be found in her embrace – not with his only 'tool/The engraver's' (Espey 78–9). Yet the hedonist had still 'noted a year late' this 'mandate/Of Eros' (*Poems* 183) he had missed:

> Mouths biting empty air,
> The still stone dogs,
> Caught in metamorphosis, were
> Left him as epilogues.
>
> (*Poems* 183)

Findley's Mauberley leaves a far different epilogue, of course; but the title of his most successful novel, *Stone Dogs*, suggests a similar threat of metamorphosis from 'the woman I had loved – as a dog loves its mistress' (376). His passion, likewise without 'mandate of Eros,' is really for the woman as an *objet d'art*, herself metamorphosed like the figure on the first Mauberley's 'Medallion':

> The sleek head emerges
> From the gold-yellow frock
> As Anadyomene in the opening
> Pages of Reinach.
>
> (*Poems* 187)

So, too, the only 'opening' for the 'heroic' bard is the aesthetic one – look but don't touch: 'Her mouth was very red; her eyes, though blue, had darkened against the intrusion of so much light and her whole face carried, even through the veil, across the fifteen yards or so of lobby like a mask. There was not a trace of emotion written there – only: *I am here and if you break me you must pay for me*' (68).

All the same, the 'heroic' aesthete's passion leads him further than Pound's Mauberley into a moment of dubious action: 'And I thought of Lucrezia Borgia, Agrippina, Messalina – while the geckoes struggled up the walls and across the ceiling, searching for a fly to kill' (373). Though 'Messalina' had so unsettled the poet Mauberley that he drifted, bewildered, uncertain, '(Amid aerial flowers) ... time for arrangements – / Drifted on/To the final estrangement' (*Poems* 183), the novelist Mauberley actually dares to kill for his Messalina, before drifting on to his own final estrangement. But first he will be impelled to confess his act of murder, if not to repent of it. Here, the style of his writing on the wall, though very different from the poet's preciousness in the '*Medallion*,' is what reveals him as a product of the same aesthetic sensibility.

Whatever one makes of the modern Messalina as an historical figure, her effect on Mauberley exposes both his ultimate identification with Pound's aesthete and the source of his aesthetic failure:

> Wallis, coming down, was like an actress in a film. She used the stairs quite consciously and made a scene of dignified bereavement. The 'star' upstairs had died, and here came the widow, walking into the future, music swelling up with every measured step she took ...

She had made a fist – and the fist was so tight I had to help her force it open.

'Thank you,' she said. And when I looked, I could see the enamel over her features had cracked.   (348)

The gesture itself is anticipated in Pound's ironic retort to the '*Ode*' in which his Mauberley had dismissed him:

> The age demanded an image
> Of its accelerated grimace,
> Something for the modern stage,
> Not, at any rate, an Attic grace.

> (*Poems* 173)

Such a gesture is not only characteristic of the moral nature of the time, but of its most popular artistic expression; for what 'The "age demanded" chiefly' was 'A prose kinema' (*Poems* 174). In this respect, Mauberley represents what to Pound was the flawed aesthetic sensibility of his age (Witemeyer 178).

Findley's Mauberley is fairly explicit about his own attempt to create 'a prose kinema' in 'his testament entirely made on walls' (58), and most of his witnesses applaud his choice of medium: 'And what a tale to tell. If I could only tell it, he thought. If there was only time and I could tell it all. Oh well. The journals; the notebooks would have to suffice. Except they were like the title cards of a silent film – without the film itself' (35). His sudden realization helps to explain, even to himself, why he has risked the safety of his journals in his panic flight from Rapallo: the huge, blank walls of the Grand Elysium Hotel are a summons from the silver screen. Even now, a glittering cast of ghostly celebrities lingers about the remembered corridors: 'Isadora Duncan, Greta Garbo, Somerset Maugham and Richard Strauss had all come up the famous tiers of marble stairs, crossing the lobbies to sign the registry and collect their keys' (22). Yet even these *glitterati* must be extras surrounding the stars of his projected show: 'Edward VIII and Mrs Simpson had danced incognito in the Winter Garden.' And dance they will again, if not on the ballroom floor, at least on the walls – in other days and climes. But first Mauberley himself will have to climb 'the great stone face of the Balkonberg' (22), thus enlarging his own image as the heroic witness.

The 'director's' image is quickly magnified to colossal proportions by his choice of an epigraph from the Book of Daniel: 'IN THE SAME HOUR CAME FORTH FINGERS OF A MAN'S HAND, AND WROTE OVER AGAINST THE CANDLESTICK UPON THE PLAISTER OF THE WALL OF THE KING'S PALACE ...' (52). Before the time of his own writing on the wall, the words from Daniel – MENE MENE TEKEL UPHARSIN – had appeared in the heavens to none other than the Windsors. But the judgment of the 'King' is not made by God, only by a sky-writing pilot whose act of terrorism makes him little different from the fascists whom he judges. What then are we to make of Mauberley's judgment of himself? Does the epigraph in fact signify a divine judgment on Mauberley? Or is it characteristic of his tendency, through myth and cinema, to inflate his own image? Might his king-sized confession even stand as monument to an ego that has unwittingly assumed its own divinity? Evidently the man whose judgment of himself is associated with divine judgment could be as capable of self-congratulation as of self-knowledge. And so Pound's epitaph for his aesthete resonates with an irony that might go unheeded in the hand-writing on the wall, though the larger question must be whether it is heeded by the frame narrator in the novel:

> Nothing, in brief, but maudlin confession,
> Irresponse to human aggression,
> Amid the precipitation, down-float
> Of insubstantial manna,
> Lifting the faint susurrus
> Of his subjective hosannah.   (*Poems* 185)

In 'Vorticism' (1914), Pound had defined 'two opposed ways of thinking of a man: firstly, you may think of him as that toward which perception moves, as the toy of circumstance, as the plastic substance *receiving* impressions; secondly, you may think of him as directing a certain fluid force against circumstance, as *conceiving* instead of merely reflecting and observing' (*Gaudier-Brzeska* 89). The first way of thinking is that of the impressionist, as defined most sympathetically by Pater in the fictional character of Marius the Epicurean: 'Had he not come to Rome partly under poetic vocation, to receive all those things, the very impress of life itself, upon the visual, the imaginative, organ, as upon a mirror; to reflect them; to transmute them into golden words?' (*Marius* I, 180–1). Pound was evidently concerned to distinguish his own 'imagism' from this aesthetic philosophy which made little more than a passive virtue of the receptive 'organ' of sight, asking only of its followers 'To keep the eye clear by a sort of exquisite personal alacrity and cleanliness, extending even to his dwelling-place; to discriminate, ever more and more fastidiously, select form and colour in things from what was less select' (*Marius* I, 33), ultimately in the hope of being 'made perfect by the love of visible beauty' (I, 32). And so Pound redefined his passive, static-sounding 'imagism' as 'vorticism.' Yet, despite its name, Pound's 'imagism' never had anything to do with the passive reception of impressions; rather, it was an attempt 'to record the precise instant when a thing outward and objective transforms itself, or darts into a thing inward and subjective':

> This particular sort of consciousness has not been identified with impressionist art. I think it is worthy of attention.
> The logical end of impressionist art is the cinematograph. The state of mind of the impressionist tends to become cinematographical. Or, to put it another way, the cinematograph does away with the need of a lot of impressionist art.   (*Gaudier-Brzeska* 89)

Hugh Selwyn Mauberley becomes, in the largest sense, Pound's own portrait of the artist as '*the type of the impressionist*, and his failure is inseparable from his aesthetic' (Witemeyer 176):

> Invitation, mere invitation to perceptivity
> Gradually led him to the isolation
> Which these presents place
> Under a more tolerant, perhaps, examination.
>
> > (*Poems* 184)

But the literary impressionist who best authorizes the type is hinted at in Mauberley's excessive fondness for a book with etchings 'Par Jaquemart' (*Poems* 182): 'When he had stretched himself on the sofa, he looked at the title-page of the book. It was Gautier's *Émaux et Camées*, Charpentier's Japanese-paper edition, with the Jacquemart etching' (*Dorian Gray* 264). Pound's Mauberley most closely resembles Wilde's impressionist *after* the murder: languorous, enervated, and quite incapable of the

action taken by his prototype. Here, Mauberley becomes a belated
Dorian Gray in his now total impressionistic passivity.

Throughout the poem, Pound characteristically defines such an
impressionist's sensibility in terms of a passive retina – 'Thus, if her
colour/Came against his gaze' – comparable to the motion-picture camera in its work of recording external impressions:

> A consciousness disjunct,
> Being but this overblotted
> Series
> Of intermittences.
>
> (*Poems* 186)

'The term "overblotted" expresses with precision Pound's view of the
impressionist mind as a *tabula rasa*' (Witemeyer 179). In this sense,
Mauberley proves by dint of constitution to be what Dorian Gray must
be by necessity, after his murder of Basil Hallward: 'overblotted,' 'dis-
junct,' trying to put off all questions of causation and responsibility in a
'series of intermittences.'

A similar impressionist aesthetics in *Famous Last Words* begins to
show up, though not with the same moral valency, in the 'cinematographical state of mind' of almost all the fictional readers within the novel.
For example, the young soldier, Annie Oakley, who guards the Kristall
Salon in the hotel stands 'like one in reverence, gazing at all the fallen
glass on the floor – conjuring the warmth and music that must have been
and the pale gold light and the famous clientele. Maybe Dooley Wilson
sitting at the piano; Ingrid Bergman over in the corner smoking a cigarette, with her hat pulled down across one side of her face; Humphrey
Bogart standing in the shadows and the music sad and perfect. Annie
pulled his gloves on tighter: watching – listening – making movies. "Well
– here's lookin' at you, kid," he said. And the music swelled ...' (*Words*
43). Bogart's line becomes, in Pound's terms, what 'the age demanded' –
the credo of a new impressionism. Bogart himself might approach near
enough to the starlet to do more than look, if he so chooses; but he speaks
in the name of an audience who, quite literally, can only watch. 'Here's
lookin' at you' is also the implicit motto of Findley's Mauberley when he
first 'lays eyes' on Wallis Simpson: *Look, but don't touch*. So impressionism, it would seem, shades cinematographically into voyeurism.

Here, Freud's idea of the stages of vision might help to define the 'perversion' of this particular 'cinematographical state of mind,' and not the inadequacy, as Pound would have it, of one of the principal art forms of our time. In 'Instincts and Their Vicissitudes,' Freud had identified

> three scenes of seeing. In the first scene, 'looking' is a gesture toward control, visual 'possession' or 'mastery' of an object ... After this initial look takes place, there is a reversal, a seemingly impossible shift from a subject's viewpoint to an object's. This shift entails a virtual 'giving up of the object' as a thing to be seen and mastered and a repositioning of 'seeing' from a different position. The looker, in effect, becomes an object ... Whereas the process starts with the power of a subject to see, the subject afterwards straddles the subject-object relationship by becoming a partial object of contemplation. In the third scene subjectivity is abandoned altogether and is replaced by an object exclusively for another's scrutiny.
>
> (Con Davis 248)

Mauberley's fate in the novel – death from an ice-pick driven through his eye – implies a fitting punishment for the voyeur who, refusing to be seen as an object, has always looked on others as objects. In this sense, there are movie-going voyeurs in the novel who are rather like him. Sergeant Rudecki, for example, who knows about Mauberley the novelist only because his *Stone Dogs* was adapted to the silver screen, is titillated by the presence of such a famous corpse. So long as the voyeur can regard him as an image, there is always something unreal, even surreal, about the celebrity. But when Rudecki sees the ice-pick in the corpse's eye, he is viscerally affected. The famous man is no longer merely an aesthetic object; Rudecki himself is implicated in the act of voyeurism.

Jacques Lacan's rereading of Freud's idea of the stages of vision makes a 'theoretical leap outside of the strictly "visual" terms of Freud's essay' to an assertion that 'seeing is but a function in a largely unconscious discourse that can be glimpsed in what Lacan calls (extending Freud's discussion) the "Gaze" – the functioning of the whole system of shifts ... The subject who looks, in Lacan's scheme, is the one who precisely is "seen" – that is, implicated – by the desire of unconscious discourse ... The Gaze, in this way, encompasses the voyeuristic wish not to be seen and the exhibitionistic wish not to be shown, and the relationship of these "perversions" (as Freud calls them) points up rather directly the positionality of visual experience *as a text*' (Con Davis 249).

Findley's movie-goers, like Private Oakley, who start 'making movies' inside their heads are not as passive or receptive as Pound would have the 'cinematographical impressionist.' Even to co-produce such 'movies' – or to respond as a reader/viewer – is to be implicated in the discourse of the primary text, or to assume a 'position' within it. But the nature of the 'Gaze' in which the reader is held has finally to be determined by the 'unconscious' of the text itself. Here, Rudecki's response to the movie *Stone Dogs* is most instructive; he is sentimentally moved to defend Bette Davis's murder of her movie husband: ' "And he deserved it, too. Son of a bitch. Everyone's always so mean to her." Rudecki got out his handker-chief and blew his nose' (151). While the screen-image of murder is not the same thing at all as the taking of a life, it is evidently used in Mauberley's 'real-life' confession to justify in advance his decision to murder for Wallis's sake: everyone, it seems, was always so mean to her too. And so the 'textual unconscious' of Mauberley's early novel becomes an apologia for his future actions; and quite as unconsciously, Findley gives him back the energy of his murderous type who, in the parodic reduction of Pound's character, had lost even the tragic dignity which continued to linger, in *Dorian Gray*, like an aura round the damned soul. In still another sense, however, the life of Findley's impressionist begins to imitate his art, just as Wilde had said it should.

At first it had seemed, to the contrary, that Mauberley's art did imitate life. The frame narrator says, 'Whatever else he was, Hugh Selwyn Mauberley was a compulsive witness. In all his life he had never been able to refrain from setting things down on paper, recording the lives of those around him, moment by moment – every word and every gesture instantly frozen in his private cipher' (21). But this sort of witness was also more inclined to be an aesthete; the narrator of George Moore's *Confessions of a Young Man* had demonstrated, in voyeuristic fashion, how life must always follow art in a sensibility inclined to gesture: 'And just as I had watched the chorus girls and mummers, three years ago, at the Globe Theatre, now, excited by a nervous curiosity, I watched this world of Parisian adventures and lights o' love. And this craving for observation of manners, this instinct for the rapid notation of gestures and words that epitomise a state of feeling, of attitudes that mirror forth the soul, declared itself a main passion; and it grew and strengthened, to the detriment of the other Art still so dear to me' (Moore 60).

Moore's narrator, of course, had also identified himself as the supreme type of the impressionist in the opening of his *Confessions*: 'I came into the world apparently with a nature like a smooth sheet of wax, bearing no impress, but capable of receiving any; of being moulded into all shapes' (49). Findley's 'witness' also seems at times to have a nature like 'a smooth sheet of wax,' depending less on judgment or critical discernment than on the receipt of impressions. As a plastic substance receiving impressions, this Mauberley, like Pound's, proves contrary to the imagist 'directing a certain fluid force against circumstance' (*Gaudier-Brzeska* 89):

> He made no immediate application
> Of this to relation of the state
> To the individual, the month was more temperate
> Because this beauty had been.
>
> (*Poems* 184)

Mauberley's disinclination to analyse the meaning of his political involvement or the nature of his attraction to it is not, however, entirely passive. Because the impressionist-as-cinematographer adapts his 'title cards' to the pictures of what happened on sixteen blank walls of 'silent film,' he is actively engaged in the other extreme 'of relations that Freud calls voyeurism and exhibitionism,' since 'exhibitionism is equally a denial of object loss; Freud sees it as an idealization of loss in the illusory form of a *thing* rather than as an acceptance of loss as a structural absence ... Exhibitionism is a positioning whose significance is always to show and never to be shown – that is, never to be shown any loss' (Con Davis 249). The fascist sympathizer as movie-director hopes by this sort of self-display to forestall the loss of his world, not to confess his 'perversion.' And so his obsession with the prehistoric image of a hand in the caves at Altamira becomes an apology for a fundamentally 'conservative' exhibitionist:

I leave you this: my hand as signature beside these images of what I knew. Look how my fingers spread to tell my name.

> Some there are who never disappear. And I knew I was sitting at
> the heart of the human race – which is its will to say *I am*.   (173)

I am is also the name, however, of the deity who writes on the wall in the
Book of Daniel. The cinematographer exhibits such a yearning for eternal life in the very script which permits him to play God by taking a life.

Such contradictions are not unusual in the 'fantastic mode of postmodern fiction' (Duffy, 'Histories' 188–9) to which the novel belongs. In
fact, the relation between postmodern and cinematic modes of narration
implies that the contradictions of voyeurism and exhibitionism might
well spring from the same 'cinematographical state of mind.' On the one
hand, the 'camera eye' wants to control a situation which mirrors the
viewer's own situation without himself being seen. On the other hand,
the exhibitionist chooses to make himself an object in order 'to resist the
passivity inherent in becoming an object for another's sight. That is, he
wishes to perform the impossible by actually directing when he will be
looked at by others and by remaining in complete control, active' (Con
Davis 254) even after his death.

There are more mundane contradictions of 'cinematic' narration, however, which help to establish a context for this reversal of looking from
voyeurism to exhibitionism. Structured scene by scene with little analysis
of any kind, Mauberley's narrative makes a number of important transi-
tions through location shots. Yet some of these scenes have an unusual
degree of local colour if they are supposed to be etchings in plaster of a
man pressed to finish his confession before he is murdered. Take, for
example, the view of the harbour at Nassau: it seems to be inscribed on
the wall just after Mauberley has locked up Estrade, his would-be assas-
sin, in the dungeon of the hotel. The next killer cannot be far behind, but
the hand of the cameraman never falters: 'The harbour at Nassau widens
opposite the town, providing mooring space for private yachts and motor
launches' (324). And so on for several paragraphs. The flouting of dramatic verisimilitude seems, in the best postmodern fashion, to call deliberate attention to the artifice of the text. Mauberley, after all, is himself
a fiction within a fiction, 'himself doubly-imaginary, the figure created
by another, very different writer' (Duffy, 'Histories' 195). And yet this
fascination with artifice encoded within the text begins to parallel Mauberley's own love of artifice, making it difficult to separate the authorial
narrator from the dramatic one. Both merge in the camera eye, creating

the sort of verisimilitude by which the eye of the viewer is comfortably located in space. Now the 'true likeness' belongs not to the dramatic moment of writing but to the cinematic mode of presentation. Thus artifice takes the place of confession.

Similarly, the use of time in Mauberley's narration proves to be cinematic rather than dramatic. His own autobiographical scenes, dated roughly chronologically, are frequently intercut with the actions of other actors, some of which the writer on walls could only imagine: '*Nauly*: September, 1936' (108), is but a typical example. Mauberley himself, as his preceding chapter suggests, is still in Paris, preoccupied with a final scene between Wallis and her husband Ernest Simpson, though we do not know this for certain until we see him arrive at Nauly for Ned Allenby's funeral. In the meantime, Charles Lindbergh converses out of earshot of the other guests at Nauly with Allenby who, we recall, had already cut Mauberley from his acquaintance several months ago and is now about to cut Lindbergh. Allenby's shout of rage is heard across the spacious lawns, though he never tells his wife or anyone else what has been said to provoke him. But we hear the whole conversation and much of what Ned is thinking. Three intercut scenes proceed to show how little Ned repeats of the conversation, now where he really goes instead of Paris, and then what are the contents of a coded telegram from von Ribbentrop to Rudolf Hess received six days later in Berlin. The next scene is the funeral at Nauly. Conspiracy, we nod knowingly. But how do we know? Who told us all these things that no single conspirator could have known?

The question of point of view is the more insistent because each of these scenes on the walls is Mauberley's. Even the story of the little girl who is murdered in the Portuguese plot against the Windsors is related by Mauberley – 'Which brings me to the end of Maria de Gama's story' (215) – though only Estrade, who murders the girl, could possibly know what happened. Of course, Estrade has tried to kill Mauberley too; but nothing in the narrative indicates that he has wrung a confession from her down in the dungeon of the hotel. The narrative inconsistencies are blatant, though one defence of them is to make a virtue of 'intermixing Mauberley's voice with the authorial narrative voice' because 'the conventions surrounding first-person narrative are [thereby] violated, thus highlighting the artificiality of the omniscience' (Shields 96). Exposing the subjectivity of such 'omniscience' might even do away with 'the pretence that we can know and judge others with godlike objectivity and certainty' (Shields 97). But it also does away with the pretence that Mauberley is in truth confessing – is trying, in other words, to take an 'objective' view of himself. The dramatic narrator and the authorial narrator remain at cross-purposes.

The only formal indication in Mauberley's narrative that he could be taking his own measure, as if from the outside, comes in the aftermath of the 'Spitfire Bazaar': 'The fire had claimed its fifty-five victims and three days later the sea yielded up the fifty-sixth: the body of Lorenzo de Broca, the young Italian poet whose words had so embarrassed Hugh Selwyn Mauberley one day' (288). Mauberley's abandonment of the first-person, however, yields no new knowledge of him; he is not even present in the Bahamas at the time of de Broca's terrorism. Perhaps it is not even possible, at this point, to tell *who* is narrating this part of the story, though it seems to be written in Mauberley's hand, since 'Quinn read again' and then left the room a paragraph later (289). The more convenient explanation would be an authorial slip of the pen.

Since Mauberley has virtually disappeared as a dramatic witness by the mid-point of the novel, he may nonetheless have a narrative reason to write about himself in the third person. For he remains as little more than the voyeuristic camera, filming the Duke and Duchess being spirited out of Portugal, the machinations and power struggles of various members of the Cabal, and finally the 'Death of Little Nell' in the Bahamas, this latter occurring two years before Mauberley even reaches the islands. The signalled parody of Dickens does not actually work to subvert sentimental conventions, however; the sudden conflation of history and fiction helps instead to sensationalize a truly grotesque sentiment: 'In the Cinema Marquee, seventy-five or a hundred people had been watching the Battle of Britain and the Fall of France. Now, in a nightmare calmly narrated by a disembodied Movietone Voice, they were caught themselves in the hordes of struggling refugees who clogged the roads on the screen while the dive bombers strafed them in the ditches down between the rows of chairs' (285). Typical of the postmodern manner, 'art' bursts through the boundary into 'life' (though this screen-'art' is really history, the 'life' fiction), collapsing any distinction between them. And yet the technique of the 'disembodied Movietone Voice' exposes the technique of the handwriting on the wall: it is meant to erase any distinctions between artifice and life in Mauberley's confession. Here, at last, the moral eva-sions of postmodern narrative technique betray the mode's hostility to ethical discriminations.

Now, narratively speaking, Mauberley himself must be the whole cabal, since he is the only one who knows everything that is going on. His own technique helps to explain his attraction to totalitarianism, just as his exhibitionism does. Perhaps de Broca's pamphlets, pronouncing 'DEATH TO FASCISTS EVERYWHERE!' (285), are even meant to announce the merited death of 'controlling' authors, since de Broca does not survive his own 'plot.' But in a bizarrely literal sense, the 'dead author' does not give up his central position in the text (as Roland Barthes had said he must). His bodily presence, his narrative omniscience, and his blurring of life/art distinctions all proclaim his continuing control.

Mauberley's point of view further declares him to be the originator, and not just the witness, of history. Getting into bed with the Duke and Duchess, the 'voyeur' ventures into the Duke's unconscious, slipping inside his very dream of mirrors. Ultimately, even his most avid reader has to admit that Mauberley's 'confession' is not personal history but 'history play': 'Quinn turned and looked at the flickering walls and shook his head. How right it was and wonderful that Mauberley should have his king confront himself in a dream. The kings in Shakespeare did the same. They always met themselves in dreams – as ghosts' (254). But Quinn does not think to ask whether Mauberley confronts himself in this dream. It is enough to watch the movie on the 'flickering walls' and assume that this king is simply an authorial projection.

Captain Freyberg is the only intratextual reader who judges that Mauberley may in fact use artifice to *conceal* his faults. He is hardly mistaken, either, to insist on the moral confusion involved in equating historical and imaginative calamities: 'And Hitler was just an actor with a moustache made up to look like Charlie Chaplin. So, when Charlie says we should all fall down – we all fall down ... Pratfalls. *Yes?* And no war. How wonderful. Just to walk out into the lobby and leave it all behind us on a giant movie screen. With the music playing and everyone applauding ... I'd like that. I really would' (53). The novel, in at least this one response, incorporates a necessary challenge to the process, as well as to the content, of Mauberley's narrative. And it is clear, in moral terms, that 'Freyberg is right: not one of [the cabal] would have any feeling to spare for him. Their moral imaginations do not extend beyond themselves' (Scobie 212). In political terms, too, Freyberg 'has the real-ism to understand that if the cabal exists, the cover-up will continue; that Mauberley's heroic testimony will be "Defaced" or "Blown up" (p. 392); and that the existence of the whole story will be denied as easily, crudely, and effectively as he denies his own blow to Quinn's stomach' (Scobie 210).

Freyberg, however, is not given the last word about the narrative status of Mauberley's confession. To Quinn falls that honour, though his sym-pathies help to make him a belated, if inadvertent, member of Mauber-ley's narrative cabal, and to deter the novel from genuine self-reflexive-ness:

Before he left the Grand Elysium Hotel to walk down the mountain, Quinn went upstairs one last time to look at Mauberley's epilogue.

Think of the sea, he read.
Imagine something mysterious rises to the surface on a summer afternoon – shows itself and is gone before it can be identified.

(395)

The camera long shot finally reveals – a vague impression. In spite of the writer's and fictional reader's experience of actual evil, both turn their backs on Pound's imagist credo – 'Direct treatment of the "thing"' (*Gaudier-Brzeska* 83). In the end, the horror of fascism is only another flickering image in a horror show.

The frame-narrator is the next to join Quinn in Mauberley's narrative cabal. His rendering of Freyberg's final challenge to Quinn's sympathy becomes a virtual parody of 'objectivity': 'You see this? You see this? You see this? You see this?' (391) the Captain screams, helpless any more to control himself. His own obsession with 'direct treatment of the thing' thus becomes a form of madness. And so the 'whole concern' of the Colonel from Munich who had Freyberg's company relieved of duty 'was with Freyberg ... Captain Freyberg himself sat up very tall in the Colo-nel's Jeep and appeared not to hear a word that was said to him. Quinn could not help but think the Captain looked like a prisoner' (393). If Mauberley should be granted the 'last word,' then, it is because he is privileged by Quinn's final impression.

Quinn, the sympathetic reader, appeals twice more to shared impressions to create another kind of empathy for Mauberley. At the outset of the novel, he can't help but idolize the figure of the artist: '*Mauberley was here; he stood right here, like me; he felt this wax; he could see the same view; he could raise the same dust as he crossed the floor.* It was a painful thought that all these things, mere things, had had the privilege of being there with Mauberley during the final days of his life and could never tell of it' (65). Yet at the end, even after Mauberley has told the worst, Quinn still 'could see the valley of the Adige and the rising mists of the spring of 1945. It made him feel very sad and he wished that he did not know how much that view had meant to Hugh Selwyn Mauberley' (394). This man, turning a piece of wax in his fingers, implicitly confesses his descent from George Moore's *Confessions*, even as Edwin Dayne proclaims his lineage in Walter Pater: 'Certainly, in my mind, these books will be always intimately associated; and when a few adventitious points of difference be forgotten, it is interesting to note how firm is the alliance, and how cognate and co-equal the sympathies on which it is based; the same glad worship of the visible world, and the same incurable belief that the beauty of material things is sufficient for all the needs of life' (Moore 166).

Pater, one recalls, had in his famous 'Conclusion' urged men to 'burn always with this hard, gemlike flame, to maintain this ecstasy' (236), precisely because 'those impressions of the individual mind to which, for each one of us, experience dwindles down, are in perpetual flight ... To such a tremulous wisp constantly re-forming itself on the stream, to a single sharp impression, with a sense in it, a relic more or less fleeting, of such moments gone by, what is real in our life fines itself down' (*The Renaissance* 235–36). And yet Pater's incurable hope that man 'must be "made perfect by the love of visible beauty" ' (*Marius* 1, 32) did not take into account the moral indifference of those who called for a literal return to pagan sensibilities: 'Mr Pater can join hands with Gautier in saying – *je trouve la terre aussi belle que le ciel, et je pense que la correction de la forme est la vertu.* And I too join issue; I too love the great pagan world, its bloodshed, its slaves, its injustice, its loathing of all that is feeble' (Moore 166). Pater's Marius, 'the humble follower of the bodily eye' (1, 241), had already found in the Roman ampitheatre the sternest test of his 'chosen philosophy ... Trust the eye: Strive to be right always in regard to the concrete experience: Beware of falsifying your impressions. And its sanction had at least been effective here, in protesting – "This, and this, is what you may not look upon!"' (I, 243). Moore's philosophy, less sentimentally aesthetic than Pater's, still did not anticipate a world fifty years away where artists and politicians alike would take him quite so literally.

Findley's Quinn, it would seem, is the true ethical heir of Pater while his Pound seems closer to George Moore in celebrating Roman *virtu* as strength. Contrary to Moore, however, the fictional Pound is also impatient with such an 'effete' idea that beauty could be sufficient to all the needs of life: 'You see? There's no place left for a man who writes like Mauberley. Mauberley's whole and only ambition is to describe the beautiful. And who the hell has time for *that*, any more' (5). And yet Findley's Pound remains unrepentant, given more to a love of killing things (83) than to any 'glad worship of the visible world.' But men like Quinn, who *are* eager for such 'glad worship,' are also sentimentally unable to look truth in the eye. An 'impression' of the panoramic view from the parapets is simply not enough to refute Pound's actual complaint, although that is what Quinn asks us to do. Whatever 'that view had meant to Hugh Selwyn Mauberley,' it means nothing beside the spectacular evidence of his moral corruption.

As Quinn's 'appreciation' shows, the novel tends to favour the 'love of beauty' or aesthetic appreciation as the only necessary saving grace. And yet Moore had already exposed the solipsism inherent in Pater's supposition that, because 'men's spirits [were] susceptible to certain influences, diffused, after the manner of streams or currents, by fair things or persons visibly present' (*Marius* I, 32), it was enough 'to meditate much on beautiful visible objects' and 'to avoid jealously, in his way through the world, everything repugnant to sight' (I, 33). Such avoidance, as Findley's Mauberley sees at last, can only be self-saving. And so he tries, in Quinn's view, to do something about evil by telling the truth about those things which are 'repugnant to sight.'

The question of truth in Mauberley's confession is still terribly complicated, in part because truth is romantically confused with beauty. Such confusion, if it is indebted to Keats, is also a logical outgrowth of the self-sufficiency of Pater's vision. For Pater's nostalgia for transient beauty turns out to be nostalgia for the vanishing eye of the beholder; it is an aesthetics which, as Pater's followers quickly saw, celebrates the virtue of narcissism. Unlike his master, George Moore was untroubled by the new aestheticism's subversion of the old 'pieties': his love of pagan bloodshed and his loathing of all that is feeble proclaims instead that beauty is strength, strength beauty; that is all ye know on earth, and all ye need to know.

While Quinn is relieved, midway in his reading, to find that 'Mauberley's only role had been to play the messenger' (148), he still must deal with the terrible truth that his 'messenger' arranges the death of Harry Oakes. And he evidently fails to see how Mauberley now side-steps tough moral questions to rest in an impressionistic cult of experience which is totally narcissistic: 'Should I write that he sat "amongst the *other* whores"? I do not know. I do know I thought it then, as I sat there on my bench all dressed in white. And it made me smile ... I smiled. I smiled because I was alive. I still had that. I could smell the bougainvillaea still, and smoke my cigarette and feel the cool white cloth of my suit against my legs – and I could watch the Airmen, still, in the marvel of their youth, the brevity of which they had no inkling of ... and I could feel their fear, their marvellous, sensual fear as they went their way to whatever beds they would find. I still had that. I still had that' (359–60).

Such narcissism is the ultimate combination of both a voyeuristic and an exhibitionistic impulse in Mauberley's character. On the one hand, he displays himself mentally and narratively as a whore, without moral qualms, yet with the sort of self-indulgent smile which permits him to retain control of the scene. On the other hand, he watches the airmen unwatched, sharing in their youth but smiling also at the impending death of Harry Oakes who first called him a whore: ' "Well, I warn you," he said. "You'd better not bring her here. I won't have any more whores underneath this roof" ' (358). Sir Harry appears to have become a double of the narrator who now must wait to be murdered himself. But by 'confessing' the Oakes murder with a smile, he can both celebrate his difference from Sir Harry – the fact that he now lives while the other does not – and accept his fear of death (or likeness to Sir Harry) as the price of having gained a few extra years.

Like Wallis Simpson, Mauberley announces, '*I want my life*' (75). And so he cannot afford to feel anything for his victim beyond the pleasure of contemplating another mirror image of himself. Even as he writes, he apparently has not got such self-knowledge as is proclaimed in the epitaph which Pound's aesthete writes for himself: 'I was/And I no more exist;/Here drifted/An hedonist' (*Poems* 186). Findley's Mauberley, more preoccupied with the 'will to say *I am*' (173) in the face of death, affirms the value of his life in the midst of his total corruption.

Heroic? 'Under a more tolerant, perhaps, examination.' For, having completed his monument to himself, Mauberley can now step back and look, not at himself watching himself, but at an apparently objectified image:

> *Wallis is sitting in my mind as I saw her first in the lobby of the old Imperial Hotel in Shanghai . . .*
> He raised the bottle.
> '*Prosit.*'
> Done. He could see himself in the mirror. Not a happy sight. Ah, well. (386)

'The juxtaposition of "Done," referring to the writing on the wall, and "He could see himself in the mirror" strongly suggest that for Mauberley the writing is a mirror' (Scobie 220). Perhaps he has even arrived, in a Lacanian sense, at the third and final stage of seeing where there is 'a new viewer ... who watches, one who takes the position left vacant by the subject who looked initially and "to whom one displays one self in order to be looked at by him" ' (Con Davis 248).

The self which judges itself should then be split, even in Lacan's terms, by this very act of looking back at the self as a viewer. And yet the text which surrounds Mauberley on so many walls is more likely a unifying image of time turned into space. 'Wallis is sitting in my mind,' Mauberley is saying even now in another moment on those walls. 'Not a happy sight,' surely, in view of the end. But the end is evidently not all that looms in sight. For the whole of Mauberley's life actually surrounds him in this image of a unitary, monumentalized self. His very project 'to salvage what [he] could of words and hold them up against the sword' (385) has thus permitted him to create the enduring self he had hoped might survive his death. 'Ah, well,' he says. In resignation, yes. But also in commendation. For the next gesture of straightening his clothing, of tidying up the room, is eloquent enough. Cleanliness, as they say, is next to godliness.

The second epigraph to Mauberley's narrative greatly complicates, in any event, the whole moral enterprise of confession: '*All I have written here,*' Quinn read, '*is true; except the lies*' (59). What, then, is the relation of 'beauty' to 'lies' in Mauberley's mind? Much less in Findley's? 'In Pound's case, the relationship was clear. Mauberley was the mask Pound might have become, and by writing about him, by making him a character in a poem that Mauberley could never have constructed in its entirety, Pound was able to make the separation complete. But why does Findley need this Mauberley he creates? Who is Mauberley to him?' (McLachlan 9). The question need only be asked in less biographical terms: why does the authorial narrator lend his support, through Quinn, to Mauberley? Or why does he ask us, in the persons of Freyberg and Quinn, to choose between truth and beauty? What is the implied aesthetic basis for this narrative privileging of 'lies' over 'truth,' since truth in the novel leads only to madness?

Perhaps the attraction of the liar is best stated in 'The Decay of Lying' and 'The Truth of Masks,' further sources not only for Mauberley's epigraph but for Pound's portrait of the decadent artist. As the figure of Dorian Gray has already suggested, Wilde would seem to be a necessary figure for anyone replying to Pound on his own terms. For Wilde had tried to establish the priority of art over life through his witty doctrine of the mask. The real misfortune of life, the decadent artist had proclaimed, was that it was so very levelling: 'It is a humiliating confession, but we are all of us made out of the same stuff.' And so the only redemption from mere copying of life – the method of realism – was a more autonomous sort of creation by means of a 'fine lie ... that which is its own evidence ... In point of fact what is interesting about people in good society ... is the mask that each one of them wears, not the reality that lies behind the mask' (*Intentions* 6, 15). The cultured liar thus stands for an ideal freedom from 'Nature's lack of design, her curious crudities, her extraordinary monotony, her absolutely unfinished condition' (*Intentions* 3). In ages past, Art had been more able to enlist 'Life in her service, and using some of life's external forms, she created an entirely new race of beings ... She clothed her children in strange raiment and gave them masks, and at her bidding the antique world rose from its marble tomb. ... History was entirely re-written, and there was hardly one of the dramatists who did not recognise that the object of Art is not simple truth but complex beauty' (Wilde, *Intentions* 23).

Mauberley himself is central to this Wildean demonstration in *Famous Last Words* of the virtue of 'complex beauty' as opposed to 'simple truth.' Not that Mauberley has always understood how a person such as

Wallis Simpson can transform herself into an aesthetic object which transcends simple truth. Only now, it seems, in the act of writing, it is 'only now – after twenty years – that I see her face as lacquered; only now that I realize she has never lived without the application of a mask ... her mouth, her eyes, her hair were masterpieces of illusion' (73). Later, he will even invent a scene of the duchess looking in 'her private mirror' at 'a face no other human being had seen. It was her midnight face, and mostly in her mind. The true face – lifted and lacquered – was the one she showed to others and the world' (191). Thus confounding usual distinctions between truth and illusion, Mauberley collapses public and private faces into the 'truth of illusion.' For the private face that Wallis cannot show the world is nothing less than 'the face of Penelope – who waits.' The illusion of glory is her public mask; but the mask of a queen is her private truth. These two masks differ, in the 'truth' of her imagination, only by degree.

Even so, does Mauberley not get a different glimpse of the truth behind the mask as he stares into the mirror of his own writing? 'Everyone in all those pictures taken then was smiling; everyone was radiant; everyone was infallible. It was all a lie, of course. The fact was, we were being used to shore up the King and his reluctant confidence – used as the symbols of the public approbation he needed so desperately ... So this was why we smiled. We were all so willing to be there; thinking ours was the ultimate face of the age' (98). The public lie and the private truth are no sooner confessed than Mauberley equivocates: 'And perhaps it was.' The tell-tale smile tells all ... that it is still the ultimate face of the age. This same smile will be used to justify the murder of Harry Oakes. So what the self-satisfied mask finally hides is nothing more than self-satisfaction. The ultimate face of the age shines with a narcissistic beauty.

What Mauberley learns from Wallis, on the other hand, about the 'truth' of the mask is how to create his own reality: 'Wallis was beaming and gleaming in a silver gown. I have rarely seen her give a better performance. Goodness, she was gay' (334). Only such performances can ever create 'complex beauty' of the sort Wilde had demanded. Wallis's performance is also akin to the beauty of 'last things' such as Mauberley finds in Schubert's piano sonata in B-flat major. For Wallis excels in the art of making the sort of exit that Mauberley will finally have to make: 'She used the stairs quite consciously and made a scene of dignified bereavement. The "star" upstairs had died, and here came the widow, walking into the future, music swelling up with every measured step she took' (348). Her exit says, *Imagine me. I know heights and depths that you will never know. Feel for me. Wish you could be me. For I cross the threshold into mystery.* Of course it is all gesture. The simple truth is, the duke has abdicated his remaining manhood. The future can only be an endless repetition of that failure. But go out with style. Raise the complex beauty of illusion to the level of truth. You owe it to your adoring multitudes. After all, you're a celebrity. One of the beautiful people, your life a mode of art.

'Obviously,' Mauberley confesses at one point, 'I was out of practice with celebrity' (334). ' "Smile," [Wallis] said. "Smile ..." – through her teeth. "Play it up, Maubie. Act" ' (335). And smile he does, right through the Holocaust. But only the war's end can perfect him in his own art of making an exit. *This is my play's last scene*, he realizes almost too late. And so he climbs toward the Grand Elysium Hotel where 'the atmosphere was mostly one of slightly giddy laughter: the joy of high altitudes, brought on by lack of oxygen and the presence of the most exciting and talked about people in the world' (30–1). Not a bad stage at all to make one's exit into mystery.

Mauberley's performance is in fact compelling. He tells enough of the simple truth to claim our sympathy – the pain, for example, he feels at Julia Franklin's merciless *exposé*: 'But – oh – the sight of oneself, caught in the eye of one who cannot lie' (129). Lies and truth can be distinct for him too, it seems. But truth is ugly, and productive only of pain. Still, pain can be converted into a complex beauty if one happens to be writing well. For beauty is the one and only object of Mauberley's confession, it turns out; the fictional Pound was right. Even the ugly truth of Harry Oakes's murder is converted into an aesthetic emotion: 'Every death I had ever seen was played before my eyes. And I thought of Beatrice in *Much Ado*: "*do you love me?*" "*Yes.*" "*Kill Claudio ...*" ' (373). For such reasons, Mauberley's 'history' is 'entirely re-written' in the Wildean manner. The body of Sir Harry Oakes becomes little more than a stage cadaver. And the Holocaust, as Freyberg rightly intuits, becomes a lovely, complex tale of 'Hansel and Gretel lying in the ovens ... and maybe somewhere a gingerbread house. Playtime. Movie time. Make believe' (54).

If the actor offers 'Nothing, in brief, but maudlin confession,' it is because he turns his back on misshapen truth for the sake of a cosmetic beauty. But not even a blaring soundtrack can now supply the beautiful emotion lacking in the actor: 'And all this while the perfect music, played by the perfect fingers of Alfred Cortot, made its perfect rhythms and made its perfect impact – Schubert's last words – endings' (386). The 'perfect ending' is hardly more than unearned sympathy, a Paterian nostalgia for life which Mauberley betrayed a long time ago. Finally, it forces an equation of 'perfect' music and performance with the 'perfect' confession of a sensibility – Wilde's revelation of a style rather than a morality. As the music swells, the 'author' follows his heroine off the stage into mystery.

Imagine me; imitate my style, Mauberley insists in conclusion. His greatest achievement lies (so to speak) in giving the age exactly what it demands: a style whose beauty seeks to shield us from the public horrors of reality and the private terrors of mortality. But his ultimate decadence is to imply the greater truth of masks than of men. Far from offering 'ideological commentary on the silence of aestheticism' (Hutcheon, *A Theory* 111), *Famous Last Words* reifies the 'triumph' of beauty over truth by letting the aesthete speak. In that sense, the novel which began as a parody of Pound's attack on the aesthete makes itself a belated target of Pound's great poem.

Post-Script

12

After Postmodernism

Canadian literature has evolved directly from Victorian into
Post-Modern ... The country that invented Marshall McLu-
han and Northrop Frye did so by not ever being Modern.
                              Robert Kroetsch, *Boundary 2*

No set of critical standards derived from only one mode can
ever assimilate the whole truth about poetry. There may be
noticed a general tendency to react most strongly against the
mode immediately preceding, and, to a lesser extent, to return
to some of the standards of the modal grandfather.
                        Northrop Frye, *Anatomy of Criticism*

An example in criticism is the neglect of the immediately
preceding New Criticism by post-modern critics, who have
jumped back to Wilde, the New Criticism's 'grandfather,' to
re-erect their theories of non-representative art.
              Paul Fussell, *The Great War and Modern Memory*

In the interlude between swathing and combining in the fall of 1962, my
grandfather David Edward Williams called a meeting of the clan to delay
my proposed entrance to journalism at the University of Western Ontario.
It was decided that I should attend Bible School for three years where I
would be inoculated against atheism, agnosticism, and secular humanism.

In the same autumn, my grandfather and parents stopped at the Bible
School outside Moose Jaw on their way to a reunion with Mom's father,
Jacob Skutevik (alias Dahl), whom she had not seen since her childhood.
I could not be excused from classes, so I was left to imagine this meeting

of grandfathers who had kept worlds apart – the one Welsh-Irish, well-to-do, and well-spoken in all his genial moral judgments, the other Norwegian, penniless, illiterate, and utterly immoral, even in his exuberant telling of tales on himself. Though his deathbed conversion would make him 'respectable' at last, Jack Dahl would leave me to occupy a troubling middle ground.

As with natural grandfathers, so too with modal grandfathers. Born between V-E Day and V-J Day and educated in a two-room school, I literally never heard of Faulkner or Hemingway until after they were dead. Joyce was a girl's name. By the time I did get away to university in Saskatoon, *Giles Goat-Boy* was proposing a *Revised New Syllabus*, and my graduate professors at the University of Massachusetts were beginning to define what was wrong with the old one. Modernism, it turned out, had erred on the side of aestheticism – in the idea that a work of art could be self-contained, free of mess and contingency, a verbal icon transcending the human muddle. The artist was convicted of taking refuge in tradition, Eliot the self-appointed hero with his finger in the dyke. Postmodernism took forceful aim at this kind of wall between art and life, tried to let chaos in again, get the reader in on the act. And yet all these dazzling reminders that our fictions were really fictions did not return us to life, only to the making of fictions. The new aestheticism, it turned out, was too occupied with its own resources to see us out of the fun house. We were invited to quest through labyrinths of voice, searching for absence, not presence.

At its best, the aesthetics of absence has proved to be a liberation movement against the dead hand of the past, designed to free us to be modern in a way that traditional modernism failed to do. Its definitive tool has been the new semiotics of French criticism, not surprisingly taken up most enthusiastically in America where revolutionary tradition has likewise hardened into authoritarianism. This new semiotics has challenged our oldest literary authorities, beginning with Aristotle and his doctrine of imitation, on grounds of an irrevocable split between signifier and signified, between word and world. If the correspondence between signs and things is purely arbitrary, then mimesis is an empty doctrine, pointing only to an absence of reality in language. Freed into speech, narrative can now avoid the tyranny of temporal progression (story as history) and the rigid control of myth (story as universal pattern). It offers only itself in the act of telling, free of any other inheritance, resisting both determination and interpretation.

The relevance of postmodern theory for western Canadian writing is fairly obvious. It refuses the political authority of the centre; it rejects the binary oppositions of two founding cultures in favour of the whole spectrum of excluded middles. In Bob Kroetsch's terms, we have resisted the temptation of the single for the allure of multiplicity. But what one finds in popular versions of our ethnic mosaic (the metaphor is the message) is a curiously static reification of central Canadian bureaucracy. At least as it is institutionalized in Folklorama or its equivalent 'festival of nations.' Island pavilions, really, where we go to share new foods and drink, and to watch the other guy's song and dance. What is more likely shared is an entrenched form of the old modernism: fragments we have shored against our ruin. The old folk-art defending against the new way of life. Québec/Canada; East/West; Wasp/Ethnic; David Edward Williams/Jacob Dahl: our inability to overcome the binary oppositions of structuralism, that ruling philosophy of the modernist era, declares at the deepest level of culture our secret allegiance to the moderns.

The abyss which separates us from the past first opened at the feet of those same moderns. They, like us, felt pulled two ways, were driven to reconcile their divided allegiances. Eliot's 'mythical method' gives a clue to what the age demanded: in 'using the myth, in manipulating a continuous parallel between contemporaneity and antiquity, Mr Joyce is pursuing a method which others must pursue after him.' Contemporaneity and antiquity: they are more than counters for a dead age of faith and a new age of uncertainty. They are binary terms in the artistic process of reconciling past and present in a 'timeless' world of myth. Though Wallace Stevens would put more faith in the imaginative act itself, his 'poem of the mind in the act of finding/What will suffice' still makes art, like myth, into a self-sufficient object transcending time. The function of such useful objects is more cunningly explained by Joyce's Stephen Dedalus in terms of what happens to his soul in the moment of aesthetic 'arrest': 'Glimmering and trembling, trembling and unfolding, a breaking light, an opening flower, it spread in endless succession to itself' (*Portrait* 172). The soul of this self-named 'priest of eternal imagination' is writ large upon the world; world is subsumed in the Word; the eternal self is all. Only trouble is, Joyce ironically exploded the solipsism of autonomous form long before the priests of New Criticism came along to put Humpty together again.

Postmodernism has now shattered this poor, patched Humpty once and for all by shoving the 'modernist' self off the wall. The 'author' vanishes in the new aesthetics of absence as authority is decentred or relocated in a plurality of readers. (Irony may also be a reader-oriented aesthetics, but it smacks of Socratic privilege, an impossible possibility, for the poststructuralist, of knowledge). The postmodern reader who shares in the imaginative process no longer has to find identification on the level of character or plot but in the 'position' of the inferred author. For author and world, like the word, are equally fictions; even history and physics are forms of saying, all subject to the contexts of discourse. What language now refers to is language, signs endlessly mirroring other signs, until fiction comes to represent itself. If this sounds like Babel revisited, well and good. The New Jerusalem was four-square anyway, self-contained. Language is where it's now at. Even if it's language which is now self-sufficient.

At its worst, postmodernism's refusal of referential language is a denial of anything but the imaginative process spreading in endless succession to itself. Even where it is truly shared with the reader, this process is not the same thing as the shared dreaming of older literature. The 'absent' character and author who are to be inferred or co-produced by the reader do not make up for the presence and force of life speaking from somewhere outside our rational consciousness. Word-games now threaten no one with possession, it is true; the authorial reader is in no danger of losing control. But language can also turn solipsistic in another way. The postmodernist's distrust of history as a coercive form of narrative makes him resist the historical meaning of words. Barthes's *l'écriture blanche* describes the postmodern writer's need to strip words of their past associations. But surely this is old hat by now: two hundred years ago, the calendar of the French Republic changed all the names to destroy the Christian associations of the Gregorian system. A significant number of Americans were likewise disappointed that the Revolutionary War had not done away with the English language (even if the next choice was only German).

The road to Babel in recent Canadian writing seems hardly so revolutionary in its ongoing pursuit of lines of ancestry. But because 'our genealogies are the narratives of a discontent with a history that lied to us,' says

Robert Kroetsch, our literature 'comes compulsively to a genealogy that refuses origin.' It is the delusory myth of American Adam, freed of history, inheritance, and the whole burden of the past, to which he does not quite refer. It has always been one way – the refused way – of overcoming our cultural stasis, our traditional fear of upsetting the balance.

Our refusal to become American leaves us none the less to drift into becoming, like Eliot, ersatz Europeans. *The Waste Land* turns into another version of 'mosaic,' a blueprint for our own uneasy national existence between past and present:

> 'I can connect
> Nothing with nothing.
> The broken fingernails of dirty hands.
> My people humble people who expect
> Nothing.'

Of course, Eliot's manipulation of myth also conceals a more fundamental motive: his fear of life as the source of his rage for order. The myths of Western tradition turn out to be about destructive passion; they have to be exchanged for a few Eastern words of wisdom. Shoring up the self becomes the only 'tradition.' In contrast to this fear of life, the Canadian postmodernist at least appears as Trickster, carting his outsize penis in a box on his back. Freeing us from the whiteman's burden. Returning us to archaic sources of energy. Promising us a more primordial America.

Trickster, in postmodern terms, is meant to keep us free of the intolerable choice of whom we are going to be. But Trickster is forced to grow up in Indian myth, and he undergoes a sea change in Sheila Watson's *The Double Hook*, the one modernist text in western Canadian literature which sees him as the figure who might really contain our opposites and so raze the walls of our ethnic isolation. Here, Thompson Indian, Métis, and European immigrant all live under the eye of this bilingual citizen who speaks the language of Indian myth and Old Testament jeremiad. At least until his people see how he oppresses them, or rather how they are divided by their own fear and self-interest. Then Trickster delivers the Word of the Psalmist's messianic prophecy. But Watson has publicly doubted that she would use Coyote if she were to rewrite the novel. Evidently he speaks the most artificial language of all in a novel about dead language. And the birth of the wordless child, the coming of the Word, makes him positively evangelized. Coyote High-Churched. This is put for that. Metonymy, when the life of the novel is metaphor. Words made one with things again, the community rejoined, by the fact of Lenchen's pregnancy. Metaphor as sexual fusion. But that fusion has not happened at the level of myth. Splendid narrative risks end in the service of tradition.

The more wily postmodernist knows that his borrowed myths can only define him in terms of the alien culture, unless he un-invents them. And so he parodies, deconstructs, unnames inherited versions. Holding to his own authority, he tells his way out of the labyrinth, turning it to child's play, like a Jack Hodgins unmasking the demon for a Rumpelstiltskin. Convinced of his own innocence, he will see no evil, do no evil, repeat no evil. Especially repeat no evil. For the myth threatens always to repeat itself. He must therefore stop short of naming a new version, of putting himself back inside any labyrinth save the maze of his own telling. And yet there are only two alternatives to repetition. Silence is one – an ultimate surrender to absence. The other is the deferment of 'meaning and other finalities,' an escape from closure, from a fatal surrender to myth. But if the postmodernist avoids entrapment, he is also avoiding ruin. Fear of life/fear of death. Modernism and postmodernism make the next binary opposition.

My own way out of this cultural labyrinth has been maddeningly slow, and mostly a failure. It's pretty clear that I surrendered to the temptation of myth in *The Burning Wood*. I wanted to find a myth, like Faulkner's second Eden in *The Bear*, that would put an end to the perverse sense of our own cultural innocence (a remarkable flying in the face of our Calvinist inheritance). But most of all I wanted a unifying myth. Grandfathers again. But also the local Chagoness Reserve and Stony Lake Bible Camp on Lake Kipabiskau. During three weeks every summer our church held Bible Camp, then two weeks of Indian Camp. The names are straight from social use – lived binaries. (I was a counsellor at both camps in 1964). But the more I tried to tell it, the less I could write it straight. Too much subversive fun in names like Joshua, in the business of letting out flats in Jericho. I knew nothing yet of theories of deconstruction, but my instincts said nothing much was sacred if it wouldn't let you laugh. So the sun dance turned into another form of carnival, though comedy taken literally could also become tragedy. The only way back to comedy, it seemed to me, was in the renewal of the myth. What I failed to see in Coming-day's death (though I kept revising it right down through the galleys) was that I had surrendered to the old myth of sin and redemption. Newly naturalized, of course. But even an open-ended subversion of Ovid couldn't change the Christ myth.

The River Horsemen was predictably more iconoclastic. According to some critics a modernist work, it marks my own fall from myths of transcendence. That could be why it was so hard to write (or to read, I've also been told). For each of the men in the novel loses his faith in some sustaining myth of his culture, at least as he defines it. The old shaman Fine-day has given up believing in the spirit world; Many-birds blasphemes a powerless Thunder Bird; Nick Sobchuk falls with his 'mad' mother out of grace into a version of her Ukrainian myth of the fallen angels humanized by grief. Even the faith-healer Jack Cann is shattered by his vision of a god who needs to be saved by man. The breaking of each myth leads, however, to new points of contact, if not to a new 'mosaic.' The technique, blamed by some on Faulkner's *As I Lay Dying*, points inversely to a shifting series of doubles by which each man glimpses his unacknowledged self. The fragmenting of narrative leaves gaps across which sparks are meant to fly, but the reader has to make such jumps for himself. Much difficult work, with little guarantee of illumination. And sometimes the leap is into silence, albeit a charged silence, latent (I hope) with new energies. Silence can even point to new namings of a myth. But the story of a man who becomes 'god' to die for the sins of godhead does not lead to an ordinary form of closure. Nor do the metaphors allow for an easy return to the fathers. They concern artists of differing types who must make their own answers to death and so free themselves to live.

Entrapment in myth was always quite immediate for me, given my family's biblical literalism. If any man shall add unto these things, God shall add unto him the plagues that are written in this book. And if any man shall take away from the words of the book of this prophecy, God shall take away his part out of the book of life, and out of the holy city, and from the things which are written in this book. End of book, end of my world. Unless I could tell another story, violate myself back into life. As it happens, the story of the end of the world is also mine by ethnic inheritance. Othin, the god of Norse myth, father of magic, the shape-changer, Trickster, could not by all his knowledge and riddling art defer the meaning of the sibyl's prophecy. I was persuaded of the necessity of endings.

Eye of the Father turns on succeeding versions of the story of a father who absents himself from endings. The flight from Europe to America, from the States to Canada, ends somewhere all the same. Apocalypse here. But the problem of defining apocalypse now becomes the problem of art and life together.

Wagner's *Ring* first proposed the terms which prevent any others: the world is to be overcome through art. The 'sin' of existence is to be atoned for in the death of men and gods alike, if in repeated performances at the Bayreuth festival. Wagner, in this sense, is the prototypical modernist, vouchsafing the world's continuance in his art. But the art that makes life does not want more than itself, and will not allow for its own succession. Even the majestic cataclysm of *Völuspá* in old Norse myth had Baldr coming back to a new throne after the end of the world. World trees and family trees continue. Only the authority of patriarchs has been ended.

Eye of the Father is mostly about fathers, then, who resist succession and so hold their families hostage to the past. Wayne Goodman evades any confrontation with his dying grandfather so that he might be free to write about him in the novel the reader is reading. But his passage in several voices through the dead centre of Wagner's 'negation of the will of life' proves to be his refusal to expose himself; the act of writing is for him an assumption of false identities. Only when he is stripped of his last mask can he be overtaken by his grandfather's story, in an act of surrender, a willed succession. The world renewed, as it always was, in the next generation, the next telling. So long as it is lived.

Nietzsche contra Wagner. We escape the bondage of the past not by refusing or resenting it but by choosing it. Wagner made the mistake of swallowing Schopenhauer's Platonism, the idea that will was the source of all suffering. But the will's secret sorrow, said Nietzsche, was its inability to will backwards. And so Zarathustra's 'postmodern' fear of recurrence had to become his laugh of joy, his learning to will the past into the future.

Becoming one's own ancestor: the heart of the story. Not to enclose the world inside the self, but to re-create the whole work of time. Making our own connections in the writing and the reading. The family tree branching into the world tree.

Post-apocalypse. What follows the deconstruction of every world of myth.

Works Cited

Alexander, S. 'The Basis of Realism.' *In Proceedings of the British Academy, 1913-1914*. Vol. VI, 279–314. London: Humphrey Milford n.d.

Alter, Robert. *The Art of Biblical Narrative*. New York: Basic Books 1981

Atwood, Margaret. *Survival: A Thematic Guide to Canadian Literature*. Toronto: House of Anansi Press 1972.

Bakhtin, Mikhail. *The Dialogic Imagination*, translated by Caryl Emerson and Michael Holquist. Edited by Michael Holquist. Austin: Univ. of Texas Press 1981

Barbour, Douglas. 'David Canaan: The Failing Heart.' *Studies in Canadian Literature* 1 (Winter 1976): 64–75

Barthes, Roland. 'The Death of the Author.' In *Image-Music-Text*, translated by Stephen Heath, 142–8. New York: Hill and Wang 1977

Becker, George J., ed. 'Modern Realism as a Literary Movement.' Introduction to *Documents of Modern Literary Realism*, 3–38. Princeton: Princeton Univ. Press 1963

Beebe, Maurice. 'Joyce and Aquinas: The Theory of Aesthetics.' *Philological Quarterly* 36 (January 1957): 20–35. Rpt. in Thomas E. Connolly, ed., *Joyce's 'Portrait': Criticisms and Critiques*, 272–89. New York: Appleton-Century-Crofts 1962

Bissell, Claude. Introduction to *The Mountain and the Valley* by Ernest Buckler. Toronto: NCL 1961

Block, Haskell M. 'The Critical Theory of James Joyce,' *JAAC* 8 (March 1950): 172–84

Bloom, Harold. *A Map of Misreading*. New York: Oxford Univ. Press 1975

Bonnycastle, Stephen. 'Robertson Davies and the Ethics of Monologue.' *Journal of Canadian Studies* 12 (Spring 1977): 20–40.

Bowering, George. *The Mask in Place: Essays on Fiction in North America*. Winnipeg: Turnstone 1982

Bradbury, Malcolm, and James McFarlane, eds. 'The Name and Nature of Modernism.' Introduction to *Modernism: 1890–1930*, 19–55. Harmondsworth, England: Penguin 1976

Braswell, William, and Leslie A. Field, eds. *Thomas Wolfe's Purdue University Speech: 'Writing and Living.'* Purdue: Purdue Univ. Studies 1964

Broadfoot, Barry, ed. *Ten Lost Years: 1929–1939.* 1973. Markham, Ont.: PaperJacks 1975

Brooker, Peter. *A Student's Guide to the 'Selected Poems of Ezra Pound.'* London: Faber and Faber 1979

Brown, E.K. Review of *As For Me and My House*. Canadian Forum 21 (July 1941): 124–5

Buckler, Ernest. *The Mountain and the Valley.* 1952. Toronto: NCL 1961

Carroll, Lewis. *Alice in Wonderland.* Rpt. in Peter Heath, ed., *The Philosopher's Alice.* New York: St Martin's Press 1974

Chaikin, Milton. 'George Moore's Early Fiction.' In Graham Owens, ed., *George Moore's Mind and Art*, 21–44. New York: Barnes and Noble 1970

Cohen, Philip K. *The Moral Vision of Oscar Wilde.* Rutherford, NJ: Fairleigh Dickinson Univ. Press 1978

Coldwell, Joan. 'Hagar as Meg Merrilies, the Homeless Gypsy.' *Journal of Canadian Fiction* 27 (1980): 92–100

Con Davis, Robert. 'Modernism: The Call for Form'; 'Depth Psychology and "The Scene of Writing": Jung and Freud'; and 'Lacan, Poe, and Narrative Repression.' In Robert Con Davis, ed., *Contemporary Literary Criticism: Modernism Through Poststructuralism*, 11–14, 217–24, 246–61. New York and London: Longman 1986

Cooley, Dennis. 'Antimacassared in the Wilderness: Art and Nature in *The Stone Angel.*' *Mosaic* 11 (Spring 1978): 29–46

Cude, Wilfred. ' "Turn it Upside Down": The Right Perspective on *As For Me and My House.*' *English Studies in Canada* 5 (Winter 1979): 469–88

Daniells, Roy. Introduction to *As For Me and My House* by Sinclair Ross. Toronto: NCL 1957

Danielson, Dennis. *Milton's Good God.* Cambridge: Cambridge Univ. Press 1982

Davidson, Arnold E. 'History, Myth, and Time in Robert Kroetsch's *Badlands.*' *Studies in Canadian Literature* 5 (Spring 1980): 127–37

Davidson, Cathy N. 'Past and Perspective in Margaret Laurence's *The Stone Angel.*' *American Review of Canadian Studies* 8 (Autumn 1978): 61–9

Davies, Robertson. 'The Deptford Trilogy in Retrospect.' In Robert G. Lawrence, and Samuel L. Macey, eds., *Studies in Roberston Davies' Deptford Trilogy*, 7–12. Victoria: English Literary Studies 1980

– *Fifth Business.* 1970. New York: Penguin 1977

- *The Manticore*. 1972. New York: Penguin 1976

Denham, Paul. 'Narrative Technique in Sinclair Ross's *As For Me and My House*.' *Studies in Canadian Literature* 5 (Spring 1980): 116–24

Derrida, Jacques. 'Structure, Sign, and Play in the Discourse of the Human Sciences.' In Richard Macksey, and Eugenio Donato, eds., *The Languages of Criticism and the Sciences of Man: The Structuralist Controversy*, 247–72. Baltimore and London: The Johns Hopkins Univ. Press 1970

Dick, Susan, ed. Introduction & Variorum Notes to *Confessions of a Young Man* by George Moore, 1–22. Montreal and London: McGill-Queen's Univ. Press 1972

Donald, David Herbert. *Look Homeward: A Life of Thomas Wolfe*. Boston and Toronto: Little, Brown and Company 1987

Dooley, D. J. 'Style and Communication in *the* [sic] *Mountain and the Valley*.' *Dalhousie Review* 57 (Winter 1977–78): 671–83

Duffy, Dennis. 'Let Us Compare Histories: Meaning and Mythology in Findley's *Famous Last Words*.' *Essays on Canadian Writing* 30 (1984–5): 187–205

- 'To Carry the Work of William James a Step Further: The Play of Truth in *Fifth Business*.' *Essays on Canadian Writing* 36 (Spring 1988): 1–21

Eliot, T. S. 'Tradition and the Individual Talent.' *The Sacred Wood*, 3d. ed., 47–59. London: Methuen 1932

Ellmann, Richard. 'The Critic as Artist as Wilde.' 1968. Rpt. in Harold Bloom, ed., *Modern Critical Views of Oscar Wilde*, 91–106. New York: Chelsea House 1985

- *Yeats: The Man and the Masks*. 1948. Rev. ed. New York: W.W. Norton 1978

Espey, John J. *Ezra Pound's 'Mauberley': A Study in Composition*. London: Faber and Faber 1955

Farrow, Anthony. *George Moore*. Boston: Twayne 1978

Findley, Timothy. *Famous Last Words*. 1981. Markham, Ont.: Penguin 1982

Fischer, Michael. *Does Deconstruction Make Any Difference?: Poststructuralism and the Defense of Poetry in Modern Criticism*. Bloomington: Indiana Univ. Press 1985

Fish, Stanley. 'Driving from the Letter: Truth and Indeterminacy in Milton's *Areopagitica*.' In Mary Nyquist, and Margaret W. Ferguson, eds., *Re-membering Milton: Essays on the Texts and Traditions*, 234–54. New York and London: Methuen 1988

Fitzgerald, F. Scott. *The Great Gatsby*. New York: Scribner's 1925

Fletcher, John, and Malcolm Bradbury. 'The Introverted Novel.' In Malcolm Bradbury, and James McFarlane, eds., *Modernism: 1890–1930*, 394–415. Harmondsworth: Penguin 1976

Forst, Graham Nicol. 'Into Silent Seas: Ideas and Images of Intellect in Kant and the English Romantics.' *Mosaic* 14 (Fall 1981): 31–44

Frank, Joseph. 'Spatial Form in Modern Literature.' *Sewanee Review* 53 (1945): 221–40, 433–56, 643–53

Frye, Northrop. *Anatomy of Criticism: Four Essays.* 1957. New York: Atheneum 1969

Godard, Barbara. 'El Greco in Canada: Sinclair Ross's *As For Me and My House.' Mosaic* 14 (Spring 1981): 54–75

Gom, Leona M. 'Laurence and the Use of Memory.' *Canadian Literature* 71 (Winter 1976): 48–58

Grace, Sherrill. 'Wastelands and Badlands.' *Mosaic* 14 (Spring 1981): 20–34

Greve, Felix Paul. 'Oscar Wilde und das Drama.' Introduction to *Vera oder die Nihilisten*, translated by F.P. Greve. Vol. 7 of *Oscar Wildes Sämtliche Werke in deutscher Sprache*, 7–102. 12 vols. Vienna: Wiener Verlag n.d.

Grove (Frederick Philip) Collection. Manuscript 2, Boxes 10–11. Department of Archives and Special Collections. University of Manitoba Libraries. Winnipeg, Manitoba

Grove, Frederick Philip. *A Search for America: The Odyssey of an Immigrant.* 1927. Toronto: NCL 1971

– *In Search of Myself.* 1946. Toronto: NCL 1974

– *Settlers of the Marsh.* 1925. Toronto: NCL 1966

Gurko, Leo. *Thomas Wolfe: Beyond the Romantic Ego.* New York: Thomas Y. Crowell Company 1975

Harrison, Dick. *Unnamed Country: The Struggle for a Canadian Prairie Fiction.* Edmonton: Univ. of Alberta Press 1977

Hehner, Barbara. 'River of Now and Then: Margaret Laurence's Narratives.' *Canadian Literature* 74 (Autumn 1977): 40–57

Hemingway, Ernest. *The Snows of Kilimanjaro and Other Stories.* 1936. New York: Scribner's 1961

Hesse, M.G. *Gabrielle Roy.* Boston: Twayne 1984

Hinz, Evelyn J., and John J. Teunissen. 'Who's the Father of Mrs Bentley's Child?: *As For Me and My House* and the Conventions of Dramatic Monologue.' *Canadian Literature* 111 (Winter 1986): 101–13

Hjartarson, Paul. 'Design and Truth in Grove's *In Search of Myself.' Canadian Literature* 90 (Autumn 1981): 73–90

– 'Of Greve, Grove, and Other Strangers: The Autobiography of the Baroness Elsa von Freytag-Loringhoven.' In Paul Hjartarson, ed., *A Stranger to My Time: Essays by and about Frederick Philip Grove*, 269–84. Edmonton: NeWest Press 1986

Holman, C. Hugh. *The Loneliness at the Core: Studies in Thomas Wolfe.* Baton Rouge: Louisiana State Univ. Press 1975

Howells, Coral Ann. *Private and Fictional Words: Canadian Women Novelists of the 1970s and 1980s*. London and New York: Methuen 1987

Hoy, Helen. ' "Dull, Simple, Amazing and Unfathomable": Paradox and Double Vision in Alice Munro's Fiction.' *Studies in Canadian Literature* 5 (Spring 1980): 100–15

Hughes, Merritt Y. *John Milton: Complete Poems and Major Prose*. New York: Odyssey Press 1957

Hutcheon, Linda. *The Canadian Postmodern: A Study of Contemporary English-Canadian Fiction*. Toronto: Oxford University Press 1988

– *Narcissistic Narrative: The Metafictional Paradox*. 1980. New York and London: Methuen 1984

– *A Theory of Parody: The Teachings of Twentieth-Century Art Forms*. New York and London: Methuen 1985

Iser, Wolfgang. *The Implied Reader: Patterns of Communication in Prose Fiction from Bunyan to Beckett*. 1972. Baltimore: The Johns Hopkins Univ. Press 1974

– *Walter Pater: The Aesthetic Moment*, translated by David Henry Wilson. 1960. Cambridge: Cambridge Univ. Press 1987

Jeffares, A. Norman. 'A Drama in Muslin.' In Graham Owens, ed., *George Moore's Mind And Art*, 1–20. New York: Barnes and Noble 1970

Jeffrey, David L. 'Biblical Hermeneutic and Family History in Contemporary Canadian Fiction: Wiebe and Laurence.' *Mosaic* 11 (Spring 1978): 87–106

Johnsen, William A. 'Toward a Redefinition of Modernism.' *Boundary 2* 2 (Spring 1974): 539–56

Joost, Nicholas. *Ernest Hemingway and the Little Magazines: The Paris Years*. Barre, Mass.: Barre Publishers 1968

Joyce, James. *A Portrait of the Artist as a Young Man*. 1916. Harmondsworth: Penguin 1976

– *Stephen Hero: Part of the first draft of 'A Portrait of the Artist as a Young Man,'* edited by Theodore Spencer; revised edition by John J. Slocum and Herbert Cahoon. London: Jonathan Cape 1956

Jung, C. G. *Aion: Researches into the Phenomenology of the Self*. Trans. R.F.C. Hull. 2nd ed. Bollingen Series XX, vol. 9, ii. Princeton: Princeton Univ. Press n.d.

Keats, John. 'Meg Merrilies.' In Douglas Bush, ed., *Selected Poems and Letters*. Boston: Houghton Mifflin 1959

Keith, W.J. *Canadian Literature in English*. London and New York: Longman 1985

Kennedy, Richard S. 'Thomas Wolfe's Fiction: The Question of Genre.' In Paschal Reeves, ed., *Thomas Wolfe and the Glass of Time*, 1–44. Athens: Univ. of Georgia Press 1971

Kenner, Hugh. 'The Cubist Portrait.' In Thomas F. Staley, and Bernard Ben-
stock, eds., *Approaches to Joyce's* Portrait: *Ten Essays*, 171–84. Pittsburgh:
Univ. of Pittsburgh Press 1976
– *The Poetry of Ezra Pound*. London: Faber and Faber 1951
– 'The *Portrait* in Perspective.' In Seon Givens, ed., *James Joyce: Two Decades
of Criticism*, 132–74. New York: Vanguard Press 1948
– *The Pound Era*. Berkeley and Los Angeles: Univ. of California Press 1971
Kermode, Frank. *Romantic Image*. London: Routledge and Kegan Paul 1957
Kertzer, Jon M. '*The Stone Angel*: Time and Responsibility.' *Dalhousie Review*
54 (Autumn 1974): 499–509
Kroetsch, Robert. *Badlands*. 1975. Don Mills, Ontario: PaperJacks 1976
– 'Beyond Nationalism: A Prologue.' *Mosaic* 14 (Spring 1981): v–xi
– *The Lovely Treachery of Words: Essays Selected and New*. Toronto: Oxford
Univ. Press 1989
Lacan, Jacques. *The Ego in Freud's Theory and in the Technique of Psycho-
analysis 1954–1955*, translated by Sylvana Tomaselli. New York: W. W.
Norton 1988
Laurence, Margaret. *The Diviners*. 1974. Toronto: NCL 1986
– *The Stone Angel*. 1964. Toronto: NCL 1968
Lecker, Robert. *Robert Kroetsch*. Boston, Twayne Publishers 1986
Lent, John. 'Wyndham Lewis and Malcolm Lowry: Contexts of Style and
Subject Matter in the Modern Novel.' In Diane Bessai, and David Jackel,
eds., *Figures in a Ground: Canadian Essays on Modern Literature Collected
in Honor of Sheila Watson*, 61–75. Saskatoon: Western Producer Prairie
Books 1978
Lessing, Gotthold Ephraim. *Laocoon: An Essay upon the Limits of Painting
and Poetry*, translated by Ellen Frothingham. New York: Noonday 1957
Levin, Harry. *James Joyce*. New York: New Directions 1960
MacDonald, Bruce F. 'Word-Shapes, Time and the Theme of Isolation in *The
Mountain and the Valley*.' *Studies in Canadian Literature* 1 (Summer 1976):
194–209
McDowall, 'Conclusions and Applications.' In George J. Becker, ed., *Docu-
ments of Modern Literary Realism*, 565–78. Princeton: Princeton Univ.
Press 1963
McLachlan, Ian. 'Not the Full Smile.' Review of *Famous Last Words*. *Books
in Canada* 10 (December 1981): 9–11
MacLulich, T.D. *Between Europe and America: The Canadian Tradition in
Fiction*. Toronto: ECW Press 1988
McMullen, Lorraine. *Sinclair Ross*. Boston: Twayne 1979
Mahaffey, Vicki. *Reauthorizing Joyce*. Cambridge: Cambridge Univ. Press
1988

Martens, Lorna. *The Diary Novel*. Cambridge: Cambridge Univ. Press 1985

Martin, W.R. *Alice Munro: Paradox and Parallel*. Edmonton: University of Alberta Press 1987

Mathews, Lawrence. 'Hacking at the Parsnips: *The Mountain and the Valley* and the Critics.' In John Metcalf, ed., *The Bumper Book*, 188–201. Toronto: ECW Press 1986

– '*Who Do You Think You Are?*: Alice Munro's Art of Disarrangement.' In Louis K. MacKendrick, ed., *Probable Fictions: Alice Munro's Narrative Acts*, 181–93. Downsview, Ontario: ECW Press 1983

Melville, A.D., trans. *Ovid: Metamorphoses*. Oxford: Oxford Univ. Press 1987

Metcalf, John, ed. Introduction to *The Bumper Book*, 1–5. Toronto: ECW Press 1986

Miller, J. Hillis. 'Stevens' Rock and Criticism as Cure, II,' *Georgia Review* 30 (1976): 330–48. In Robert Con Davis, ed., *Contemporary Literary Criticism: Modernism Through Poststructuralism*, 416–27. New York and London: Longman 1986

Monaghan, David. 'Metaphors and Confusions.' *Canadian Literature* 67 (Winter 1976): 64–73

Monier-Williams, Sir Monier, et al. *A Sanskrit-English Dictionary*. Oxford: Clarendon Press 1960

Monsman, Gerald Cornelius. *Pater's Portraits: Mythic Patterns in the Fiction of Walter Pater*. Baltimore: The Johns Hopkins Press 1967

– *Walter Pater's Art of Autobiography*. New Haven and London: Yale Univ. Press 1980

Moore, George. *Confessions of a Young Man*, edited by Susan Dick. Montreal and London: McGill-Queen's Univ. Press 1972

Munro, Alice. *Lives of Girls and Women*. 1971. Scarborough, Ontario: New American Library 1974

– *Who Do You Think You Are?* 1978. Scarborough, Ontario: New American Library 1979

Murdoch, Iris. 'Against Dryness: A Polemical Sketch.' *Encounter* 16 (January 1961): 16–20

– 'The Sublime and the Beautiful Revisited.' *Yale Review* 49 (December 1959): 247–71

Murray, Glenn. 'Who Killed Boy Staunton: An Astrological Witness Reports.' *Studies in Canadian Literature* 2 (Winter 1977): 117–23

New, William H. 'Sinclair Ross's Ambivalent World.' *Canadian Literature* 40 (Spring 1969): 26–32

Newman, John Henry. *Apologia Pro Vita Sua*, edited by Dwight A. Culler. 1864. Boston: Houghton Mifflin 1956

- *An Essay in Aid of a Grammar of Assent*. 1870. Notre Dame: Univ. of Notre Dame Press 1979

Nietzsche, Friedrich. 'Twilight of the Idols.' In *The Portable Nietzsche*, translated by Walter Kaufmann. New York: Viking Press 1954

O'Sullivan, Vincent. *Aspects of Wilde*. London: Constable and Company 1936

Otis, Brooks. *Virgil: A Study in Civilized Poetry*. Oxford: Clarendon Press 1963

Pache, Walter. 'The Dilettante in Exile: Grove at the Centenary of his Birth.' *Canadian Literature* 90 (Autumn 1981): 187–91

Pater, Walter. *Marius the Epicurean: His Sensations and Ideas*. 1885. 2 vols. London: Macmillan 1910

- *The Renaissance: Studies in Art and Poetry*. 1873. London: Macmillan 1910

Peterman, Michael. *Robertson Davies*. Boston: Twayne 1986

Poe, Edgar Allan. 'The Philosophy of Composition.' In Edward H. Davidson, ed., *Selected Writings of Edgar Allan Poe*. Boston: Houghton Mifflin 1956

Poulet, Georges. 'Phenomenology of Reading.' In Robert Con Davis, ed., *Contemporary Literary Criticism: Modernism Through Poststructuralism*, 350–62. New York and London: Longman 1986

Pound, Ezra. *Gaudier-Brzeska: A Memoir*. 1916. New York: New Directions 1970

- *Selected Poems*. Edited by T.S. Eliot. 1928. London: Faber and Faber 1948

Proust, Marcel. *Remembrance of Things Past*, Vol. 3, translated by C.K. Scott Moncrieff, and Terence Kilmartin. 1981. Harmondsworth: Penguin 1983

Radford, F.L. 'The Great Mother and the Boy: Jung, Davies and *Fifth Business*.' In Robert G. Lawrence, and Samuel L. Macey, eds., *Studies in Robertson Davies' Deptford Trilogy*, 66–81. Victoria: English Literary Studies 1980

Ricou, Laurence. 'David Canaan and Buckler's Style in *The Mountain and the Valley*.' *Dalhousie Review* 57 (Winter 1977–78): 684–96

Riquelme, John Paul. *Teller and Tale in Joyce's Fiction: Oscillating Perspectives*. Baltimore and London: The Johns Hopkins Univ. Press 1983

Robertson, George. 'An Artist's Progress.' *Canadian Literature* 21 (Summer 1964): 53–5

Roper, Gordon. 'Robertson Davies' *Fifth Business* and "That Old Fantastical Duke of Dark Corners, C.G. Jung."' *Journal of Canadian Fiction* 1 (Winter 1972): 33–9

Ross, Sinclair. *As For Me and My House*. 1941. Toronto: NCL 1957

Roy, Gabrielle. *Enchantment and Sorrow: The Autobiography of Gabrielle Roy*, translated by Patricia Claxton. 1984. Toronto: Lester and Orpen Dennys 1987

- *The Road Past Altamont*, translated by Joyce Marshall. 1966. Toronto: NCL 1966

- *Street of Riches*, translated by Henry Binsse. 1957. Toronto: NCL 1967
Rubin, Louis D., Jr. 'Thomas Wolfe: Time and the South.' In Leslie A. Field, ed., *Thomas Wolfe: Three Decades of Criticism*, 59–83. New York: New York Univ. Press and London: University of London Press 1968
St Pierre, Paul M. 'Rounding the Ovoid.' *Mosaic* 11 (Spring 1978): 127–35
Scobie, Stephen. 'Eye-Deep in Hell: Ezra Pound, Timothy Findley, and Hugh Selwyn Mauberley.' *Essays on Canadian Writing* 30 (1984–85): 206–27
Shewan, Rodney. *Oscar Wilde: Art and Egotism*. New York: Barnes and Noble 1977
Shields, E.F. ' "The Perfect Voice": Mauberley as Narrator in Timothy Findley's *Famous Last Words.*' *Canadian Literature* 119 (Winter 1988): 84–98
Solecki, Sam. 'Some Kicks Against the Prick: John Metcalf in his Essays.' In John Metcalf, ed., *The Bumper Book*, 207–23. Toronto: ECW Press 1986
Sontag, Susan. *On Photography*. New York: Farrar, Straus and Giroux 1977.
- *Under the Sign of Saturn*. New York: Farrar, Straus, Giroux 1980
Spanos, William V. 'Modern Literary Criticism and the Spatialization of Time: An Existential Critique.' *Journal of Aesthetics and Art Criticism* 29 (Fall 1970): 87–104
Spengemann, William C. *The Forms of Autobiography: Episodes in the History of a Literary Genre*. New Haven: Yale Univ. Press 1980
Spettigue, Douglas O. FPG: *The European Years*. Ottawa: Oberon 1973
Stich, K.P. 'Grove's New World Bluff.' *Canadian Literature* 90 (Autumn 1981): 111–23
Sutherland, Ronald. 'The Relevance of Robertson Davies.' *Journal of Canadian Studies* 12 (Spring 1977): 75–81
Thomas, Clara. *The Manawaka World of Margaret Laurence*. 1975. Toronto: NCL 1976
Thomas, Peter. *Robert Kroetsch*. Studies in Canadian Literature, No. 13. Vancouver: Douglas & McIntyre 1980
- 'Robert Kroetsch and Silence.' *Essays on Canadian Writing* 18–19 (Summer-Fall 1980): 33–53
Thompson, Anne. 'The Wilderness of Pride: Form and Image in *The Stone Angel*.' *Journal of Canadian Fiction* 15 (Autumn 1975): 95–110
Tonkin, Boyd. 'Hitler's Understudy.' Review of *Famous Last Words*. *New Statesman*, 27 March 1987: 33
Trehearne, Brian. *Aestheticism and the Canadian Modernists: Aspects of a Poetic Influence*. Kingston, Montreal, London: McGill-Queen's Univ. Press 1989
Wainwright, J. A. 'Fern Hill Revisited: Isolation and Death in *The Mountain and the Valley.*' *Studies in Canadian Literature* 7:1 (1982): 63–89
Walser, Richard. 'The Angel and the Ghost.' In Paschal Reeves, ed., *Thomas*

Wolfe and the Glass of Time, 45–67. Athens: Univ. of Georgia Press 1971

Whicher, Stephen E., ed. *Selections from Ralph Waldo Emerson*. Boston: Houghton Mifflin 1957

Wilde, Oscar. *De Profundis*. 1905. Vol. 12 of *The First Collected Edition of the Works of Oscar Wilde*, edited by Robert Ross. 15 vols., 1908–22. Rpt. London: Dawsons of Pall Mall 1969

– *Intentions*. 1891. Vol. 3 of *The First Collected Edition of the Works of Oscar Wilde*. London: Dawsons 1969

– *The Picture of Dorian Gray*. 1891. Vol. 4 of *The First Collected Edition of the Works of Oscar Wilde*. London: Dawsons 1969

Witemeyer, Hugh. *The Poetry of Ezra Pound: Forms and Renewal, 1908–1920*. Berkeley and Los Angeles: Univ. of California Press 1969

Wolfe, Thomas. *Look Homeward, Angel*. 1929. New York: Scribner's 1957

Woodcock, George. 'Don't Ever Ask for the True Story; Or, Second Thoughts on Autobiography.' *Essays on Canadian Writing* 29 (Summer 1984): 16–25

– 'The Plots of Life: The Realism of Alice Munro,' *Queen's Quarterly* 93 (Summer 1986): 235–50

Yeats, W. B. 'Lapis Lazuli.' In M.L. Rosenthal, ed., *Selected Poems and Two Plays*. New York: Collier 1966

York, Lorraine M. *'The Other Side of Dailiness': Photography in the Works of Alice Munro, Timothy Findley, Michael Ondaatje, and Margaret Laurence*. Toronto: ECW Press 1988

Young, Alan R. 'The Genesis of Ernest Buckler's *The Mountain and the Valley*.' *Journal of Canadian Fiction* 16 (1976): 89–96

Index

- 'Retrospect' 58
decadence: defined 6–7, 8; in Davies
30, 58, 73; and fear of nature 27;
in Findley 257–9; in Grove
29–30, 43–6; in Joyce 7–8, 20–2,
27–8, 29; in Laurence 87–8, 100;
in Moore 13–14, 17–19; relation
to modernism 6; to postmodernism 9–10; in Wilde 6–7, 9–10,
27–8, 43–6, 257
deconstruction 8–10, 11; and decadence 9–10; in Hodgins 268; in
Kroetsch 268; see also Derrida,
Jacques; Lacan, Jacques; Miller, J.
Hillis; Munro, Alice: undecidability in Who Do You Think You
Are?; postmodernism
Defoe, Daniel 108
Denham, Paul 105, 106, 136, 137
Derrida, Jacques 8–9, 11, 209–10,
211
diary: communicative triangle in
122; as confessional mode 32,
105, 112; conventions of irony
110–11; conventions of narrative
control 113, 114, 116, 121–2;
conventions of prospective plot
109–10; conventions of secrecy
105, 122; conventions of temporal
incompletion 108; difference from
memoir 110; from monologue
107, 111; historical examples of
108; as novel form 105, 107, 110;
used by Defoe 108; by Gide 107;
by Sartre 107
Dick, Susan 18, 19
Dickens, Charles 250
Dooley, D.J. 148, 161, 164
Dowson, Ernest 27
dramatic monologue 106–7
Duffy, Dennis 56, 57, 84, 248

Eliot, T.S. 3, 180, 188, 189, 264;
mythical method of 265, 267

- 'J. Alfred Prufrock' 107
- 'Tradition and the Individual
Talent' 3, 33, 188, 189
- Waste Land, The 8, 267
Ellmann, Richard 7, 86
Emerson, Ralph Waldo 62; and self-
reliance 62, 157
Espey, John J. 238, 239

Farrow, Anthony 18
Faulkner, William 150, 152, 264; As
I Lay Dying 269; The Bear 268
Findley, Timothy 36; relation to
Moore 36, 246–7, 253, 254, 255;
relation to Pater 36, 242–3,
253–4, 260; relation to Wilde 36,
244, 246, 257–8, 259, 260
- Famous Last Words 36, 237–60;
as apologia 238, 246, 247, 258;
and the beautiful 254–5, 257–8,
259, 260; and cinema 241–2,
244–9, 250, 251, 252; as confession 238, 240, 242, 248, 249,
250, 251, 254, 255, 256–7, 259,
260; decadence in 257–60; exhibitionism in 246, 247–8, 255;
impressionism in 36, 244, 246,
247, 252–3, 254–5; masks in 240,
258–9, 260; narrative problems of
249–52; as parody of Pound 36,
237–44, 260; reader/viewer-
response in 238, 244–5, 246,
251–5; reverse mimesis in 246,
259; self-knowledge in 238, 242,
255; voyeurism in 244–5, 247,
248, 250, 251, 255
Fischer, Michael 8, 9–10, 12, 211
Fish, Stanley 11–12
Fitzgerald, F. Scott 81, 162; The
Great Gatsby 81
Flaubert, Gustave 20–1, 136, 145;
Madame Bovary 137
Fletcher, John 136, 141, 143, 145
Foucault, Michel 227